Professional Services Automation

Professional Services Automation

OPTIMIZING
PROJECT & SERVICE ORIENTED
ORGANIZATIONS

Rudolf Melik

Ludwig Melik   Albert S. Bitton   Gus Berdebes   Ara Israilian

John Wiley & Sons, Inc.

Published by John Wiley & Sons, Inc., New York
Published simultaneously in Canada.

This publication is designed to provide accurate and authoritative information in regard to the subject matter covered. It is sold with the understanding that the publisher is not engaged in rendering professional services. If professional advice or other expert assistance is required, the services of a competent professional person should be sought.

ISBN 0-471-23018-9

Printed in the United States of America

10 9 8 7 6 5 4 3 2

Contents

To the Honourable Céline Hervieux-Payette, P.C., Senator
for her support and encouragement

and

To the employees and customers of Tenrox,
without whom none of this would have been possible.

Foreword

This book describes a new suite of software applications designed specifically for organizations whose work is project-based and human resource intensive, to make their operations more efficient and their resources more productive. While these applications currently are referred to using many acronyms—the three most widely used being Professional Services Automation (PSA), Service Process Optimization (SPO), and Enterprise Services Automation (ESA)—they all have one common goal: to improve the workflow surrounding the management and delivery of project-based services. The true test of value for these applications lies in their ability to either reduce costs or increase services revenue for the end user.

Gartner Dataquest defines these products as software designed to track and allocate the major resources of externally focused services companies or internally focused services departments, namely, people, intellectual capital, and time to their output. Examples of externally focused services companies include IT professional services providers, engineering and construction companies, and health care providers. Alternatively, examples of internally focused services departments include the IT department of any large enterprise or the research and development arm of a pharmaceutical company. Some market observers have likened these applications to ERPs for service-based organizations.

These applications first emerged in the North American market in 1998 and were primarily targeted toward IT professional services providers. In fact, many of the vendors who now create and sell these applications actually worked for IT professional services firms where they witnessed firsthand the need for a tool to improve their ability to manage and deliver IT professional services. This need stretched far beyond the capabilities of available project management software.

Over the past two decades the IT services market has marked the emergence of more specialized professional services providers who have moved from simply integrating software and communication systems, to creating IT solutions that help manage an enterprise, to business process solutions that manage an entire business process workflow. What is truly fascinating about this transformation is that IT professional services providers are directly responsible for making many of these firms more efficient and profitable, yet they have largely not used technology as an enabler to increase their own internal business processes.

As these applications gained traction, and given the somewhat limited size of the IT professional services market, a number of vendors began targeting new market segments, specifically the internal IT departments of enterprises and other embedded services-based departments. This new marketing focus began in earnest around the second quarter of 2000. Again, the purpose of these applications, in this instance, is to improve the workflow of specific business processes related to internal service delivery. In the future these two new segments will likely represent the greatest market opportunity.

In terms of market validation for these applications there are three points to consider:

1. Some of the largest internally and externally focused services organizations have deployed these applications. Two of the largest deployments to date include two IT professional services providers with approximately 6,000 users and 75,000 users, respectively.

2. Numerous large enterprise software vendors see tremendous opportunity in this space and have developed—or are in the process of developing or acquiring—competitive applications.

3. Gartner Dataquest projects that the worldwide market for new software licenses will grow from $177 million in 2000 to $1.2 billion by 2005, at a CAGR of 46%.

Looking ahead the following four scenarios are likely to play themselves out:

1. Industry analysts as well as software vendors will increase their evaluation and analysis of the ROI delivered by these applications. This market has matured to the point where the proposed workflow efficiencies of these applications can now be measured on a broader scale.

2. To date there are approximately 28 software vendors who claim to have an PSA/SPO/ESA product, which has created a very crowded playing field. In order to stand apart from the crowd, most software vendors will differentiate their products by focusing on solving the services management and delivery inefficiencies of specific vertical markets (i.e., IT professional services, engineering and construction, and pharmaceuticals).

3. Even with a new focus on differentiation via verticalization, the market is unlikely to sustain approximately 28 software vendors. Should this hold true, the market will see an increase in mergers, acquisitions, and in some cases company closures.

4. Over the next few years the bulk of functionality offered by these applications will become relatively commoditized, particularly around time and expense capture, resource management, and project management. As such, leading software vendors will likely focus a significant amount of investment on improving three key areas of functionality: portfolio management, knowledge management, and the strategic sourcing of external resources.

No matter what name is assigned to these applications, if you are an executive or project manager in a services organization, chances are this software can help improve your business process efficiencies. While some may believe that these applications will provide them with a competitive advantage, Gartner Dataquest believes that these applications will soon be viewed as a competitive necessity for services organizations. Never before has there been a fully integrated suite of products that centralizes all the key data points for the management and delivery of services. The following pages offer a detailed look at the genesis of these applications and the specific business workflow inefficiencies they address for both internally and externally focused services organizations. Anyone interested in learning more about these applications will find this book an excellent resource.

TED KEMPF
Principal Analyst,
Gartner Dataquest

Preface

This new class of business software goes by many confusing acronyms: PSA (Professional Services Automation), SPO (service process optimization), SRM (service relationship management), and many other variations.

> PSA, SPO, SRM ... software whose ultimate goal is to maximize the performance of project- and service-oriented organizations (PSORGs).

They all essentially refer to the same idea—a solution that provides an *Enterprise Resource Planning* system for primarily white-collar project/service organizations (PSORGs). The principal aim of this class of software is to make such organizations more efficient, and to use mechanization to streamline their increasingly complicated processes. They are primarily focused on creating bottomline benefits by putting powerful software tools into the hands of the people generating project and service revenue for the enterprise.

The primary focus of traditional Enterprise Resource Planning (ERP) systems is the blue-collar world of factory automation and the world of accounting systems, where the raw data tends to be rolled up and summarized into the organizational structures that were built to conform to the accounting view of the enterprise. These accounting views are useful in the production of general ledgers and other high-level accounting snapshots of the enterprise, but they usually bear little relationship to the dynamic way project-focused organizations are structured and continually restructured around new projects.

This new breed of software solutions called PSA focuses on

servicing the needs of PSORGs, and is evolving to become the *optimized* and *specialized* ERP for these types of enterprises. (Project/service-oriented organizations are the main focus of this book, and we often use the terms PSORGs, *organizations,* or *enterprises* interchangeably, as we are always referring to the same type of organization.)

The ultimate goal of these systems is to maximize the performance of PSORGs. These solutions automate and integrate core business processes with the intent of increasing the efficiency of how projects are planned, budgeted, created, staffed, scheduled, implemented, and billed in the real world.

The challenges for these organizations include evaluating their own processes and determining what has to be optimized, as well as selecting among the numerous PSA vendor offerings. The objective of this book is to assist the reader in identifying the key concepts of PSA solutions, their principle features, criteria for selecting them, and their implementation requirements.

Many medium- to large-sized enterprises use traditional single-vendor ERPs to help centralize and mechanize their traditional core business processes. Enterprise resource planning software automates many of the basic business processes that most enterprises need to implement—for example, accounting, human resources, inventory control, procurement, and order processing. Most of these processes are provided in modules created by the ERP manufacturer or from their strategic partners. In many ways, ERPs eliminate the enterprise's burden of selecting its own best-of-breed[1] solutions, and substitute the expertise of the ERP manufacturer. The major benefits provided by ERP solutions are the best practices[2] expertise of the ERP manufacturer and the integrated nature of the application modules.

ERPs have focused on traditional business processes within traditional industries.[3] Project- and service-oriented organizations

---

1. *Best of breed* refers to the best solution or product available to perform a given function. Compare this concept to that of buying generalized software such as ERPs.

2. *Best practices* are practical approaches and techniques gained from experience that have shown to produce best results.

3. Some examples of these industries include manufacturing or distribution, which may be very competitive and dynamic, but are generally well understood and mature; their basic core business practices have been heavily mechanized for some time already.

have had to rely on solutions that do not meet their particular needs, and more often than not are crude combinations of non-integrated systems, such as stand-alone project management tools, simple spreadsheets, in-house custom-built systems, and paper-based methods to manage their core business processes. The result has often been a state of less-than-impressive efficiency.

> **ERP systems have not focused on project and service oriented organizations.**

Like more traditional businesses, PSORGs are under constant pressure to maximize revenues, minimize project costs, produce more measurable results, improve efficiency, and increase customer satisfaction. Continued reliance on productivity solutions that have not been tailored to their needs, such as general-purpose ERP systems, stand-alone project management tools, in-house–created applications, spreadsheets, and paper, is not an effective method of increasing productivity and profitability for such companies. These project-focused organizations have their own unique business processes that require optimization. Mechanized solutions intended to streamline business processes for such companies must naturally focus on the life cycle of the companies' own products, namely service and project engagements.

Some of the unique requirements for PSORGs are dictated by whether their projects are for cost centers (nonbillable and based on budgets) or profit centers. Most IT departments are engaged in internal software development, engineering, R&D, product design and only serve internal *clients.* The projects and services implemented for these internal clients are based on corporate budgetary constraints and is non-billable work. On the other hand, some PSORGs perform work for external *clients,* and usually perform their billing based on various rating algorithms.

Very few PSORGs efficiently deliver their projects or services. Due to increased industry complexities and inefficient corporate processes, service workers are not focusing on their

> **Very few PSORGs efficiently deliver projects or services.**

key responsibilities. Instead, they are being bombarded with increasing numbers of administrative tasks, technology issues, unmanageable workloads, and either a lack of useful information or an inundation of useless detail (or both). There is a great need and an increasing demand for software applications to make PSORGs more productive and more profitable. PSA applications, or the many other aforementioned similar acronyms, describe a set of software solutions that have been designed to achieve such a goal.

PSORGs are ridden with inefficient processes and unstructured behavior. Resources are not utilized at their optimal capacities, collaboration is less then ideal, billing cycles are lengthy, project status is based on outdated information, and project costs are not managed or known with certainty—all of which leads to a less-than-productive organization and to decreased profitability. PSA solutions address these inefficiencies in much the same way that generic ERP solutions address the business processes within manufacturing organizations.

As a rising number of organizations operate under project- and service-oriented methods, establishing a streamlined and more productive approach to their core business processes is no longer optional, it is a necessity. Professional Services Automation solutions and PSA vendors are therefore addressing this need by leveraging, complementing, and enhancing the best features of customer relationship management (CRM), human resources (HR), project management, accounting, knowledge management (KM), business intelligence (BI), and ERP systems in order to deliver an integrated approach to increasing service efficiency.

The core processes that are found within most project and service engagements can be summarized in the following five-step process:

1. Manage and report demand.

2. Schedule and plan.

3. Track and charge actuals.

4. Collaborate and analyze.

5. Integrate.

These five steps can be further broken down into the following core business processes:

➤ Managing demand for projects or services

➤ Searching for, assigning, and scheduling resources

➤ Managing projects

➤ Tracking work actuals

➤ Billing or charging back

➤ Acquiring knowledge, collaboration, and communication

➤ Managing requests and other process workflows

➤ Requisitioning purchases

➤ Integrating

➤ Reporting and analysis

PSORGs have traditionally been inconsistent in evaluating their performance metrics. Are billing rates used in an optimal way? Can project costs be managed more effectively? Are resources used effectively? Can billing cycles be shortened to reduce accounts receivables (A/R) and increase cash flow? The challenge for PSA solutions is to provide functionality that delivers identifiable and measurable results to these organizations.

The return on investment for PSA solutions can be impressive and is usually realized in a short period of time. Measurable PSA results are often realized more quickly than are those obtained from implementing traditional ERP systems. The following are some of the key measurable concepts associated with implementing a PSA solution:

> **Return on Investment for PSA solutions is quick and large.**

➤ More efficient client invoicing, thus reducing A/R and increasing cash flow

➤ Improved resource utilization, productivity, and efficiency

➤ Accurate revenue recognition methods

➤ Efficiently tracking project costs for R&D or capitalization purposes

➤ Improved reporting and analysis capabilities, leading to more effective decision making

All organizations can benefit from automating their basic business processes by implementing PSAs. To gain the full benefit from their installation, it is likely that a PSORG will have to evaluate its internal processes.[4] Before evaluating external software, an organization needs to ensure that its internal business processes receive fine-tuning.

An evaluation of a PSA solution should not be focused on its features alone. The product's technology is certainly a crucial factor in determining how effective, in terms of both usability and costs, the solution will be. For example, is the solution offered with Internet capabilities? Are integrations and customizations efficient and cost effective? Does the vendor provide an SDK/API (software development kit/application programming interface)[5] in order to ensure a more efficient method of developing enhancements to the product? What databases does the vendor support? Addressing technology questions as a key focus in a PSA evaluation will lead to a better-informed decision.

Each type of PSA solution has its own strengths and limitations. One solution is not necessarily better than any other. However, some certainly shine in specific areas. Determining which areas are important to your business is key in selecting the most effective solution. In addition, evaluating all benefits, costs, and corporate risks associated in implementing a PSA solution is crucial. (Please refer to Appendix B, "Professional Services Automation Request for Proposal Template," for a template request for proposal that can be used when searching for a PSA solution.) Ensuring that your organization has effective processes already in place will assist you in implementing a PSA solution and getting the highest return on investment. Enterprise software solutions are much

> **Each type of PSA solution has its own strengths and limitations.**

---

4. Professional services automation solutions are very flexible; however, mechanizing poor internal processes may not result in an optimal organization.

5. *Software development kit* refers to a package that a vendor supplies to help the customer (usually its IS/IT organization) create interfaces, modify screens, and so on, without having to depend on the PSA vendor. Application programming interface (API) refers to entry points, or hooks, that the PSA vendor provides to the customer's IT organization to interface the PSA to the organization's own in-house systems.

more effective when the organization's business methodologies and practices are well thought-out. Many PSA vendors can provide assistance in the required business analysis and restructuring methodologies that can improve internal processes to help your business benefit the most from mechanized solutions.

We would love to hear your feedback, questions, and comments on this book. Please e-mail us at feedback@psabook.com.

Acknowledgments

This book grew out of the surprising realization that there was a lack of published information in the marketplace about the new and exciting subject of Professional Services Automation (PSA).

Working in this fast-changing area since its beginning, and working with our customers to implement these great solutions, we naturally assumed that this subject had already attracted a wide body of published work to help people navigate among the competing products, vendors, terminology, and technology.

We were surprised when we could not find much material available, so we decided to do something to correct this deficiency.

The enthusiasm to help people was contagious and quickly infected a number of our colleagues at Tenrox, who insisted on somehow finding the time during their seven-day work schedules to contribute their expertise to this project.

All of us are industry practitioners, most with management, engineering, or other technical background, so the book deliberately has a practical orientation toward helping people in our industry.

We would particularly like to thank the following people for their major contributions:

- ➤ Edwin Badalian, VP of development, and one of the founders of Tenrox, who contributed his expertise in systems development

- ➤ Rafat Hilal, chief technology officer (CTO) and one of the founders of Tenrox, who contributed his technology expertise

➤ Dave O'Brien, integration project manager, who contributed his expertise in system integration and implementation

➤ Richard Yeghiayan, director of finance, who contributed his financial expertise

➤ Thomas Kupracz, senior account executive, who offered his expertise pertaining to ERP and PSA systems

➤ Knar Laleyan, senior software engineer, who did extensive work and research on the resource management chapter

➤ Randy Urquhart, sales manager, who provided insight and guidelines for many sections of the book

➤ Edna Badalian, Eric Plouffe, and Mary Ivancic, graphic designers, for their artistic contribution to the book cover and all of its diagrams

➤ Business Objects, for reviewing and commenting on the performance analysis chapter

We would also like to thank our final prepublication reviewers Claudio Cervini, Neil Stolovitsky, Gianni Pellecchia, Mariam Saad, Johnatan Zakaib, Trisha Reid, Armine Saidi, and Noam Schnitzer, who assisted extensively with proofreading and content reviews.

Everyone else at Tenrox helped in some way with the preparation of this book, and we would like to thank them all.

Finally, we would like to thank our families for putting up with our having to spend even more time away from them to work on this new project.

Professional
Services
Automation

Part

1

What Are PSA, SPO, ESM, SRM, ESA, and BPA?

> **PSA solutions automate and integrate core business processes with the intent of increasing project productivity and profitability.**

Regardless of the acronym used, whether it is PSA, SPO, SRM, or any other variation, they all refer to the same thing. Their ultimate goal is also the same: Maximize the performance of project- and service-oriented organizations (PSORGs) and their staff.

These solutions automate and integrate core business processes with the intent of increasing project productivity and profitability for these specialized organizations. The challenge for PSORGs in evaluating such solutions lies not only in understanding the need to streamline their own processes, but also in analyzing the software solutions from the many vendors offering different variations of PSA solutions.

BPA	Business process automation
ESA	Enterprise service automation
ESM	Enterprise service management
PSA	Professional services automation
SPO	Service process optimization
SRM	Service relationship management

PSA solutions streamline the processes of winning the business or contract, staffing the project, managing the engagement, successfully implementing the project, and finally collecting payment for services rendered.[1]

This book's goal is to assist readers in identifying the key concepts of PSA solutions and the features these solutions provide in order to deliver measurable results to organizations that implement them.

---

1. Often the engagement also has an ongoing component because additional work is often required after the project is formally completed. This includes support and periodic enhancements, which must also be sized, managed, and billed.

Chapter *1*

Managing the Service Supply Chain

■ INTRODUCTION

A considerable amount of literature and software is available regarding supply chain management (SCM), enterprise resource planning (ERP), and customer relationship management (CRM). Enterprise Resource Planning and SCM are primarily back-office applications that focus on accounting, inventory, order processing (fulfillment) and procurement, whereas CRM software mostly addresses front-office needs such as opportunity management, marketing campaigns, call center management, and customer service.

PSA software provides the tools, techniques, and technology that enable project- and service-oriented organizations (PSORGs) to manage personnel, resources, projects, and clients.

Many medium- to large-sized companies utilize single-vendor software systems called ERPs to centralize and manage some of their core business processes. Enterprise Resource Planning software provides accounting, human resources (HR), inventory, procurement, and order-processing functionality. The major benefit of an ERP system is that it provides an integrated solution that can be used in conjunction with reporting tools to gain insight into the company's operations.

The major ERP vendors tend to be perceived as having different strengths and weaknesses when compared with each other (e.g., some emphasize their strength in the industrial sector, whereas others focus their strength in providing HR department functionality). In some cases, major enterprises have installed *multiple* ERPs to gain the benefit of some of these features—that is, they try to get the best features from each offering. In these cases, as we shall see later, these enterprises are essentially following what we call the best-of-breed approach to software solutions.

Traditional enterprise systems such as ERPs and SCMs have focused on the manufacturing and distribution sectors where they originated. The dramatic expansion of the service industry in the last decade has led to many service organizations' trying to apply these traditional ERPs outside of their conventional homes (which is typically in accounting and HR departments) often with mixed results.

This situation has often created the worst of all possible worlds, in which the enterprise is running powerful and expensive ERP systems for the accounting or HR departments, leaving the revenue-producing parts of the organizations like professional services to mechanize themselves in a haphazard manner with spreadsheets and paper, or to attempt building an in-house system. This can lead to situations in which the back-office costs are increasing due to the expensive systems the functional support groups like finance are running, while the front-line groups (who are the ones generating the revenue) suffer from an almost complete lack of productivity and mechanization tools. Essentially, these organizations have produced a situation in which the back-office functions and systems are driving the front-line, revenue-producing part of the organization, instead of the other way around—not an optimal situation. Please refer to Appendix D, "Professional Services Automation and Enterprise Resource Planning," for more details.

> The enterprise is running powerful ERP systems for accounting or HR departments, while the revenue producing teams, like professional services, mechanize themselves in a haphazard manner with spreadsheets and paper.

Due to the continued aggressive adoption of information technology (IT), increased competition, increased customer expectations, globalization, scarcity of skilled resources, and technological innovations, service organizations are under constant pressure to maximize revenues, minimize project costs, produce more measurable results, improve productivity, and increase customer satisfaction. In addition, using systems such as ERPs, independent project management tools, in-house applications, spreadsheets, or paper-based systems are no longer to be viewed as effective methods for increasing productivity for PSORGs.

Much like manufacturing or distribution companies, service organizations have their own unique business processes. If software applications are to be implemented in order to streamline such processes, then the functionality these applications adopt must focus on the project life cycle.

Some of the unique requirements for PSORGs are dictated by whether their projects are for cost centers (nonbillable and based on budgets) or profit centers. Most IT departments are engaged in internal software development, engineering, R&D, and product design, and they only serve internal *clients*. The projects and services implemented for these internal clients are based on corporate budgetary constraints and is nonbillable work. Some PSORGs perform work for external *clients,* and usually perform their billing based on various rating algorithms.

> Some of the unique requirements for PSORGs are dictated by whether their projects are for cost centers (nonbillable and based on budgets) or profit centers.

Regardless of whether the work is being done for internal or external clients, the focal point is on implementing the project or service; as such, several questions need to be addressed. How can organizations

➤ Manage to deliver projects on time and within budget?

➤ Ensure that proper resources are in place to deliver such projects?

➤ Effectively report on project information in real time?

➤ Ensure that project information is accessible at all times by anyone?

➤ Ensure that employees focus on core responsibilities rather than administrative tasks?

➤ Efficiently manage the life cycle of a service or project engagement?

➤ Streamline their key service or project processes for greater productivity?

The fact is that very few PSORGs efficiently deliver their services. Due to increased industry complexities and inefficient corporate processes, service workers are not focusing on their key responsibilities. They are instead being bombarded with increasing amounts of administrative tasks, technology issues, unmanaged workloads, and lack of information. There is therefore a great need and an ever-increasing demand for software applications that can render PSORGs more productive and more profitable.

For a discussion of deploying a commercially available PSA solution versus building it in-house, please refer to Appendix C, "In-House Software."

■ PRESENTING PSA SOLUTIONS

Professional Services Automation (PSA) describes a set of software solutions that have been designed specifically for PSORGs. These solutions streamline business processes for these organizations. They automate and integrate core business processes so that organizations within these industries can increase productivity and profitability.

> **Professional services automation streamlines, automates, and integrates the delivery of projects and services.**

Project- and service-oriented organizations are ridden with inefficient processes and behavior (see Figure 1.1). Resources are not utilized at their optimal capacities, collaboration is less than ideal, billing cycles are lengthy, project status is based on outdated information, and project costs are not managed or known with certainty—all of which lead to a less-than-productive organization and decreased profitability. Professional Services Automation solutions address these inefficiencies

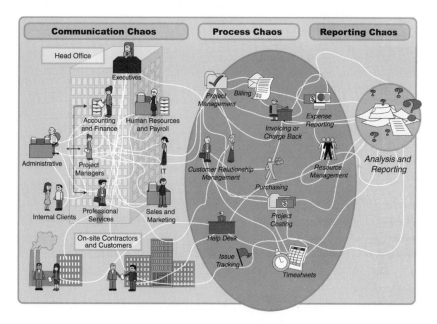

Figure 1.1 Before Professional Services Automation

in much the same way that ERP solutions address the business processes for more traditional industries.[1]

As an increasing number of organizations operate under project- and service-oriented methods,[2] establishing a streamlined and more productive approach for core business processes is no longer simply nice to have, it is a necessity. Professional Services Automation solutions and vendors are therefore addressing this need by leveraging, complementing, and enhancing the required or best features of CRM, HR, project management, and accounting or ERP

---

1. Enterprise resource management solutions are generally used for the most stable back-office functions, such as general ledger creation and other basic accounting functions. Their implementation is also often tailored to the sponsoring department, often finance. Having an ERP customized to service finance needs is a problem for PSORGs, which require a more responsive information system to manage their project engagements.

2. Project-oriented methods often refer to organizing work, budgets, and human resources around the concept of delivering a project as a mission, then disbanding immediately after the project is completed.

systems in order to deliver an integrated approach to service efficiency.[3]

■ BENEFITS

Because PSA solutions streamline the life cycles of project and service engagements, how can executives determine the benefits and measurable results their organizations can derive from implementing a PSA solution?

PSORGs have traditionally been inconsistent in evaluating their performance metrics. Are billing rates used in an optimal way? Can project costs be managed more effectively? Are resources used effectively? Is employee collaboration optimal for improved project results? Can billing cycles be improved in order to reduce accounts receivable? Organizations implementing projects and offering services are focusing on corporate and process efficiency more than ever. Both areas are essential because services comprise an enormous portion of many modern businesses, and the pressure for high performance and efficiency is higher than ever.[4] The challenge for PSA solutions is to provide, in a quick fashion, functionality that delivers positive, identifiable, and measurable results to these organizations.

> The challenge for PSA solutions is to provide in a quick fashion functionality that delivers positive, identifiable, and measurable results

The ultimate benefits of PSA solutions are increased productivity and profitability within a short period of time. The ability to achieve such benefits is based on the productivity of the company's resources and the technology used in order to perform projects or services more effectively. Specific benefits include the following:

---

3. Professional services automation solutions are optimized to deliver the functionality required by PSORGs.

4. In the last decade, there has been constant pressure to increase performance and profitability. Enterprises are constantly reducing and reorganizing staff during good times and especially during bad times. Tools that enhance productivity are always required.

➤ Increased employee productivity through more focused work

➤ More opportunities due to improved resource management

➤ More effective resource utilization and retention

> The ultimate benefits of PSA solutions are increased productivity and profitability within a short period of time.

➤ Improved client satisfaction due to quicker and more complete billing and lower project costs

➤ Overall operational efficiency

➤ Maximization of billable revenues

➤ Improved reporting capabilities for more effective decision making

➤ Quicker measurable results

All such benefits lead towards greatly improving profitability.

■ HOW CAN MY ORGANIZATION BENEFIT FROM A PSA SOLUTION?

All organizations can benefit from automating their basic business processes (see Figure 1.2). Internal business processes such as opportunity management, resource management, project management, purchasing, expense reporting, timesheet management, and many others are not fully mechanized in most organizations. To gain the full benefit of this mechanization, the organization will have to review its processes and structure them so that mechanization is not inhibited. As can be seen from the ROI sections that follow, significant savings are to be realized in *non–re-engineered organizations.*[5]

---

5. If PSORGs were actually re-engineered, the corresponding benefits would be that much greater, because some of the mechanized benefits would not be squandered on inefficient manual organizational processes.

The following chapters further examine the large return on investment and benefits that result with the introduction of PSA solutions in PSORGs.

In evaluating how an organization will benefit from a PSA solution, certain key questions should be asked. How will the organization benefit from

➤ Increased employee collaboration to deliver projects and service clients?

➤ Capturing all project-related costs quickly and accurately?

➤ Accurately and quickly generating billable information at a level of detail and format demanded by clients?

➤ Streamlining project-related business processes so that clients can be serviced more efficiently?

➤ Improved management of project portfolios (e.g., resource allocation and utilization, status, costs, billings)?

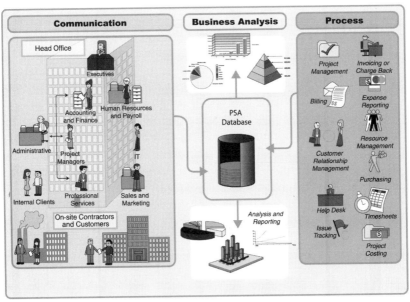

Figure 1.2 After Professional Services Automation

As can be seen from the figure in the introduction to the next part, showing the complete Professional Services Automation cycle, the services provided by a PSA solution cover the whole range of service and project delivery.

One of the key benefits associated with implementing a PSA solution is the improvement of billable cycles. Increasing billing efficiencies reduces A/R days and improves financial liquidity, which is a clear benefit to most organizations.[6] Another key benefit is the improved management and utilization of resources. Ensuring that resources are scheduled and utilized on appropriate projects is also a clear benefit to all PSORGs.

---

6. This topic is covered further in later chapters. The ability to bill faster on a sustained basis will be seen to result in considerable savings to PSORGs providing billable services.

Chapter 2

Streamlining Business Processes

Professional Services Automation solutions streamline business processes for PSORGs. This section describes the core processes that are found within most service engagements and ways in which PSA solutions go about streamlining them.

Which processes are improved?

> *Managing demand for projects or services:* The first process in any service engagement is the management, identification, and tracking of potential projects, opportunities, leads, and proposals. PSA solutions enable organizations to better manage, qualify, and prioritize demand for projects and services.

The processes of managing demand, resource management, project management, tracking actuals, billing or charge back, knowledge acquisition, tracking requests, purchases, integration, and reporting are improved.

> *Searching for, assigning, and scheduling resources:* After requirements have been identified for approved projects, the next step is to match the requirements with the resources necessary to satisfy them. This is a complicated process; PSA solutions provide improved tracking, deployment, skill matching, availability

matching, and prioritizing of resources to a given service engagement.

➤ *Managing projects:* PSA solutions ensure that information pertaining to project status, tasks, assignments, objectives, and time frames is easily accessible and measurable by authorized personnel. These solutions enable increased collaboration and communication; they also improve management and tracking of overall project status.

- *Tracking work actuals:* During any service engagement, the ability to accurately capture and track time and expense information and their associated approval is very valuable. These *actuals* provide the information necessary to determine and analyze project profitability and efficiency. Professional Services Automation solutions significantly streamline these traditionally labor-intensive and error-prone processes, thereby rapidly improving productivity, cash flow, and compliance with enterprise and industry rules and regulations. The more efficient this tracking process becomes, the greater the positive impact on efficient project delivery and financial liquidity.

- *Billing*: After actuals have been accumulated, the process of accurately and efficiently converting billable time and expenses into detailed invoices follows. Professional Services Automation solutions streamline this process by enabling actuals to be converted into professional invoices at the level of detail required by the customer. The PSA not only facilitates this information to be quickly and accurately captured and assigned, but also makes all this information completely auditable. Thus, mechanization allows clients (be it internal or external) to receive detailed, accurate invoices quickly.

- *Acquiring knowledge, collaboration, and communication:* Within an organization, and certainly during service engagements, the accessibility of information, documents, best practice methodologies, templates, libraries, and other pertinent information improves performance and produc-

Streamlining Business Processes ➤ 15

tivity. A PSA solution enables a streamlined approach to capturing, sharing, and retrieving relevant documentation.

- *Handling requests:* Within a service engagement, unforeseen issues and requests appear regularly.[1] The manner in which organizations typically process these requests is through a combination of e-mail messages, calendar to-do lists, phone calls, and voice mails. This style of communication is neither methodical nor traceable, and therefore results in lowered productivity and effectiveness. Certain PSA solutions streamline this process by managing all requests and issues pertaining to a service engagement. Requests can be prioritized, resolved, alert-triggered, approved, and analyzed efficiently, thereby improving productivity and performance.

- *Purchase requisitions:* During a service engagement, purchase orders are usually required to ask for additional staff, training, equipment or material. Some PSA solutions offer purchase workflows to reduce the administrative costs of creating and approving purchase requests, issuing the purchase orders, and getting the orders filled.

- *Integrating:* In most large organizations, PSA systems do not exist in a vacuum. Often, other important information systems must be integrated with PSA systems, in particular CRM, HR, project management, accounting, and ERP systems. Often, multiple *brands* of each of these systems[2] may be within a single enterprise, making the integration

---

1. Some examples include requests for increased scope, increased complexity, additional reporting, recycling of requirements, and so forth.

2. Some enterprises have consciously implemented multiple-vendor ERPs to take advantage of the best characteristics of some of them. In particular, some ERPs are considered better for their mature HR functionality, whereas others are known for their well-developed financial modules. In addition, enterprises that engage in corporate acquisitions can also end up with mulitvendor ERP installations, as well as multiple installations of the same vendor's ERP, that are configured in such a vastly different way that they appear to be completely different products with completely different user interfaces, workflow rules, procedures, and so on.

of the PSA system, and indeed all applications, nontrivial. This complexity is especially prevalent in organizations that grow by acquisitions; in such organizations, multiple and incompatible systems are acquired, integrated, discarded, and modified on a regular basis.

- *Reporting:* The difficulty for most organizations is not in acquiring the data, but rather is in creating knowledge out of the large amounts of data being collected. Most organizations with unsophisticated reporting capabilities can only access bits and pieces of project information. For example, often important cost information is not easily related to project status, customer contractual SLA (service level agreement) requirements, or actuals versus forecasted information. PSA solutions provide real-time access to business metrics pertaining to project status, activities, utilization, clients, requests, revenues, costs, or any other information. PSA solutions also offer the flexibility of generating detailed reports through popular report writers and business intelligence, online analytical processing (OLAP) tools. Organizations easily access real-time and detailed project information in either a graphic or textual format, enabling more effective decision-making

■ USER BENEFITS

This section describes the benefits of modern PSA solutions for PSORGs from the perspective of the various communities inside and outside the enterprise, including clients, sales staff, customer contact staff, administrative staff, professional services staff, finance staff, project managers, IT teams, and executives. All these groups have different needs, and PSAs have evolved to provide each group with the right amount of functionality to ensure the efficient execution of their tasks. For example, they minimize the amount of overhead imposed on the individual professionals in having to enter data into the PSA system, while providing a great amount of status-reporting power to project managers, and a great amount of analysis power to the executive community.

Professional Services Automation tools have evolved into state-of-the-art, easy-to-use, and full-featured scalable solutions that can be used by large or small enterprises.

Modern PSA products offer a wide feature set, including the following:

➤ Opportunity and engagement management

➤ Resource management

➤ Purchasing, revenue, and cost accounting

➤ Timesheet management and expense reporting

➤ Invoicing and charge back

➤ Problem reporting and tracking

➤ Performance analysis

> **Professional services automation solutions offer a wide range of specialized functionality to key groups involved in product and service delivery.**

Clearly, PSAs offer benefits to almost every functional area of any enterprise.

Providing functionality to so many groups within the organization presents a great opportunity to increase the communication and accuracy of the information everyone shares. Conversely, it also raises the importance of having accurate information and well-integrated systems; this confirms the importance of proper selection, installation, and integration of a best-of-breed software that interoperates with the organization's internal production systems.

The principal user communities of a full-featured modern PSA are the following:

➤ Sales and customer contact staff

➤ External and internal clients

➤ General administrative staff (nonbillable resources)

➤ Professional services staff

➤ Finance department

➤ Project managers

➤ IS/IT department

➤ Executive staff

➤ Sales and Customer Contact Staff

Modern PSA solutions offer sales staff the ability to create and manage their opportunity pipelines. They make it possible to log customer contact information, track estimated value of an opportunity, assign probabilities, track sales staff, deal status, track related notes or e-mails, attend to other opportunity details, and calculate time frames.

Like all other PSA information, this data is securely stored in a central database, which is easily updated and accessed by sales staff, sales managers, and business unit leaders, as well as by managers and all other authorized personnel.

> **Professional services automation offers a consolidated and centralized customer view over the whole project life cycle.**

Having the PSA solution used from the start of the sales process provides a central point for all customer information to be stored. As more information is collected, it is automatically cross-referenced to the existing data and made immediately available for querying and reporting.

This process allows a fully consolidated customer view that is always available to all authorized users during the ongoing relationship with a customer or throughout the entire life cycle of a customer relationship, from the initial discussion stages to contract signing, project planning, implementation, and support, as well as any vendor-initiated follow-ups.

This type of integration provides the sales team and executives an extensive and comprehensive view of customers, especially the most important ones—Who are they? What engagements are outstanding with them? What revenues and costs are associated with the customer? What are the problems reported and their resolutions? Who are the key contacts? The list goes on and on.

In addition, because the centralized PSA data repository is already tracking the customer from the first sales call to final implementation of a solution, it is natural for the customer contact or help desk personnel to also use it, and therefore to also benefit from this same consolidated customer view. For example, the customer contact representatives can quickly retrieve the complete customer record (or at least all of the information they are authorized to see) and update the new customer request, as well as create tickets.[3]

This ticket is automatically cross-referenced to existing customer data, and it becomes immediately available to other interested parties within the PSORG, such as the following:

➤ Account managers, who are usually interested in any important occurrences relevant to their customers

➤ Professional services managers, who may be delivering functionality or performing integration for the customer

➤ Product development staff, who may be interested in failures or problems that the customer is experiencing with the product or services

➤ Clients

Professional Services Automation clients can actually be external clients to the enterprise that must be billed periodically, or internal clients who pay for the professional services they consume via an internal corporate budgeting process.

> **Professional services automation provides functionality for internal clients (such as other divisions/departments) and external clients.**

For both types of customers, PSA solutions offer the same level of centralized tracking and reporting. In most cases, opportunity management, engagement management, and cost and revenue accounting will probably not be used for internal clients. However, most of the other PSA functions are likely to be equally important for both categories of organizations.

---

3. A *ticket* is a record that tracks the customer request through the whole cycle, from initial contact to problem resolution. It is often created by an inbound call center's customer relationship management (CRM) software system in response to a customer-reported problem.

External Clients

External clients are being granted increasing access to their own information, principally to tickets the PSORG call center created for them. For example, they can sometimes examine the status of their requests, problems, bugs, and so on. However, the main interface between and PSORG and its external clients continues to be the billing functions of the organization's PSA solution.

A PSA solution allows the service provider to collect all relevant charges accurately. In addition, it provides the rating flexibility required to properly calculate the professional services invoice.

Professional service invoicing can represent a complicated and involved exercise that may have to use a variety of *rating rules* to calculate the proper billing. For example, rating may depend on the following:

➤ The activity

➤ The project

➤ The client

➤ The task

➤ The employee

In addition, the charges may be based on the following rates:

➤ Project fixed rates

➤ Activity fixed rates

➤ User custom rates

➤ User daily rates

➤ User fixed rates

As described previously, a lot of rating information potentially must be taken into consideration before the PSORG could properly invoice the external client.

Because of the increasing complexity and specialized nature of the rating challenges associated with professional services, PSA solutions have evolved to include sophisticated rating and billing capabilities.

In addition to performing all the proper invoicing calculations, the software also provides a mechanized *invoicing workflow*[4], one of the many customizable workflows PSAs offer to ensure that the invoice is always properly created, approved, and issued. This workflow ensures that all the individual steps required to process the invoice are properly followed.

A PSA solution is in a position to bill the external client accurately by providing the exact amount of detail requested.

Internal Clients

Internal clients of the professional services organization can usually be offered extensive project information because there are few (if any) security concerns, and in fact there are often organizational directives requiring the enterprise's central project management office (PMO),[5] as well as its business unit's PMO, to have full access to all project status and cost information.

Among the most important internal clients of PSAs are the PMOs of semi-autonomous business units that have profit and loss responsibility; they require information from a wide variety of corporate sources. A PSA offers these PMOs powerful control and reporting capability interfacing to all of the important sources of information, principally ERPs and legacy applications.

The internal client PMO groups are often very sophisticated and fully utilize almost all of PSA functionality.

> **Among the most important internal clients of the PSA are the project management organizations of semiautonomous business units that have profit and loss responsibility.**

---

4. A *work flow* is a mechanized series of steps that the process must follow before it is completed. At key steps in the work flow, various people (usually managers) have to approve the process before the work flow is allowed to progress to the next step.

5. Often, a large organization has multiple project management offices (PMOs). Typically, every large department or business unit has its own, which feeds and receives data from the corporate-level PMO, which reports to the senior corporate executives.

These PMO business units are also among the heaviest users of business intelligence (OLAP) functionality; this is not surprising because they are juggling internal deliverables to and from various departments (e.g., their internal IT), as well as managing external suppliers, all for the purpose of providing a product or service to an external client that will be charged for the work.

Internal clients of PSORGs, at a minimum, are provided with project charges, deliverables, and milestones; in practice, however, they often demand and acquire much more information.

➤ General Administrative Staff

Nonbillable resources with administrative duties reap significant benefits from a PSA solution. Without a PSA solution, the general administrative (GA) staff has to deal with laborious, repetitive, manual, error-prone, and paper-intensive processes that often lead to high overhead costs, frustrations, unmotivated employees, delays, and bottlenecks.

Professional Services Automation solutions eliminate most (if not all) of the repetitive tasks and alleviate the need to use paper or e-mails for entry or approval processes, leading to a more motivated, organized, and agile administrative team.

General administrative staff role changes from paper shuffling, e-mail processing, and repetitive data entering to the more sophisticated role of educating users, defining policies, identifying best practices, and automating administrative work using the PSA solution.

➤ Professional Services Staff

The professional staff of an organization is the department that actually delivers the service to the internal or external clients. This necessary activity often results in paying the professional (employee or consultant), as well as billing the client; this is particularly important when dealing with external clients.[6]

Professional Services Automation provides the staff with the

---

6. In some cases, the employee delivering the services would be better called administrative or nonprofessional staff. Regardless of classification, however, the organization's interest would lie in minimizing data entry and other overhead associated with the staff using the PSA solution for time and expense capture.

most powerful functionality available on the marketplace to help ensure that the required project information is captured accurately, punctually, and with a minimum of overhead.

Professional Services Automation makes this task as easy as possible by providing access from a variety of data entry devices, including e-mail, browsers, wireless phones, and PDAs (personal digital assistants).[7] The intent is to provide access from almost anywhere in a secure and efficient manner.

> **Professional services automation makes it possible for the professional staff to enter the required data from anywhere.**

The service delivery users can bill for completed work, and they are automatically reminded to close and submit their timesheets and expenses promptly following whatever cycle has been agreed upon with the client. In addition to the service delivery, professionals can be granted access to the details of the engagements and projects, or to a subset created by their manager. These approved work items and activities automatically appear on their schedules, where they can view the items the instant they log into the system.

Professional staff simply have to log into the PSA solution, and they are provided with a list of the approved activities to which they are assigned. On such a list they can quickly update the status and charges, and immediately return to the essential tasks at hand.

A PSA tool conceals a considerable amount of complexity from the professional staff. Certainly a simple project with a minimal list of activities and managed by a single project manager for a single user, in which the staff is charging all of their time to a single budget, does not offer much complexity.

However, it is not unusual to have staff members work on a number of activities across a number of projects, with different project managers, with variable charges, and with different budgets.

In this case, as in the simple situation, the professional staff again only has to log into the PSA and fill in all the automatically presented information regarding all of the preconfigured projects,

---

7. Personal digital assistants come in many styles and with many capabilities. Some of the most powerful for this type of use would have wireless connectivity.

activities, and so on, to which they have been assigned by their project managers.

► Finance Department

The finance department is an important beneficiary of modern PSA solutions. The benefits span the whole finance organization, with particular impact on the billing and payroll groups. The dramatic reduction in actual physical paper necessary to track, approve, and archive information is a great benefit.

> **Professional services automation offers important benefits to finance groups— reduction in paperwork, accurate data, and mechanized interfacing to accounting systems.**

The PSA system provides an automated method to enter data for time and expenses for exactly the correct project activity; the data is then routed automatically via their own workflow for proper approval, in turn updating the central database of project charges. Therefore, errors and delays associated with such things as manual activities, rekeying, manual rating, and calculations are eliminated.

Because a modern PSA also provides numerous methods for submitting the data (e.g., Internet access, mechanically readable e-mail forms, wireless access), the user is provided with ample means to enter the information accurately and promptly.

In addition, because only approved project items may be billed, and all time (e.g., misappropriated time, unexplained absenteeism, unreasonably long lunches, late arrivals, early departures, charges to the wrong project) must be accounted for, misused time is greatly reduced.

Because the PSA system is tailored and optimized for PSORGs, it is preconfigured to carry the data at the level of detail that project managers, customers, and PMO groups require.[8] The data is then summarized properly to the usually much higher level required by the finance group and their accounting or ERP systems; this benefits all parties involved because the project-delivery and revenue-generating professional services teams have what they need to

---

8. Project delivery teams must have access to the level of detail *they* need to do their jobs, as well as a billing system that provides the rating and summary capabilities to provide the customers with the invoicing they demand.

carry out their projects, whereas the finance groups do not have to disrupt or reconfigure their accounting and ERP systems to provide the flexibility and details the professional services teams require in their PSORG tracking and support systems.

➤ Accounting Department

Because the organization is not dealing with any paper and because all information is formally approved via workflows, the database containing time and charges (among other things), can be trusted as precise. It can be safely used to feed other mechanized systems, and can be used for automated reconciliation, accruals, financial reports, and revenue recognition, as well as to speed up month-end and quarter-end processing.

In addition, because all the information related to activities is mechanized rather than paper-based, any archiving requirements related to government, taxes, research and development credits, special funding, regulations, or other legal requirements can be easily implemented.

The accounting group derives great benefit from being able to properly bill external clients quickly and accurately. In addition, having all the raw information in a central database allows mechanized accounts receivable systems to perform whatever validation is required.

Professional Services Automation software allows the invoice history to be tracked so that accurate and timely information can be provided to finance, sales, marketing, and project management groups regarding the billing status for any customer quickly and easily. In addition, because modern database and reporting, including OLAP tools, are being used, the information is reported in a visual, friendly, and usable manner.

The PSA database also allows easy centralized tracking of any issues that arise that may affect customer satisfaction and billing; it also allows these issues to be quickly forwarded to the responsible group for resolution, and makes it possible for that group to update the central repository with the resolution. Essentially, the organization is using modern technology to eliminate paperwork; to validate all documents and data used for decision making, auditing, and billing; and to ensure that any client, partner, or employee issues are recorded and resolved. The data can then be quickly exported into the organization's accounting or ERP system if necessary.

➤ Payroll Administrators

The payroll group within finance has its responsibilities greatly simplified by a modern PSA solution. They can eliminate the cumbersome task of manipulating paper, spreadsheets, or e-mail timesheets and expense reports. All the data is collected, validated, and entered into the PSA database; it is then sent to the payroll system with minimum to no manual intervention.

Out of the box, modern PSA systems provide for automatic reconciliation of payroll to submitted time; they also validate all required business rules, such as auditing, holidays, and administrative tasks, as well as work, shift, and overtime policies. PSA solutions should also ensure that timesheets, expense reports, and all other corporate documents conform to government regulations (e.g., the United States Defense Contract Audit Agency (DCAA), European time directives, France's Loi des 35 heures, California wage laws and Quebec Government Horaire Variable and FDA's Code of Federal Regulations (CFR) 21 Part 11).

Payroll administrators are able to control exceptions such as making adjustments, and also able to enforce corporate overtime rules, pager/on-call policies, and other such rules. The data can then be quickly processed by the internal payroll system or sent to a payroll outsourcer.

➤ Project Managers

Project managers are key users of a PSA system. They are the ones who define and manage critical parts of the organization and work breakdown structures, as well as plan and track the work of service professionals. They define the budgets that will fund the activities, validate and approve time and expenses, and are the resources that approve purchases required for the projects (within their budget and authorization limits).

> **Project managers are key PSA users— projects are planned, budgeted, tracked, reported on, and billed using the PSA solution.**

In those situations in which it makes sense for the system to automatically generate predefined data and make automatic submissions, project managers have the functionality available to make it happen.

In addition, in places where many project managers are sharing the same set of service professionals, each manager has the ability to approve or reject items at the activity level (also known as line item approval) that belong to their respective projects.

Naturally, all the information submitted, accumulated, and stored in the PSA database is accessible by project managers at any time. In addition, because the software is tightly linked to other internal enterprise tools such as office tools, ERPs, and payroll systems, the typical paperwork load that burdens most project managers is dramatically reduced.

Therefore, PSA solutions provide project managers with sophisticated project tracking and reporting capabilities while dramatically reducing the amount of time and paperwork required for day-to-day management, follow-up, and operations.

➤ Information Technology Department

The IT department is the group that provides computer services to the enterprise. It is usually budget driven and achieves minimal to no billable work outside of the enterprise. Therefore, it is usually a very large and visible cost center. It is usually under pressure to *do more with less,* and do it quickly; this includes doing less in-house custom development, which has a history of being both difficult to produce on time and expensive to maintain. Often the first installation of a simplified PSA solution is for the IT organization itself to manage and control its own projects' costs.

> IT departments do not do any external billable work, but are often the first group to implement a PSA — to manage their projects/resources.

A PSA solution offers the IT department an opportunity to rapidly deliver advanced, cost-effective functionality, while using the department's own limited personnel on assignments that directly add to the organization's primary business or *core competency.*[9]

---

9. Most enterprises do not like spending money or time on doing anything outside their identified *core competency,* which usually refers to that enterprise's main business focus. They also often require their internal IS/IT staff to concentrate their efforts and take advantage of the very competitive marketplace in prepackaged commercial applications.

Information technology departments cannot be expected to be domain experts in all software the enterprise deploys, and certainly not for solutions that are evolving as rapidly as PSAs. Using a commercial solution, the IT personnel can instead concentrate on mastering the PSA's business intelligence (OLAP) tools or its software development kit (SDK) to customize and integrate the solution with existing production applications, ensuring that all the required data can be captured, all the required reports made, and OLAP analysis produced. In this light, the internal systems group can concentrate on producing results for their end users, rather than embarking on a multiple-year development effort to reproduce something that can be simply purchased commercially.

In addition, because IT is usually not the primary focus of many organizations, systems engineers are often faced with limited career opportunities, thereby leading to frequent IT staff changes. Using commercial solutions for its noncore functions allows an enterprise to protect itself by deploying its limited number of senior resources to its most critical, or *core*, areas.

Furthermore, many advanced PSAs offer knowledge management functions that allow IT staff to very quickly gain more expertise in managing the application, and they often provide self-service functionality directly to the end user.

For a discussion of deploying a commercially available PSA solution versus building in-house, please refer to Appendix C, "In-House Software."

➤ Executives

Executives and others with a profit and loss responsibility are among the heaviest users of PSA business intelligence (OLAP) functionality. Naturally as the span of control and financial responsibility grows, it becomes increasingly important to quickly identify and manage trends, slipping financial indicators, customer satisfaction, opportunity closings, billing issues, revenue timing overhead, margins, and so forth.

> Executives with profit and loss or budget responsibility are heavy users of business intelligence-OLAP tools.

In many cases, especially in large enterprises, specialized tools will be already in place to perform some of this financial modeling, executive information reporting, profitability analysis, head-count analysis, project status, exception reporting, and so on. Very often, all these inputs are packaged for the executive and referred to as an *executive dashboard.*

Often these tools are so customized to the business and culture of the enterprise that they are custom-built systems, using what were powerful tools—back when the systems were first assembled (surprisingly, they are often based on spreadsheets, are time consuming to generate, and provide inconsistent and out-of-date information). In any case, PSA solutions can be configured to be the core executive dashboard, or to provide feeds into other enterprise systems.

Of course, modern systems have a lot to offer: the data that reside on relational databases can be easily loaded into OLAP systems, providing many preprogrammed or ad hoc views of the data, from individual small projects to enterprise-wide results.

Modern PSA solutions provide today's enterprises with numerous tangible and intangible benefits throughout the organization. They can track a customer from the initial contact stages, to concluding a contract, to installation, to production and support. They integrate with call center, customer relationship management and ticketing systems, and in some cases provide their own CRM and ticketing functionality.

They minimize administrative overhead and maximize the billable time of service professionals that carry out the work. The systems provide a wide variety of means for professionals to submit time, expenses and statuses using the Internet, wireless communication, and e-mail. Numerous predefined and custom-created workflows can ensure that all charges, documents, budgets, and activities are approved by the proper managers, even if approval is required at the line-item level and by multiple managers.

They offer the professional service provider with sophisticated rating capability as well as powerful bill- or charge-back preparation functionally to ensure accurate and detailed invoicing; at the granularity, the customer requires it.

Finally, PSAs provide powerful business intelligence (OLAP) capability that allows managers (especially senior managers) with profit and loss responsibility to gain insight into the operations of their enterprise.

■ HOW PROFESSIONAL SERVICES AUTOMATION SOLUTIONS FIT VARIOUS INDUSTRIES

Professional services automation solutions have served to optimize an increasing number of consulting organizations and internal IT divisions or departments. PSA solutions are broadly designed systems with many modules and features. Just like ERP solutions, PSA solutions are not equally powerful in every module; organizations that are looking for such a solution should determine which PSA components are important to them and which will yield the most savings and efficiencies.

Professional services automation software can be a powerful tool for organizations operating in many industries. The following section describes how PSAs fit within each industry, as well as the key benefits and features of a PSA that help an organization streamline and optimize its business processes.

Professional Services Automation solutions have the two following primary objectives:

1. Automate companies that perform services for external clients by mechanizing the process of data collection, approval, reimbursement, payable tracking, resource management, and invoice generation.

2. Make internal divisions and departments of larger organizations operate like business units. These departments then charge back the parent organization for the work performed.

Ultimately, PSA solutions allow organizations to reduce the effort required for invoicing (or charge back) by maximizing resource usage and cutting administrative overhead. This results in substantial productivity, efficiency, and profitability gains. PSA solutions automate business processes by implementing workflows to better track and deliver engagements.

The distinction between invoicing and charge back is described in the following section on key features. The industry sections specify whether PSA use within an industry would be for invoicing, charge back, or both.

Every industry must conform to a myriad of rules and regulations. Professional Services Automation solutions help organizations automate, streamline, enforce, and validate their compliance to these regulations. In addition, by using powerful built-in reporting and analytical tools, organizations are able to efficiently prepare for audits, improve the decision making process, and perform hypothetical analysis.

The following industries are covered: content creation and delivery, energy and natural resources, financial services, health care, high tech, pharmaceuticals, professional services, public sector, and telecommunications.

➤ Energy and Natural Resources

The energy sector routinely experiences large price fluctuations and sudden increases in supply or demand depending on politics, regulations, economic conditions, and seasonal effects. Because energy-related revenue is influenced by many external factors, organizations operating in this space need to pay close attention to their operating overhead and project-related expenses.

Organizations operating in this sector include the following:

- ➤ Fossil fuel energy: exploration of oil and gas, oil and gas refineries, oil drilling or planning, petroleum products, operation of gas fields, coal producers

- ➤ Nuclear energy: nuclear power plants

- ➤ Renewable energy: organization involved in developing solar/thermal, wind, and hydropower energy production

- ➤ Electric utilities

Key Benefits

PSA software has the following benefits for energy and natural resource enterprises:

- ➤ Identifies and decreases project expenses and purchases

- ➤ Optimizes the hiring of staff and project related purchasing process by using web-based technologies

- ➤ Reduces overhead by automating administrative tasks and redundant activities

➤ Increases project and purchasing visibility

➤ Tracks spending and monitors AFE (accredited financial examiner) and budget adherence

➤ Uses data visualization tools to pinpoint problems, to identify trends and best practices, and to make forecasts for strategic planning

Key Features

The following are the primary PSA modules that can help streamline an energy or natural resources organization:

➤ Staff and project purchasing

➤ Cost and revenue accounting

➤ Timesheet management, labor management, expense reporting

➤ Charge back

➤ Request tracking

➤ Help desk duties

➤ Document management

➤ Knowledge management

➤ Performance analysis

➤ Integration

➤ Financial Services

Globalization and deregulation are just some of the sweeping changes in the financial sector. Globalization of financial services implies support for multicurrency, multiregional taxation, and other local features by the organization's enterprise software. With the emergence of large new competitors from nontraditional market sectors, financial services organizations have to respond even more quickly to market changes and customer trends.

Financial services include accounting, banking, insurance, brokerages, financial advisors, mutual fund companies, tax preparation, and audit services.

Key Benefits

PSA software has the following benefits for the financial sector:

➤ Cuts costs by eliminating or automating administrative tasks such as timesheet collection, repeated data entry, paper-intensive expense reports and purchases, and inefficient approval processes

➤ Maximizes productivity of billable and internal IT resources

➤ Identifies and decreases off-project expenses and purchases

➤ Eliminates inaccuracies caused by paper-based processes, manual work, and human error

➤ Enhances and accelerates communication with customers, partners, and employees using Internet technologies

Key Features

The following modules are the primary PSA modules that can help streamline a financial services organization:

➤ Resource management

➤ Staff and project purchasing

➤ Cost and revenue accounting

➤ Timesheet management, labor management, expense reporting

➤ Charge back

➤ Request tracking

➤ Help desk duties

➤ Document management

➤ Knowledge management

➤ Performance analysis

➤ Integration

➤ Health Care

Health care organizations have to balance providing outstanding patient care, scheduling staff, and safely delivering service while reducing costs, complying with reporting and regulatory bodies, and being prepared to handle emergencies.

The type of health care organizations that can benefit from a PSA solution include the following:

➤ Health care providers: integrated delivery networks, hospitals, and academic medical centers

➤ Managed care providers and payers: health maintenance organizations (HMOs), preferred provider organizations (PPOs), and traditional health insurance providers

➤ Ambulatory providers: Long-term care and assisted living facilities, physician networks, specialty care centers (such as sports medicine and rehabilitation facilities), home health care agencies, and medical clinics

Key Benefits

PSA software has the following benefits for health care providers:

➤ Reduces costs while maintaining safety standards

➤ Optimizes and maximizes utilization of health care professionals

➤ Generates alerts as an early warning and notification mechanism—for example, to indicate budget overruns; to warn of incomplete, unprocessed, or late documents; to remind managers to schedule or hire required staff

➤ Provides live data visualization reports that enable management to detect trouble spots, identify best practices, and make better informed decisions

➤ Enables a health care organization to comply to regulations, including health insurance portability and accountability act (HIPAA) and Joint Commission regulations

➤ Helps the organization hire and keep the best employees

Key Features

The following modules are the primary PSA modules that can help streamline a health care organization:

➤ Resource management

➤ Project management (for internal IT teams)

➤ Staff and project purchasing

➤ Cost and revenue accounting

➤ Timesheet management, labor management, expense reporting

➤ Charge back (for internal departments)

➤ Document management, knowledge management

➤ Performance analysis

➤ Integration

➤ High Tech

The high-tech sector has been the key engine of growth and efficiency over the last several decades. Companies operating in this space are used to extremely short product development and life cycles, time to market is an issue of survival, and manufacturing quality and speed a necessity.

High-tech organizations include software companies, semiconductor manufacturers, contract manufacturers, electronic device makers, personal computer original equipment manufacturers (OEMs), component distributors, and research and development (intellectual property) companies.

Key Benefits

PSA software has the following benefits for the high-tech sector:

➤ Maximizes resource utilization (reduce resource gaps)

➤ Increases resource efficiency (by reducing time spent by precious resources on administrative tasks and other noncore activities)

➤ Increases project visibility and reduces project scope creep

➤ Cuts costs and improves productivity

➤ Enables accurate tracking of R&D spending (in terms of time, expenses, and purchases) and can generate extensive reports for auditing purposes

Key Features

The following modules are the primary PSA modules that can help streamline a high-tech firm:

➤ Resource management

➤ Project management

➤ Staff and project purchasing

➤ Cost and revenue accounting

➤ Timesheet management, labor management, expense reporting

➤ Invoicing or charge back (for internal departments)

➤ Problem reporting and request tracking, help desk duties

➤ Document management and knowledge management

➤ Performance analysis

➤ Integration

➤ Media

Creating and delivering content involves the management and planning of expensive and scarce resources such as directors, actors, special effects experts, and postproduction editors. In today's digital and fast-paced economy, content creators and presenters are under pressure to deliver substantially high-quality projects in exceedingly smaller budgets and time intervals.

Media organizations include web production, graphic design, art production, audio-visual production, music production, and broadcasting companies.

Key Benefits

PSA software has the following benefits for media organizations:

➤ Maximizes resource utilization by reducing resource gaps

➤ Increases billable hours by reducing time spent by billable resources on administrative tasks and other nonbillable activities

➤ Compresses invoice cycle time through automation of data collection, approval, and invoicing

➤ Increases project visibility and reduces project scope creep

➤ Cuts costs and improves productivity

Key Features

The following modules are the primary PSA modules that can help streamline a content creation organization:

➤ Resource management

➤ Project management

➤ Staff and project purchasing

➤ Cost and revenue accounting

➤ Timesheet management, labor management, expense reporting

➤ Invoicing or charge back (for internal departments)

➤ Problem reporting and request tracking, help desk duties

➤ Document management and knowledge management

➤ Performance analysis

➤ Integration

➤ Pharmaceuticals and Biotechnology

Organizations in this sector are faced with numerous internal and external challenges. External challenges include competition from traditional and generic drug manufacturers, evaluating partnerships and mergers, dealings with health care organizations, and compliance with changing regulatory requirements. Internal challenges include controlling and cutting costs, result-oriented research and development, efficient manufacturing, and marketing activities.

Key Benefits

PSA software has the following benefits for pharmaceutical and biotechnology industries:

➤ Reduces costs while maintaining safety standards

➤ Optimizes and maximizes utilization of health care professionals

➤ Generates alerts as an early warning and notification mechanism—for example, to indicate budget overruns; to warn of incomplete, unprocessed, or late documents; to remind users to schedule or hire required staff

➤ Provides live data visualization reports that enable management to detect trouble spots, identify best practices, and make better informed decisions

➤ Enables a health care organization to comply to regulations including HIPAA and Joint Commission regulations

➤ Helps the organization hire and keep the best employees

➤ Provides compliance with government and regulatory regulations such as FDA 21 CFR Part 11

➤ Enables accurate tracking of R&D spending (in terms of time, expenses, and purchases) and can generate extensive reports for auditing purposes

Key Features

The following are the primary PSA modules that can help streamline an organization in this sector:

- ➤ Resource management

- ➤ Project management (for internal IT teams)

- ➤ Staff and project purchasing

- ➤ Cost and revenue accounting

- ➤ Timesheet management, labor management, expense reporting

- ➤ Charge back (for internal departments)

- ➤ Document management and knowledge management

- ➤ Performance analysis

- ➤ Integration

➤ Professional Services

Professional services are challenged by fierce global competition, profit margin pressure, high turnover, a highly mobile workforce that is difficult to track and supervise, and customers that expect fast response times, instant feedback, and status updates on their projects.

Professional services firms that can benefit from a PSA solution include consulting organizations, staffing agencies, professional services business units or IT departments, as well as IT, software, engineering, architecture, marketing, advertising, public relations, legal, accounting, construction, security, and business services.

Key Benefits

PSA software has the following benefits for professional services:

- ➤ Maximizes resource utilization by reducing resource gaps

- ➤ Increases number of billable hours by reducing time spent by billable resources on administrative tasks and other non-billable activities

- ➤ Compresses invoice cycle time through automation of data collection, approval, and invoicing

- ➤ Increases project visibility and reduces scope creep

- ➤ Ensures projects remain within budget constraints

➤ Cuts costs and improves productivity

Key Features

➤ Opportunity management and engagement management

➤ Resource management

➤ Project management

➤ Staff and project purchasing

➤ Cost and revenue accounting

➤ Timesheet management, labor management, expense reporting

➤ Invoicing or charge back (for internal departments)

➤ Problem reporting and request tracking, help desk duties

➤ Document management and knowledge management

➤ Performance analysis

➤ Integration

➤ Public Sector

Public sector organizations are under constant pressure to reduce costs and reduce bureaucracy while offering increasing responsiveness and high-quality services to the public. Poor quality of public services not only impacts the service organizations themselves, but may also have an effect on the political leadership at the local, state, and federal levels. In addition, because some of the services delivered affect public security; efficiency and effectiveness may be extremely important because they can increase the amount of service delivered with the same monetary expenditure. PSA solutions can offer significant cost savings and other benefits to this highly service-oriented industry.

Public sector organizations include law enforcement, government contractors, government offices, school districts, colleges, government-owned corporations, and not-for-profit organizations.

Key Benefits

PSA software has the following benefits for the public sector:

➤ Helps control spending and establish budgets, policies, and thresholds for all spending and purchases

➤ Generates alerts as an early warning and notification mechanism—for example, to indicate budget overruns; to warn of incomplete, unprocessed, or late documents; to remind users to schedule or hire required staff

➤ Provides live data visualization reports that enable the detection of trouble spots, identification of best practices, and the making of better informed decisions

➤ Helps the organization hire, manage, and keep satisfied employees

➤ Provides compliance with government and regulatory regulations such as Defense Contract Audit Agency (DCAA), Fair Labor Standards Act (FSLA), Loi des 35 heures, and other regulations regarding work and overtime policies

Key Features

The following are the primary PSA modules that help streamline a public sector organization:

➤ Resource management

➤ Project management (for internal IT teams)

➤ Staff and project purchasing

➤ Cost and revenue accounting

➤ Timesheet management, labor management, expense reporting

➤ Charge back (for internal departments)

➤ Document management and knowledge management

➤ Performance analysis

➤ Integration

➤ Telecommunications

The rapid growth of the Internet, the increasing demand for more bandwidth at rapidly falling prices, intense global competition, and changing technologies are business as usual for telecommunications firms. Although telecom companies spend substantial resources on automating their manufacturing and production facilities, they focus little attention on the productivity and efficiency of their workforce. PSA solutions address this vital need by tracking time and costs and by analyzing project performance from a project/service delivery (rather than inventory) perspective.

Telecom organizations include network device manufacturers, telecommunications providers, optical network makers, wireless device makers, and wireless network providers.

Key Benefits

PSA software has the following benefits for the telecommunications industry:

➤ Maximizes resource utilization by reducing resource gaps

➤ Increases resource efficiency by reducing time spent by precious resources on administrative tasks and other noncore activities

➤ Increases project visibility and reduces scope creep

➤ Cuts costs and improves productivity

Key Features

The following modules are the primary PSA modules that can help streamline a telecommunications firm:

➤ Engagement management

➤ Resource management

➤ Project management

➤ Staff and project purchasing

➤ Cost and revenue accounting

➤ Timesheet management, labor management, expense reporting

➤ Invoicing or charge back (for internal departments)

> ➤ Problem reporting and request tracking, help desk duties

> ➤ Document management and knowledge management

> ➤ Performance analysis

> ➤ Integration

➤ Summary

This section has described how PSA solutions can help organizations in various industries streamline their operations, deliver better and higher quality services at lower costs. PSA solutions are designed to optimize PSORGs. A complete PSA solution addresses the entire service cycle, from opportunity to engagement to delivery.

It is also important to note that given the unique needs and requirements of every industry and organization, completely out-of-the-box closed PSA solutions are not likely to provide the right fit. It is imperative that such solutions offer open systems with an extensive software development kit, documented and open data model, and plug-in programming interfaces that help an organization customize some screens, reports, and functionality to fit its specific organization and industry.

Please refer to Appendix B–PSA RFP Template, for a template RFP that can be used when searching for a PSA solution.

■ POTENTIAL RETURN ON INVESTMENT

The ROI of PSA solutions can be impressive; it is based on increasing efficiencies throughout the numerous stages of a service engagement. The ROI results are often very substantial for PSORGs of almost any size.

Return on investments from implementing PSA solutions are usually realized in a rather short period of time, much shorter than are ERPs. This advantage is primarily due to the tailored nature of the solution (focused on PSORGs), quick implementation of full-featured relevant functionality, modern user interface demanding minimal user training, and lower purchasing and ongoing maintenance costs of PSA solutions.

The ROI is impressive when you include staff size as part of the equation. For example, a 1,000-person PSORG that increases its

> **Small percentage improvements in productivity translate into *significant* dollar savings.**

billable utilization by just five percent will increase the number of fully billable resources by 50 people, or 10,400 hours per year. At a billable rate of $200 per hour, this yields an increase in revenue of over $2 million annually—most of which goes directly to the bottom line! For a corporate IT department, this correlates to an effective increase of 50 people to its staff.

A number of ROI calculations are presented in following chapters. They can all be found on the companion website (psabook.com). In all cost savings and ROI calculations throughout this book, cost of PSA system acquisition and maintenance has not been taken into account; reduce savings accordingly after this information is available.

Part **2**

Section A.
Professional Services
Automation Components

As can be seen from the following table, PSA functionality can be divided into multiple core components, which are usually present in most PSAs, as well as extended components that are more specialized and only a select handful of vendors provide. Figure P2.1 illustrates the PSA cycle.

The core components include performance analysis, resource management, project management, revenue and cost accounting, and timesheet management. The extended components include collaboration and HR management. The following chapters describe all of the aforementioned components.

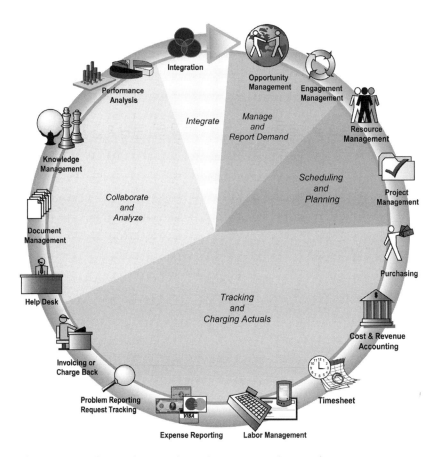

Figure P2.1 The Professional Services Automation Cycle

Core Components	Description
Performance analysis	Executive reporting, OLAP-based multidimensional data analysis, ROI, and decision support. Quick and customizable home, portal, and dashboard views and peer reviews.
Operations	Organization breakdown structure (OBS) management, site management, scoping, business rules, component-based security profiles, access rights, audit trails, general ledgers, and terminology settings.
Resource management	Skills and expertise assessment and matching. Resource allocation, search, scheduling, leveling, forecasting, and availability
Project management	Work breakdown structure (WBS) and engagement tracking. Multiple levels for budgeting amounts, duration, schemes, thresholds, and estimate to complete (ETC). Project scheduling, quality control, and R&D claim management. Seamless integration with major project management applications.
Revenue & cost accounting	Cost and billing rate engine, support for dependencies, history, custom rules, fixed, hourly, daily, custom, WBS, and split billing settings. Multicurrency support, tax category and jurisdictions. Invoicing and payroll wizards and payment processing.
Timesheet management	Timesheet submission, validation, and approval, compliance reporting, supervisory controls, automatic approval, notes, document attachments, and work assignment. Regional holiday, overtime, and administrative tasks processing, constraints, validations, and usage rules. Adjustment, status indicators, and mass update. Compliance to regulations for governmental and regional guidelines.
Expense reporting	Expense submission, validation, and approval, compliance reporting, markups, business rules, document/receipt attachment thresholds, foreign currency conversions, supervisory controls, automatic approval, and work assignment. Offline expense reports and multiple expense report views from which to choose.

Core Components	Description
Knowledge management	Hierarchical view of the entire organization, knowledge repositories, document management, full text searches, best practice templates, keyword searches, advanced queries, company policies, corporate handbooks, and collaboration.
Strategic sourcing	Requisitions, purchase orders, suppliers, customizable workflow engine, document attachments, staff purchasing, and receipts.
Request and issue tracking	Call tracking and escalation, change and process management, help desk, classification, notes, document attachments, and a customizable workflow engine.

Extended Components	Description
Customer and partner relationship management (CRM and PRM)	Some PSA solutions include CRM and PRM functionality. CRM includes customer self-services, contact management, marketing campaigns, and a more sophisticated demand management system. PRM automates the workflows and processes of finding, training, and managing partners.
Human resource management (HR)	HR systems process the staff requisition, purchasing, and recruitment process.
Complete enterprise accounting	Invoices, accounts payable/receivable, revenue recognition, and other such information generated by a PSA solution is exchanged with the organization's accounting system.

Chapter 3

Opportunity Management

■ INTRODUCTION

Opportunity management (OM) provides the ability to identify and track potential projects, opportunities, leads, and proposals. It enables organizations to better manage, qualify, and prioritize project and service demand. Opportunity management should include proposal management, pipeline analysis, forecasts of revenue and resource requirements, competitive analysis, win-loss reports, and performance statistics.

If the goal of PSA solutions is to maximize the performance of PSORGs, then one key element within a PSA solution for increasing such performance is the management and tracking of project and service demand. The lifeblood of any PSORG is its billable service revenues. The lifeblood of an IT (or other internal service) department is the manner in which it manages the work or projects being requested. In either case, the ability to manage project and service demand with increased efficiency will lead to better results, more projects, better-managed engagements, and a superior view of future resource requirements for the organization's complete project portfolio. The scope of this chapter includes identifying and describing the key concept of demand management within a PSA solution and the benefits derived from implementing it.

One process streamlined by PSAs is that of demand or opportunity management. A concept well known within the CRM market, it can include sales funnel or pipeline analysis, work requests, proposal management, and win-loss reporting. How an organization manages, evaluates, and prioritizes service or project requests/demand will certainly determine future productivity and profitability. The manner in which work demand is managed depends on whether the work is to be done by internal departments (such as IT departments), thus implementing work for internal needs, or by professional services organizations implementing projects for clients, thus doing billable work.

■ THE PAIN

Internal or IT departments and professional services firms receive numerous amounts of work requests, bug fixes, project leads, and issues from clients on a daily basis. Most organizations have a relatively reactive approach and a difficult time managing incoming requests, prioritizing work, assigning resources, or tracking and reporting on that work. In addition, there are limited ways to judge whether the investment was worthwhile. This mismanagement leads to an inefficient approach that will not only lead to delays in projects or increases in costs, but also lost client opportunities, poor customer or internal department satisfaction, and as a result, lower productivity and profitability. This mismanagement is primarily caused by a lack of a support system for tracking of work requests or customer leads. Most organizations do not have effective tracking systems to manage, prioritize, and track such demand.

■ THE NEED

What requests or projects need to get done for this month or the next three months? Who is requesting such work? Which work should have priority? Which client project is estimated to be more profitable? Are there enough resources to take on such a project? Is the sales pipeline filled with enough potential to meet revenue targets? These are only some of the questions that should be answered in order to manage the demand for work more effectively. For professional services firms, billable services are the primary stream of revenues. The management and tracking of sales opportunities is therefore a crucial part of their success. However, many of these activities are important to the internal IT group, which also has to manage their project portfolio, their incoming projects, their staff loads, and so on.

■ THE REMEDY

PSA solutions enable organizations to better identify, qualify, quantify, prioritize, and manage demand for services and projects by automating and streamlining the process. Response to work requests is quicker, project engagements are prioritized, customer leads can be followed and managed through the sales pipeline, quantifying future demand is more precise, and resources can be forecasted more effectively to meet that demand. Successfully streamlining the process will lead to increased efficiencies and thus the need for demand/opportunity management functionality within any PSA solution.

■ CORE FUNCTIONALITY

➤ Demand/Opportunity Management Capabilities

The following capabilities are usually incorporated within demand/ opportunity management functionality:

- ➤ Managing marketing opportunities in order to create and track demand initiatives
- ➤ Managing incoming work requests in terms of profiling the request, prioritizing, and evaluating
- ➤ Managing proposals, including proposal and quote templates
- ➤ Determining ROI and win-loss analysis
- ➤ Contract and agreement templates
- ➤ Pipeline forecasting and analysis
- ➤ Evaluating and planning resource capacity based on forecasted work

➤ Demand/Opportunity from Two Points of View

Information Technology or Internal Departments

The focus of IT or internal departments is on organizing, managing, and executing incoming project requests from various departments within the organization.

- ➤ Capturing and qualifying requests through help desk, bug tracking, issue tracking, departmental projects, and so on
- ➤ Prioritizing the requests based on urgency and ROI importance
- ➤ Forecasting and anticipating demand for requests and associating to resource capacity, training, and possible recruitment
- ➤ Reporting and analysis in real time

➤ Professional Services Organizations

The focus is on organizing, managing, and executing incoming project opportunities from clients in order to generate billable revenue.

- ➤ Tracking leads
- ➤ Using proposal templates, and organizing, qualifying, and managing them through the pipeline
- ➤ Prioritizing projects based on profitability, ROI, resource capacity, or other metrics
- ➤ Forecasting demand and associating it to resource capacity, training, and possible recruitment
- ➤ Reporting and analysis in real time

■ DEMAND/OPPORTUNITY WORKFLOW

Figure 3.1 shows a sample opportunity workflow. The workflow should be completely customizable; administrators should be able to define notifications for various state transitions (e.g., send e-mail

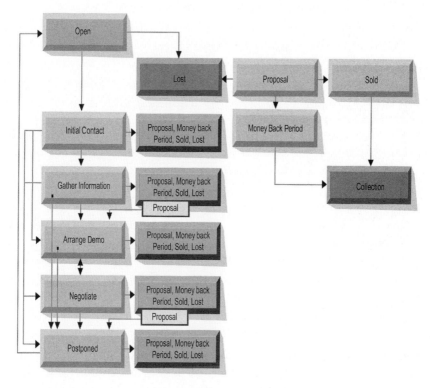

Figure 3.1 Sample Opportunity Management Workflow

to accounting when a sale is closed). Administrators should be able to add, delete, and edit states, transitions, and notifications in order to map the workflow to their own sales process.

➤ The Demand/Opportunity Management Process

The following table highlights some of the requirements of IT or Internal Departments, versus Professional Services Organizations involved in billable activities.

■ EXTENDED FUNCTIONALITY

Many PSA solutions offer variations on the theme of demand/opportunity management. However, beyond the core functionalities previously described, you should look for specific functionalities in

	For IT or Internal Departments	For Professional Services Organizations
Creation, identification, qualification of demand	Record data such as departmental requests, resource requirements, work descriptions, and contact infomation, as well as help desk service, bug tracking, and issue tracking.	Tracking of marketing campaigns to generate demand. Tracking customer leads and recording information such as customer profiles, preferences, work descriptions, revenue potential, time lines, and other contact information. Manage and deliver proposals as potential clients move through the sales pipeline.
Knowledge management	Capture, share, analyze, modify, and save documentation pertaining to work requests, such as bug reports, technical specs, proposals, and other documentation or approvals.	Capture, share, analyze, modify, and save documentation pertaining to service demand, such as technical specs, proposals, quotation templates, or other documentation. Ensure information on competitors is available and managed in order to compete effectively.
Evaluate demand	Evaluate the validity of work requested based on the ROI for the company. ROI can be based on costs, time spent, productivity improvements, or effect on revenues to the organization. An evaluation of in-house implementation costs versus outsourcing the work request should also be performed.	Evaluate the validity of project bids based on the ROI for the company. ROI can be based on revenues, costs, profitability, or time spent. Project revenue and profitability scenarios can be evaluated in order to obtain more precise forecasting. Determine the probability of winning the project and thus revenue and pipeline forecasts.
Prioritize demand	For IT departments it is essential to focus on work with the greatest ROIs. Not to do so would render an organization inefficient, costly, and profitably ineffective. Prioritizing the work is crucial. • Prioritize based on importance and urgency. • Prioritize based on costs and potential ROI analysis. • Prioritize based on resource capacity. • Prioritize based on the organization's objectives.	For billable organizations, it is essential to focus on work with the greatest ROIs. Not to do so would render an organization inefficient and would not maximize its profitability. Prioritizing the work is a crucial process. • Prioritize based on revenue or profitability scenarios. • Prioritize based on win probability. • Prioritize based on resource capacity. • Prioritize based on the organization's objectives.

	For IT or Internal Departments	For Professional Services Organizations
Resource capacity	Demand management functionality enables IT departments to view work requests and upcoming tasks easily. IT departments can therefore evaluate resource requirements for projects in a straightforward way and then proceed to ensure resource capacity; either by recruiting and hiring or by adapting existing resources to meet the new work schedule	Opportunity management functionality enables billable organizations to view work requests and upcoming work easily. PSOs can therefore evaluate resource requirements for a project in a straightforward way and then proceed to ensure resource capacity; either by recruiting and hiring or by adapting existing resources to meet the new work schedule.
Analyze performance	By incorporating business intelligence & reporting capabilities, an IT department can review work request information at its smallest detail and share the results with those who require it. Information such as the amount of work and costs incurred by department, by user, by corporate site, by team, by geography, or by any other metric can be measured. This will result in precise, real-time analytical information enabling an organization to make better decisions on project delivery. More projects will be delivered on time and on budget, thus ensuring department or end user satisfaction and improved corporate effectiveness.	By incorporating business intelligence and reporting capabilities, a PSO can review project opportunities at the smallest detail and share the results with those who require it. Information such as win-loss records versus competitors, pipeline forecasts, opportunities by client, by project type, by revenues, by geography, or by any other metric can be measured. This will result in precise, real-time information enabling an organization to make better decisions on project prioritization, client budget restrictions, project potential, or project delivery. Projects with larger ROIs will be focused on more often, resource requirements can be forecasted efficiently, more projects will be delivered on time and on budget, thus ensuring client satisfaction and improved profitability. Answer the question: Where is the greatest sales opportunity?

order to properly evaluate a PSA solution offering demand/opportunity management.

➤ Integration

The level of integration strongly influences the usability of PSA solutions in real corporate environments. Look for significant integration features within any PSA solution.

> ➤ *CRM integration:* For some organizations, demand/opportunity management within a PSA solution may not be needed. Some PSORGs may have already invested in traditional enterprise applications such as a CRM, of which many already incorporate demand/opportunity management functionality. Therefore, implementing a PSA solution, which also incorporates such functionality, would not be an option for such organizations, because they have already invested considerable amounts into implementing the solution and training on it. However, having PSA solutions that seamlessly integrate with their CRM applications will provide the essential functionality these firms require. Ensuring that a PSA vendor offers seamless integration with leading CRM applications will enable PSA clients to manage their initial project tracking processes more effectively.

> ➤ *Integration with the rest of the PSA application:* Here, we are looking at integration with resource management, project management, and budgeting features. This will enable a work request, after it is approved, to go seamlessly from the demand/opportunity management module to reserving available resources to the building of project teams, to assigning activities and adopting budgetary scenarios without manual intervention or the need to key in information several times.

➤ Reporting and Business Intelligence

Extensive reporting capabilities for demand/opportunity management functionality across the entire application are required, such as numerous canned reports, a customizable reporting engine, OLAP capabilities, support for business intelligence tools, and the

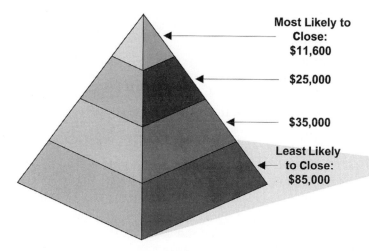

Most Likely to
Close:
$11,600

$25,000

$35,000

Least Likely
to Close:
$85,000

Figure 3.2 Revenue Potential and Profitability of Close

ability to drill up and down on data. Effective business intelligence will enable users to capture information on buying habits and client preferences, thus building valuable client relationships; analyze sales-force efficiency and performance by team, by user, and by geography; pinpoint sales trouble areas more quickly; and share pertinent information with your team and clients.

Business intelligence capabilities enable faster, more accurate identification of information in order to implement more effective decision making. As you can see in Figure 3.2, there are many more analysis reports that can be envisioned using the business intelligence and OLAP tools.

➤ Access

Total accessibility of information is another key feature—especially extended Internet access, e-mail access, wireless communication, and Windows-based entry. Accessing service requests or opportunity leads over the web or through a wireless device will result in a more efficient use and management of resources. Requests and leads could then be approved, commented on, analyzed, and edited from remote locations. The corporate workforce is becoming more mobile; thus, such capabilities are not only necessary but also crucial in order to compete more effectively.

➤ Customization

No application provides a 100% fit for a sophisticated organization. Customizable applications enable increased usage and return on investment. Such is the case for PSA solutions and their demand/opportunity management functionalities. A well-documented software development kit (SDK) and API (application programming interface) will enable the development of enhancements and extensions to the application. The SDK can be used to extract and manipulate data from a local or remote database, and it can exchange data with other third-party applications. It can also be used to develop import/export plug-ins, enhancements to the core product, customization of base functionality, the user interface or look, and tight integration with third-party software.

■ SUMMARY

Tracking, managing, and reporting on project demand in a more efficient way will lead to improved results in productivity and profitability, both for service firms that generate billable revenues and thus require a better look into their opportunity funnel or pipeline, and for internal IT or service departments managing their project portfolios.

Chapter

4

Resource Management

■ INTRODUCTION

Resource management enables improved tracking, deployment, matching, and prioritizing of resources based on skills, interests, location, availability, and business practices for a given service engagement. As a key component within a PSA solution, resource management enables improved resource utilization.

Complex projects require massive ongoing efforts to communicate objectives and plans, define milestones, schedule tasks, and allocate resources. An organization that handles multiple complex projects in parallel has the added burden of making sure that resources are optimally utilized. For PSORGs, it is very costly to have high-skilled resources on standby due to scheduling issues or poor planning. This situation can sometimes result in a significant loss of profitability for the team and for the enterprise.

Resource management (RM) software can efficiently manage and allocate resources across all engagements. Resource management allows managers to track resource skills, interests, and availability. Furthermore, RM enables managers to reserve and schedule resources based on availability, skill/interest matching, project priority, overloading, and other factors. This section defines RM, its key benefits, and its workflows. In addition, it outlines important features to look for in an RM application and examines the benefits of using an RM system.

Many organizations use spreadsheets, a shared calendaring system, or even paper to reserve, track, and manage resources and

> Resource management is a key PSA component that involves the selection of the required resources based on their type, skills, proficiencies, and availability in order to carry out a project.

projects. Sometimes a project management tool, may be used for such purposes. The inherent costs associated with this highly manual, inaccurate, and inefficient process go unnoticed in the initial phases of a project, but are more visible as the project gets well underway. Without the right software tools, management lacks visibility, is unable to make decisions based on accurate data, and cannot establish the relationship between many business variables in order to detect developing trends early enough to be proactive. Instead they must react after the fact, and even then their information systems may be so poor that they still may not be able to make the required changes.

■ CURRENT SITUATION

In an organization without a formal RM process, project managers are engaged in an *art* rather than a *science:* They must make decisions based on intuition, what they may know, one-on-one communication, hearsay, meetings, and informal analysis. Managers use

> Without software tools, resource management is more art than science.

these inefficient and flawed techniques to determine what resources are allocated to which projects and engagements. This informal and unmanaged process can lead to overloading of resources, as well as cause resource gaps, unforeseen resource shortages, and other scheduling/reservation problems that can significantly impact the cost, outcome, and delivery dates of any project.

The following is a list of the issues that arise without proper resource management:

> ➤ Inaccurate method of determining resource gap and inability to adjust accordingly

➤ Difficulty of ensuring that the appropriate resources are engaged on a project in a timely manner

➤ Inability to determine optimal resources and workloads effectively, which can jeopardize project completion date

➤ Inability to assign and track work easily

➤ Inability to determine resources that need to be hired, and at what point in time they should be hired

➤ Difficulty in the selection process of resources or in determining which candidates are most qualified given skill set, availability, and priorities

➤ Inability to avoid congestion and conflicting priorities during peak demand

➤ Difficulty in performance assessment

➤ Poor skill and interest matches

➤ Mix-ups in resource reservation and assignment

➤ Difficulty in specific talent search and scheduling

➤ Inability to forecast accurately future resource needs and requirements

■ WHAT IS RESOURCE MANAGEMENT?

Resource management involves the selection of required resources based on their type, skills, interests, proficiencies, and availability in order to carry out a project. Resource management software includes modules to manage resource calendars (availability) and skill sets, details on project engagements including required skills per task, task dependencies, task start and end dates, and proficiencies. Resource management software also has the ability to run RM queries using user-created scenarios based on parameters such as project priority, start/end date, importance of skill matching/availability, interest, location, and the ability to *overload* resources.

Forecasting staffing needs requires one to determine the following:

➤ Estimate demand for resources by engagement (contract), project, or activity.

➤ Find qualified resources based on skills, interests, and proficiencies.

➤ Compare the availability of required skills to the schedules and deadlines.

➤ Search for qualified resources by skills, interests, and availability when assigning work.

➤ Engage new resources from an external source (as a last resort).

➤ Reduce risk when committing to project schedules and deadlines.

Standardizing and benchmarking these steps allows management to do the following:

➤ Have a central directory of resource skills, proficiencies, and profiles.

➤ Track and report on resource utilization.

➤ Report on resource skills, interests, calendars, project milestones, requirements, and critical paths.

➤ Plan in terms of capability and availability to meet future needs.

➤ Optimize utilization and hiring of resources.

➤ Generate a comprehensive resource plan that highlights resource gaps (known as gap analysis: in this context, the gap occurs when a resource is idle). Gaps can be used to take on additional engagements or can be used for training purposes.

Maximizing the use of limited and precious resources will ultimately result in substantial efficiencies, higher profit margins, faster response times, customer satisfaction, and improved employee retention and morale.

■ BENEFITS

The benefits of implementing RM can be summarized as follows:

➤ Improvements in scheduling capability

➤ Powerful and user-friendly systems that allow managers to perform matching resources to projects based on expertise, interest, and availability

➤ Ability to streamline and automate resource management process, thus avoiding gaps

➤ Enhancement of resource and employee productivity by minimizing uncertainty and waste

➤ Ability to quickly take action to pursue profitable engagements

➤ Minimization of overloading, overbooking, and underutilization

■ SOME DEFINITIONS

Due to the casual use of various terms and concepts, RM is a complex topic that is often poorly understood. The following table briefly describes the key terms and concepts.

Concept or Term	Description
Activity	A project-specific task, which has a start and end date.
Assignment	A specific resource assigned to a particular activity.
Assignment policy	Specify, (1) the policy that specifies whether to reserve the resource if the activity is assigned, and (2) the applicable reservation hours per day.
Availability	The indication of when and how much of a resource's time can be scheduled for assigned work.
Availability score	The level at which the resource is available for work (measured in units)—for example, at 50%, 90%, or 100% of full time.
Calendar	A template calendar that specifies reserved, available, and unavailable time.

continued

Concept or Term	Description
Engagement	A contract; an agreement between two or more parties for a set of specified deliverables, usually with predefined milestones.
Group	A set of resources.
Proficiency	The degree of excellence in a skill or the desired standards in a project.
Project	A plan with a set of tasks and resources that need to be scheduled, assigned, and tracked.
Reservation	The booking of a resource.
Reservation policy	Specify policy to auto assign work if resource is reserved and the applicable default number of hours reserved per day.
Resource	The people used to complete tasks in a project.
Resource calendar	A calendar that specifies working and nonworking time for an individual resource. Resource calendars are used to track holidays, vacations, working days, shifts, and reservations.
Resource breakdown structure (RBS)	Hierarchical organization of resources that facilitates both roll-up reporting and summary resource scheduling by enabling one to schedule at the detailed requirement level, and roll up both requirements and availabilities to a higher level.
Resource gap analysis	The assignment and reservation of available resources or plan to hire required resources.
Resource leveling	The process of rescheduling activities so that the requirement for resources on the project does not exceed resource limits. The project completion date may be delayed in the process.
Resource management	The indication of when and how much of a resource's time can be scheduled for assigned work.
Resource management queries	Queries that can be named and saved for future reference.
Resource smoothing	The process of rescheduling activities so that requirements for resources on the project do not exceed resource limits. In smoothing, as opposed to resource leveling, the project completion date may not be delayed. Activities may only be delayed within their float.
Resource utilization	The extent to which resources are put to practical use. Calculated by the number of work hours of a resource over a period of time.
Scheduling	The timing and sequence of tasks within a project.

Concept or Term	Description
Site	Organization's location.
Skill	Qualification.
Skill score	The value expressed as the percentage of resource proficiency and selected proficiency for a specific skill.
Total score	The average of skill score and availability score, taking into consideration the importance of the skill and the availability.

■ RESOURCE MANAGEMENT PROCESS

The resource management process involves the following steps, illustrated in Figure 4.1:

➤ Engagement management: Define contract/engagement, gather specifications, and define associated projects.

➤ Define skills/proficiencies: Define generic skills, which can be assigned to resources and tasks (e.g., web design, accounting, marketing).

➤ Define projects/activities/tasks: Create projects, activities, and tasks that are required to be performed for a specific engagement.

➤ Define RM queries: Create RM queries to search for skilled resources based on various criteria such as availability, project

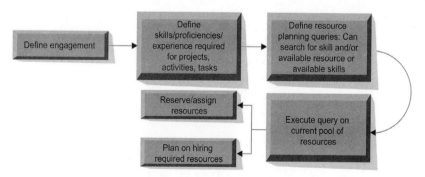

Figure 4.1 Resource Planning Process

priority, resource overload, experience level, and proficiency. Managers can create multiple queries to evaluate various alternatives (e.g., whether to overload current resources or hire additional ones).

➤ Reserve and assign resources: After RM finds resources that match the criteria, managers can reserve and assign resources accordingly.

➤ Strategic sourcing: In addition to being able to search for available resources, a complete RM application should include the ability to search for available skills. For example, search for 300 hours of web design work; if the current resource pool cannot handle the request, then mechanisms should be set in place to schedule and initiate hiring of new resources.

■ RESOURCE MANAGEMENT SETUP

Resource management setup includes the following steps, illustrated in Figure 4.2:

➤ Define reservation/assignment policy: For some organizations, assignment of an activity to a resource (to do actual work) may be not be the same as reserving a resource, whereas for another organization, reservation may automatically imply work assignment. The reservation/assignment policy defines this relationship and also lets the administrator specify the default number of hours for reservation.

➤ Define base calendars: Administrators should be able to define base calendars; the base calendars can be associated to sites and groups. Users created within a specific group automatically default their users' calendars to their group calendar. The user calendar can then be initialized to include the user-specific availability and agenda.

➤ Define regional holiday sets: Larger geographically or structurally dispersed organizations have multiple physical and virtual sites. The employees of such an organization may have various holiday calendars. The RM system must take this regional availability into account when booking resources.

➤ Manage sites: Define and configure the physical or virtual sites that represent how the organization is structured.

➤ Define skills and proficiencies.

➤ Associate skills to tasks and activities.

➤ Associate skills to users and specify interest levels.

➤ Set up users.

• Associate holiday set: Specify user's holiday set; user's calendar should automatically be updated with the holidays defined within the set.

• Associate sites: Set user's master (the user's home office) and active site (where the user currently works).

• Set user calendar: Select an alternate base calendar if the group base calendar does not apply to this user. Also, set availability of the user for various date intervals.

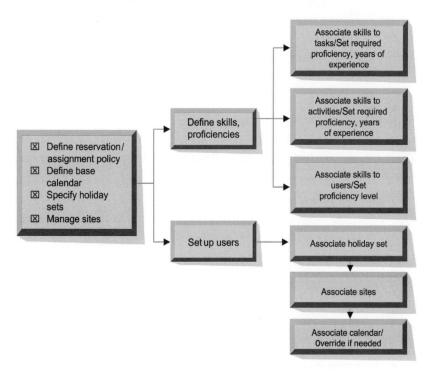

Figure 4.2 Resource Planning Setup

■ SCHEDULING TECHNIQUES

RM systems also have the option to automatically schedule a project based on the information provided. Various techniques exist for generating a project schedule. This section describes the most widely used techniques.

> **Resource planning systems provide various scheduling techniques: critical path method, leveling, smoothing, PERT, and others.**

➤ Critical Path Method

Critical path method (CPM) is a project management technique that is used to schedule project tasks so that the project is completed as fast as possible. This technique relies on accurate task estimates, earliest start date and latest finish date per task, and task sequence (task dependencies); CPM does not take into account resource availability. The techniques that follow improve on CPM by considering availability.

➤ Resource Leveling

Tasks are moved within their minimum and maximum start-finish dates in order to maximize resource utilization; as a result, project completion date may be delayed.

➤ Resource Smoothing

Resource smoothing is also known as time-limited resource scheduling. Tasks are moved within their minimum and maximum start/finish dates in order to maximize resource utilization; unlike resource leveling, with this technique the project completion date cannot be delayed.

➤ Resource-Limited Resource Scheduling

Project start and finish dates reflect expected resource availability. The final project schedule is always limited by the availability of resources.

➤ Program Evaluation and Review Technique

Program evaluation and review technique (PERT) is a project management technique that uses probabilities to schedule a project.

Each activity is assigned a best, worst, and most probable completion time estimate. These estimates are used to determine the average completion time. The average times are used to compute the critical path and the standard deviation of completion times for the entire project.

■ QUERIES

Using an RM query, one can do the following:

➤ Search for qualified, available, or qualified and available resources.

➤ Search for available skills.

➤ Filter by site(s) or by group(s).

➤ Select projects or activities to use for skill matching.

➤ Define minimum skill, availability, and total scores (to prevent overloading or overworking).

➤ Specify importance of skill and availability.

➤ Search for Qualified Resources

Perform skill matching by specifying skills, keywords, or aliases without considering availability. Additional configurable parameters should include the following:

➤ Select proficiencies that are equal, higher, or lower than a certain specific level.

➤ Select years of work experience.

➤ Search for a specific set of skills and proficiencies.

➤ Specify interest level (e.g., very interested, career goals).

➤ Search for Available Resources

Search for availability without considering qualifications. Additional configurable parameters should include the following:

➤ Ignore availability based on project/activity state and priority.

➤ Ignore interests.

➤ Allow overload based on project/activity state and priority.

➤ Reassign work to match resource availability based on project/activity state and priority.

➤ Look for resources that are willing and able to travel and/or relocate.

➤ Search for Qualified and Available Resources

Combine both qualified and available search options; this should include the same configurable parameters.

➤ Search for Available Skills

This query is an accurate method of determining resource gap and the ability to take action accordingly. For example, an engagement is known to require 200 hours of marketing, 100 hours of PR work, and 300 hours of call center management. A search for available skills results in resource shortages as follows: 50 hours of PR and 250 hours of call center management. The strategic sourcing system should allow the manager to set up the necessary notifications and reminders so that the resources are made available when required through reassignment from other sites or by hiring additional resources. Optionally, the strategic sourcing RM system can be integrated with the HR system to automatically initiate requests for additional staff.

■ NOTIFICATIONS

Notifications are a key component of any RM system. The following is a list of key notifications that should be provided:

➤ Display warning (or send e-mail) if no resources have been allocated (assigned) to an engagement; the notification can be set to be automatically triggered a certain number of days before the engagement starts.

➤ Send e-mail to a project manager to inform that resource R1, R2, . . . RN have been reserved for a project but they have not been assigned to work on the project.

➤ Send e-mail to engagement manager if previous queries failed to find sufficient resources to work on the engagement. In this case, the engagement manager would have to follow up with HR to ensure resources are hired.

➤ Set up notifications that warn when critical resources are overbooked or are underutilized for extended periods of time.

■ RETURN ON INVESTMENT

The ROI calculations shown in the following table demonstrate the cost savings that can result by increasing resource utilization in PSORGs.

These figures do not include the benefits associated with optimizing the workforce, project reporting, resource management, budgeting, forecasting, and automating administrative and other manual processes.

The average billing rate per hour is $50 per hour and the average nonbillable resources salary is $30,000, respectively.

	20	50	100	200	1,000	10,000
Total number of resources	20	50	100	200	1,000	10,000
Total number of billable resources	6	15	30	60	300	3000
Total number of nonbillable resources	12	35	70	140	700	7000
Additional revenue gained with increased utilization	$12,480	$31,200	$62,400	$124,800	$624,000	$6,240,000
Yearly savings in nonbillable resources	$3,600	$10,500	$21,000	$42,000	$210,000	$2,100,000
Estimated annual billing	$418,080	$1,045,200	$2,090,400	$4,180,800	$20,904,000	$209,040,000
Savings in cost of capital	$458	$1,145	$2,291	$4,582	$22,908	$229,080
Total annual return	$12,404	$32,134	$64,268	$128,537	$642,681	$6,426,810

Weighted average cost of capital (WACC), defined as the average rate for the company to raise or borrow additional funds, is set at 10 percent. The WACC can vary among companies, depending on their ability to raise capital through debt or equity.

Productivity improvement in days for invoicing and payment cycle is calculated to be four days based on the nonbillable resources productivity's being improved by one percent.

Total annual return is calculated at 75% for first year as three months are allotted for site planning, implementation, and rollout. Calculate your own ROIs online on resource management by visiting the psabook.com/roi/ru.htm web site.

➤ Resource Management Return on Investment

Figure 4.3 shows graphically the tabular data that is presented in the previous table on ROIs. It shows the total annual recurring savings that can be expected from applying the standard savings to organizations of various sizes.

■ SUMMARY

Resource management is a key PSA component that is of special interest to consulting organizations or to any organization that has precious and limited resources that are assigned to various engagements.

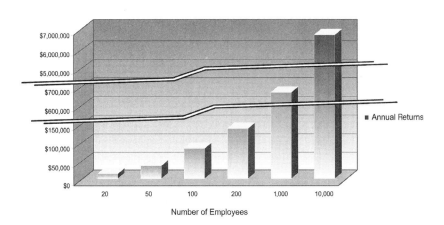

Figure 4.3 Annual Return Diagram

Until recently, RM has been a complex technology that was available only to the privileged few. Significant global competitive pressures, the advent of the Internet, and many other technological factors have contributed to making this and other enterprise technologies available, affordable, and intuitive to use.

Using RM software can significantly improve resource utilization. By minimizing resource gaps and maximizing resource utilization, the organization can deliver more projects in a cost effective, profitable, and timely manner, and it can do so by using the optimal amount of required resources.

Chapter 5

Project Management

■ INTRODUCTION

Project management ensures that the information pertaining to project status, tasks, assignments, objectives, and time frames are easily accessible and measurable by authorized personnel. It increases collaboration, communication, management, and the overall accuracy of project status reporting. It also should include work breakdown structure (WBS), engagement tracking, multiple levels for budgeting amounts, durations, schemes, thresholds, and certainly integration with readily available popular scheduling tools.

Project management software can centralize mission-critical data in all project areas. Centralized data enable managers and team members alike to communicate, collaborate, report on, and track project progress. This section outlines the details of applications with project management features and their ability to greatly simplify and improve project management efforts by providing the tools necessary to track, analyze, and report on project performance.

When investigating software offerings available in the marketplace to help automate the project management process, a potential buyer can quickly become overwhelmed by the many features and options provided by these products. To help in the decision-making process, the first step is to outline the information that is required to be tracked in a project.

Any software application that is to be considered must at a minimum contain the feature set to effectively track and report on all project phases, have the tools to optimize resources, and finally have the ability to reduce inefficiencies.

■ A BRIEF HISTORY OF PROJECT MANAGEMENT APPLICATIONS

Project management applications have been around for over 40 years; the first few appearing in the 1960s provided the most basic functionality such as finding the fastest path from project start to completion (critical path). The dawn of the PC age in the 1980s made project management applications accessible to all members of a team, allowing them to share project information. Today, every member of the team can connect to a centralized database and provide their updates electronically from anywhere in the world.

■ PROJECT SCOPE MANAGEMENT

A project's scope is the clear identification of the work required to successfully complete or deliver a given project. One of the project manager's responsibilities is to ensure that *only* the required work (the *scope*) will be performed and that each of the deliverables can be completed in the allotted time and within budget.

> **A project's scope is the clear identification of the work required to successfully complete or deliver a given project.**

Project scope management is commonly broken down into five separate processes: initiation, scope planning, scope definition, scope verification, and scope change control. Each of these processes is briefly described in the following discussion and illustrated in Figure 5.1.

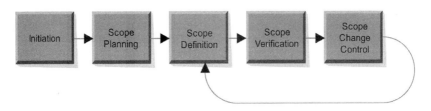

Figure 5.1 Project Management Flow

➤ Initiation

In the initiation process, an organization must recognize that a new project exists or has the need to exist. The need for a project can be sparked from a number of places, most often a customer need or a market demand. The initiation process typically includes a feasibility study or a plan including high-level goals with the intention of getting management or customer approval to create a more formal plan.

➤ Scope Planning

Developing a written scope statement is the key element to the scope planning process. The written statement of the project's scope will serve as a way to measure whether a deliv-

> Scope control: control the planning, definition, verification, and change control for the scope in writing.

erable (or the project as a whole) has been completed successfully by detailing the project's justification, objectives, and deliverables. Scope statements can be created either by the members of the team or by the entity commissioning the project.

➤ Scope Definition

The major deliverables of a project must be broken down into easily manageable phases or subprojects. This process helps to ensure that resources can be more clearly assigned to their areas of responsibility, so that resources, time, and cost can be more accurately estimated and detailed.

➤ Scope Verification

Scope verification (simply put) is the acceptance by the entity commissioning the project of the project's scope and work. During this process, the results of the work that has already been completed, as well as all related documentation, must be ready for review so that the project may proceed.

➤ Scope Change Control

It is an undeniable fact that most projects experience changes to their scope during their life cycles. When a change occurs, the primary concern of the project manager is to ensure that the impacts caused by changes are factored into the scheduling and allocation of resources, as well as time and cost estimates.

➤ Project Scope Management Tools

The management of each of these processes and their related data can be accomplished in a number of different ways, such as centralizing documents in a version control system and/or a change management system that has the ability to attach documents. Tools adopted must have the ability to easily share and review documents, as well as to associate any documents containing scope changes to the appropriate project activity.

■ WORK BREAKDOWN STRUCTURE

A project manager must have the ability to specify the work content of the project in terms of its deliverables and the activities that must be performed for each deliverable. One of the principal tools used for controlling the work contents of a project is the work breakdown structure (WBS; illustrated in Figure 5.2).

Work breakdown structure is a grouping of work elements, such as clients, engagements, portfolios, projects, phases, tasks, and activities, that organizes and outlines the total scope of a project. Each descending level in the WBS represents an increasingly detailed definition of a project component. The WBS defines the work ele-

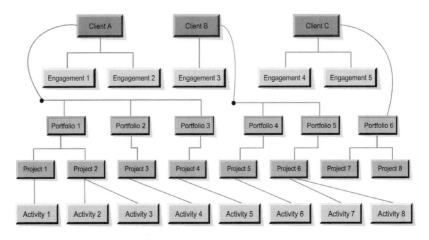

Figure 5.2 Work Breakdown Structure

ments and should not be confused with the organization breakdown structure (OBS), which organizes the staff or resources that perform the work.

A well-planned WBS allows project managers to reap many benefits, including the following:

> **Work breakdown structure is a grouping of project elements, such as clients, engagements, portfolios, projects, phases, tasks, and activities, that organizes and outlines the total scope of a project.**

➤ A consistent method and procedure for data collection, analysis, and reporting

➤ Aid in the planning and estimating of similar work for future projects

➤ Help in the organization of tasks so that responsibility can be assigned to appropriately skilled resources and easily tracked

➤ WBS Tools

For a software application to help simplify a project manager's duties, its foundation must revolve around its ability to properly display the WBS of a project. It should display information about clients, engagements, projects, phases, and activities. Each of these items is related to the other, should be displayed in a tree format, and should support easy navigation and various search options (i.e., by name, ID, keywords, type, or some form of grouping).

➤ Cost/Benefit Analysis

Performing a cost-to-benefit analysis involves estimating the investment (costs) and returns (benefits) of various project alternatives, and then applying a standardized formula such as an ROI calculation to explore alternatives that help in the decision-making process.

■ CHANGE MANAGEMENT

Change management may be used in one of two ways. In the first sense, it refers to making changes in a managed or systematic fashion. The changes typically lie within the responsibility and control of the project manager. However, in some cases, changes might have been triggered by events or individuals originating outside the project. Hence, the second way in which change management may be used is in responding to changes over which the project manager exercises little or no control (e.g., shifting economic tides, end customer modifying project scope, etc.).

It is imperative that a project manager properly manages any data that could have a positive or negative impact on cost or schedule. Change management is the process for accommodating change and keeping requirements clear, concise, and valid. Every project manager needs this capability, regardless of what terminology may be used to refer to this process.

➤ Change Management and Configuration Management Tools

A change management application must have the ability to adapt to the changing needs of projects and project teams. It should allow for multiple configurable workflows, each workflow containing its own set of states to track changes. It should optionally send automatic e-mail notifications based on criteria defined by the project manager or members of the team. Finally, it should support attachments of project-related documents and links.

■ COST

The costs incurred by human resources working on a project can be computed in several different ways.[1] Hourly rates are calculated by multiplying the number of hours worked by an hourly cost rate. Fixed rates are calculated based on a fixed dollar amount between two dates, regardless of the number of hours of work performed. Daily rates are based on a fixed dollar amount for the work performed in one workday, regardless of the number of hours worked. Custom rates are also a possibility for calculating rates on special days such as weekends or statutory holidays.

---

1. For this and other discussions, we are focusing on calculating personnel costs in terms of hours worked. In some industries an important alternative is used that relates to piecework or unit work. Because most professional costs are calculated by the hour and most PSA solutions easily handle piecework, we will not be focusing on piecework calculations.

Project Budget

Whereas a smaller project may be carried out without a fixed budget, larger projects usually require the development of a formal budget. Budgets are extremely important for project managers, simply because if there is no budget, then it is very difficult for the managers to control the scope. When a budget is defined, it should include the cost of each task, as well as the costs being incurred for expenses and materials. Using project management software makes this process much easier during the initial planning stages and continues to add more significant benefits as it fulfills the ongoing need to track and reflect the cost of changes in status reports.

> **Budgets help control project scope.**

Project Budgeting Tools

The following table shows the potential difference (or delta) between the project's original budget, its current estimate, and its actuals.

	Budget	Estimate	Actuals	Budget Δ	Estimate Δ
Time (hours)	100	85	90	10	−5
Cost ($)	10,000	8,500	9,000	1,000	−500
Revenue ($)	15,000	12,750	13,500	1,500	−750

An application that is going to be used for project budgeting must allow the project manager to input budgeted time, cost, and revenue amounts and compare it to the actuals. A notification system should automatically inform the project manager, perhaps by sending e-mail, if the project's budget or an activity's budget has been exceeded. Integration with a timesheet system is a definite advantage, as it would allow project activities to optionally become automatically suspended if a budget has been exceeded.

Estimate to Complete

Having team members provide an estimate to complete for each major activity or deliverable can prove to be an invaluable tool for the project manager. By evaluating each team member's estimate to complete (ETC) and totaling the ETCs for a project activity, a project manager can evaluate whether the project's budget remains accurate, or whether adjustments should be made.

► Estimate to Complete Tools

Allowing each member of a team to specify the amount of time they estimate to completion of an activity is a great way for a project manager to ensure that the original budget is still adequate.[2] The ETC must have the ability to be turned on or off on a per-activity basis, and it must be easily accessible to a project manager for reviewing up-to-date information.

► Earned Value Reports

Earned value reporting is the most commonly used tool for measuring performance, simply because it considers three key project elements: a project's scope, schedule, and cost.

To help you understand how the earned value for a project can be calculated and reported on, we must review the following terms:

- ► *Budget* is the portion of the approved cost estimate that has been allocated for expenditure on one or more project activities with predefined start and end dates.

- ► *Actual cost* is the total of direct and indirect costs (such as overhead) incurred in accomplishing one or more activities with predefined start and end dates.

- ► *Earned value* is a percentage of the total budget proportional to the percentage of the work that has been completed.

It is with these three variables that a project manager is able to measure the performance of a team.

► Expenses

In addition to tracking and reporting on the time for resources in-

---

2. Naturally, this assumes the team members have the adequate skill to estimate the ETC for their activities. Poor ability in this area will lead to inaccurate results.

volved in performing work, a project manager must also consider expenses incurred and materials purchased by those resources to obtain the true cost of a project.

➤ Time

Using project-oriented time management (PTM) a project manager can do the following:

- ➤ Track time that resources spend on various activities (so that they can ensure a project is delivered on time and on budget).

- ➤ Track nonwork time (e.g., breaks, vacations, leaves of absence), a process that, without software, all too often is an inefficient and paper-intensive administrative task.

■ PROJECT SCHEDULING

> **The most commonly used project scheduling types are the milestone schedule, deliverable schedule, activity schedule, and Gantt chart.**

Project scheduling is the determination of start and end dates for project activities. Various types of schedules are used by project managers, each having its own unique purpose. The most commonly used schedules are the milestone schedule, the deliverable schedule, the activity schedule, and the Gantt chart. Each is described in further detail in the following discussion and illustrated in Figure 5.3.

➤ Milestone Schedule

A milestone schedule should be created when the project team evaluates its progress toward the final deliverables. The milestone schedule helps the team by determining the sequence of the project's major accomplishments and the time in which they need to be completed.

Milestones are recorded on the project timeline, between the first milestone, which is the project start date, and the last milestone, which is the project finish date. All other milestones such as the completion of major deliverables will fall between the start and

Need   **Schedule Type**

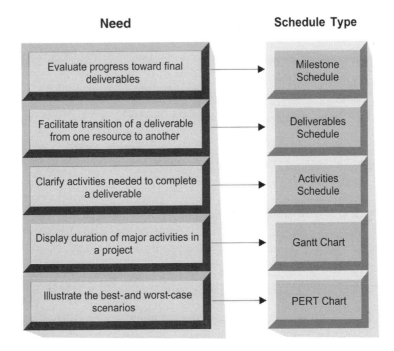

Figure 5.3 Project Scheduling Diagram

finish milestones. It is strongly recommended that the number of milestones in a given project timeline is kept to 10 or less.[3]

➤ Deliverable Schedule

A deliverable schedule should be created to facilitate the transition of a deliverable from one person to another. It shows the sequence of deliverables to be created, from first to last, and who is accountable for meeting the delivery dates for each.

Typically, a deliverable is depicted as a subproject of the main project. It is commonly displayed in a treelike structure within a WBS. Each deliverable can be further broken down to show the activities that need to be performed by various resources in order to complete the deliverable.

---

3. Only the major deliverables are shown, in order to keep the high-level view of the project plan simple(r) and uncluttered.

ID	Task Name	Start	End	Duration	Sept.2001										
					16	17	18	19	20	21	22	23	24	25	26
1	Task 1	9/17/2001	9/21/2001	5d											
2	Task 2	9/24/2001	9/26/2001	3d											
3	Task 3	9/17/2001	9/19/2001	3d											
4															

Figure 5.4 Sample Gantt Chart

➤ Activity Schedule

An activity schedule should be created to schedule and clarify the activities needed to complete a deliverable. By having an activity schedule, the project manager and the team are able to make sure that each activity is completed on time, which in turn ensures that the deliverable is completed on time.

➤ Gantt Chart

A Gantt chart (see Figure 5.4) is used to display the duration of each task within a project. Its purpose is to help people inside and outside of the project team understand each of the major activities and milestones, as well as the current project status. Bars with arrows between each major activity help to illustrate the timeline that is required from the start of a new activity to its completion. Some Gantt charts may also display additional information, such as the percentage completed or actual hours worked on each activity.

➤ PERT Chart

Program evaluation and review technique (PERT; see Figure 5.5) was developed by the United States Department of Defense as a management tool for complex military projects. Through PERT, complex projects can be blueprinted as a network of activities and events.

PERT charts can demonstrate best- and worst-case project scenarios. Most PERT charts identify three time estimates: most optimistic, most pessimistic, and most realistic. PERT charts are very useful in large, complex projects, in which overlooking details may create unresolvable problems. PERT charts are frequently used within a project for detailed evaluation planning. The critical path of a PERT chart highlights important deadlines (such as major deliverables) that must be met if the overall project is to be completed on time.

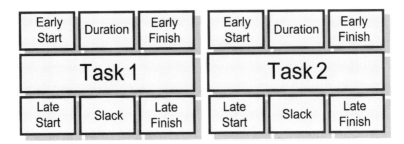

Figure 5.5 Sample PERT Chart

➤ Project Scheduling Tools

Project scheduling tools must provide an extremely rich feature set that touches on many areas. The ability to specify start and finish dates for one or more projects and activities that have been outlined in the WBS is critical. The ability to prevent members of the team from continuing to charge time to these categories by automatically suspending them upon the end date is a definite asset.

■ RESOURCE MANAGEMENT PROCESS

Resource management is the process of determining what people, materials, or equipment—and what quantities of each—are required to carry out a project.

➤ Resource Identification

In order to identify what resources are required to complete a given project, a project manager has several options available. Reviewing the plan of a completed project of similar nature can provide insight into which projects have been completed successfully and which could have been optimized. Should the project manager not have a prior example to which he or she can refer, a close examination of the WBS can provide an excellent guideline.

➤ Resource Management

Resource management involves identifying, documenting, and assigning project roles and responsibilities, as well as reporting relationships. Roles, responsibilities, and relationship reports may be assigned to individuals, groups, or teams. Prior to acquiring the resources needed for a project or activity, the project manager must first assess which skills are required for each part of the project, and when will those skills be required.

➤ Staff Acquisition

Staff acquisition involves getting the resources needed assigned to specific duties and beginning the work. The process of acquiring and assigning resources involves several considerations such as prior experience, personal interests, personal characteristics, and resource availability.

➤ Resource Management Tools

Tools that are to be used for resource planning should possess the ability to match the skills of one or more resources to the skills needed for an activity so that an informed decision can be made as to who should perform the work. Additionally, the ability to indicate which qualified resources are available during the required timeframe and the ability to reserve them helps to complete the missing pieces of the resource-management process.

■ PROJECT PROCUREMENT

➤ Procurement Planning

Procurement planning is the process of identifying what requirements can best be met by purchasing products or services outside of the organization. In some cases, it can be more cost effective to procure services, materials, or some work by subcontracting out to a team of people with the necessary skills.[4]

> Procurement planning is the process of identifying what requirements can best be met by purchasing products or services outside of the organization.

➤ Source Selection

Source selection involves the receipt of bids or proposals and an evaluation to ensure that the best vendors are selected. Decisions on

---

4. Outside help is often sought when special expertise is required, and increasingly for the bulk of the project team itself, especially when the PSORG experiences a high demand for its services and cannot meet all the staffing requirements internally. Often internal staff is kept to an absolute minimum, and external contract resources are used for many project activities.

awarding a contract may be made based on several factors, such as quality, time frame, and cost. It has become commonplace to put together a request for proposal (RFP) which details the specifications of the product or service required. Using an RFP ensures that all vendors bidding on the contract are, at a minimum, able to provide the product or service as it has been detailed in the RFP. (Please refer to Appendix B, "Professional Services Automation Request for Proposal Template," for a template RFP that can be used when searching for a PSA solution.)

➤ Purchasing Administration

Purchasing administration is the process of ensuring that the source or supplier's product or service meets the level of quality outlined in the contract. The main tasks of someone performing the duties of a purchasing administrator are to do the following:

➤ Ensure that the correct details of the product or service required are indicated in the contract with the source that has been selected.

➤ Ensure that the product or service provider is delivering the results outlined in the contract.

➤ Manage any changes to the contract for the product or service.

➤ Process invoices to ensure that the product or service provider's invoices are paid in a timely manner.

➤ Project Procurement Tools

In order to fulfill the most basic needs for procurement, the selected application should be able to accommodate multiple contracts for the procurement of goods or services and should have the ability to be associated with a supplier. The list of contracts should be maintained in a treelike structure so that they can be logically grouped and reported on.

■ SUMMARY

A project management solution must deliver a wide variety of features that include document management and sharing, timesheets, expense reports, cost and revenue accounting, planning and scheduling, and a powerful and flexible WBS. A project management application is ideal for PSORGs that wish to automate these aspects of their operational processes

> A project management solution must deliver a wide variety of features that includes document management and sharing, time sheets, expense reports, cost and revenue accounting, and a powerful and flexible WBS.

while allowing for the information collected to be seamlessly integrated with their accounting and payroll systems.

Chapter 6

Purchasing Workflows

■ INTRODUCTION

This PSA component provides workflow capabilities to streamline the purchase of resources, be it human resources, material, or equipment. Benefits include reduction in administrative costs, the automation of requisition tracking, purchase order (PO) processing, shortened fulfillment cycles, and a streamlined approval process. Some features include supplier integration, customizable workflow engine, routing requisitions for approval, applying business rules, e-mail notifications, document attachment, receipt attachment, and integration with expense and invoicing modules.

> **Purchasing work flows streamlines the purchase of resources, be it staff, material, or equipment.**

Often, the price of a piece of equipment or a resource is considered the only cost of making the purchase. However, the cost of processing the purchase itself can be very high, especially for purchases requiring complicated or time-consuming research, elaborate paper-based approval procedures, a choice of many possible suppliers, quality control issues, and associated services and guarantees,

> **Benefits include reduction in administrative costs, the automation of requisition tracking, PO processing, shortened fulfillment cycles, and a streamlined approval process.**

especially when multiplied by the number of times such activities are conducted.

Furthermore, in purchases by organizations, typically a number of individuals are involved: the requester, the approver, the person who sets budgets, the purchasing agent, and the person receiving the goods. All these individuals require communication with one another until a purchase takes place. The larger the organization, typically the more items are purchased, the more people get involved in the process, and therefore the more expensive the process becomes.

Like any other nontrivial process in an organization, the purchasing process requires a structure, a flow, and an efficient means of communication between the parties involved (see Figure 6.1 for an overview of the process). A streamlined purchasing application (PApp) can eliminate enormous amounts of redundant inter-departmental communication, as well as allow administrators to embed enterprise policies, rules, and thresholds at every step of the process.

With the omnipresent use of e-mail as the communication tool

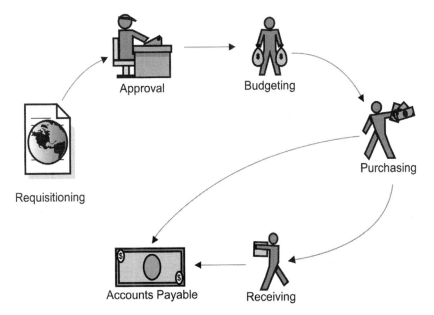

Figure 6.1 Overview of the Requisitioning/Purchase Process

of choice, submitting an e-mail about almost anything has become a simple task, and is often the first tool that comes to one's mind for requesting anything. It is, after all, paperless, and can be forwarded to an unlimited number of people, an infinite number of times. If e-mail has become the *magic bullet* to communicate, why spend money on buying software that passes a request from one person to another? Moreover, why spend even more money on training staff on how to use yet another new piece of software? Why not just designate a person in the organization as the primary contact for making purchases and establish a policy by which everyone e-mails that contact for his or her purchasing needs?

Whether it is a trivial item such as a work lamp, sophisticated manufacturing equipment, or software, predefined steps are often involved in making a purchase, and many of these steps are usually poorly documented, poorly understood, and rarely followed. For example, the purchaser may not have gotten the proper number of competitive quotes, did not use the preferred supplier, did not get the contracted price, did not seek proper approval, did not have the budget, and so on. As a result, inefficiencies develop, and these inefficiencies lead to higher costs.

One of the first steps involved in making a requisition is to determine the initial contact to receive the request. Lack of this knowledge results in the lengthening of the requisition process—an employee is obligated to make a request to his or her manager, who in turn is supposed to refer to the appropriate parties for processing. Many times the wrong people end up receiving the request. Consequently, the request is sent back and forth and rerouted to yet another person. This unnecessary communication takes away time and concentration from many people.

Another issue is the authority level of the person approving purchases. Often, depending on the cost of an item, its type, or both, different people can authorize the purchase. Yet again, with a manual request processing system, many requests end up in the hands of the wrong people who have to either reroute or authorize a request

> **Nonmechanized purchasing involves heaps of paper, a virtual blizzard of e-mails, or worse.**

without having the authority to do so. This often results in a virtual blizzard of e-mails.

Even in cases in which manual processing is successful, the person who made the request has no way to determine the status of the requisition. To find out, that person must once again initiate another chain of queries that propagate through the same channels. Nowadays it is expected that when a simple parcel is given to a courier, the sender can inquire as to its exact location at every stage of the delivery process. For organizations to apply a similar standard to their purchasing process, an automated tracking system is required—a system that can automatically report on the status of the transaction throughout the entire process from start to finish, and do so without human intervention.

In addition, there is the dilemma of clearly detailing the specifications of the items to be purchased. Typically, employees issuing purchase requests tend to be careless in providing the necessary requirements. For example, one may request a new computer and specify the RAM, CPU, and hard-disk parameters, but may not specify the operating system. At this point, two scenarios can occur:

1. When the request reaches the purchasing agent, the unspecified parameter may be noticed and the agent can send the request back to the sender and ask for the missing information. This, of course, results in unproductive recycling.

2. The request reaches the purchasing agent, the missing parameter is not noticed, and the order is processed. As a result, the system that the manufacturer ships may come with an operating system that is not what the requester needed, resulting in wasted time and frustration.

On the other hand, deploying a software application to process purchase requests ensures that employees follow a set of rules where they have to specify all important required items as determined by the organization's purchasing policies. This will ensure that the user cannot submit the request prior to specifying the required fields.

■ GENERIC APPLICATION

A PApp should be generic enough to accommodate the needs of acquiring any type of item. Even in vertically integrated organizations, many different types of items need to be purchased. For example, in a semiconductor manufacturing company, not only wafers and manufacturing parts are purchased, but various items ranging from equipment, furniture, and soft drinks to staffing requests and training for employees also may be requested and delivered. Therefore, if PApp is too specialized, it cannot be used for general purposes, and additional purchasing applications/processes would be required.

> **Purchasing solutions should be as generic as possible; otherwise they won't cover all of the enterprise's needs.**

Although the core infrastructure behind PApp should be domain independent, one should be able to customize and enhance the system to cater to an industry's and organization's specific requirements.

When the term *purchasing* is used, the acquisition of physical objects comes to mind. However, we don't only need equipment and material to be ordered for a project; we also often need human resources of various types, such as computer specialists and trainers. The process of making a requisition for human resources is not much different from acquiring equipment: the requester still has to build a case for making the request, the budget has to be approved, the research has to be done, various options have to be considered, and a final decision has to be made to select the appropriate resource.

A PApp should allow the user to define different workflows and fields for each type of acquisition. For example, the workflow for defining computer purchases should incorporate its own specific parameters such as operating system type. Similarly, staff purchasing should incorporate its own unique fields such as specifying areas of expertise, level of experience, and salary range. Furthermore, each purchase type should have its own unique flow so that the appropriate manager approves the purchases. For example, a computer purchase may have to be approved by the project manager, whereas a staff purchase would have to be approved by the HR department.

■ USER-DEFINED WORKFLOWS

The making of a purchase request and the subsequent steps are typically sequential. The user submits a request, it is approved, an order is made, and the goods are received. Different categories of items typically go through different processes: A high-priced item may require multiple levels of approval; a specialized piece of equipment may need to be further specified by the domain expert, whereas a request for an intern may need to be handled by the human resources department versus the usual purchasing group.

PApp should provide the means for defining a workflow for each of these scenarios (see Figure 6.2 for a sample workflow). Each workflow must have its own defined states, with every one of them having its own set of user-defined fields. At any given point in the workflow, there may be one or more subsequent states to which the user can go; in other words, the application should guide the user to the possible next step(s). Therefore the organization is depending on the mechanized system to ensure that the proper procedures are followed rather than the fallible memory of the actual user.

> General-purpose purchasing applications must support configurable work flows—depending on the product or service being purchased.

This introduces the concept of transitions between states. The transition corresponds to the action that the user takes when he or she wants to move the request to the next state. For example, a requisition can have a state called Initial and another state called Approved. The person approving a request selects the approve action. The approve action sends the request to the next stage, the approved state. The administrator defines the action as the transition moves from one state to the next.

■ SUPPLIER INFORMATION

Searching for vendors in yellow pages or other directories is another area in which unnecessary time is spent when making a purchase. Most organizations have preferred suppliers; however, the list of suppliers and other pertinent information is usually scattered or difficult to access. Furthermore, new staff may never find this information. As a result, every qualification process requires the individual responsible for this task to start the search from scratch, resulting in substantially repetitive and unproductive activities. The abilities of a PApp to show the organization's approved supplier list

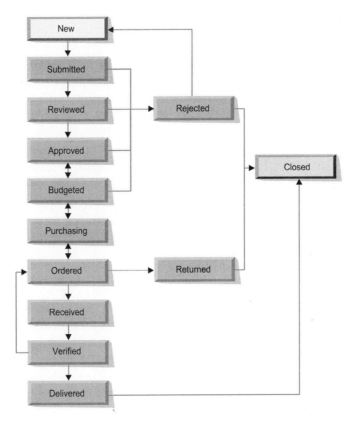

Figure 6.2 Sample Enterprise Purchase Order Workflow

and perform online access to their product catalogs with *their own* pricing[1] are great time savers in preparing purchase requests.

■ USER-DEFINED FIELDS

No matter how many fields an application can have for any feature, an organization will always need additional custom fields to be associated to certain modules. Although many applications offer the

---

1. This refers to the increasingly common trend of vendors' providing custom pricing in their product catalogs (typically online) to their customers, so that the customers always see the prices that have been negotiated for them by their corporate purchasing departments.

user the capability to define fields, all such fields are usually compiled into one long list without the option to classify them. Such lists very quickly render themselves useless due to their lack of grouping, as well as the difficulty of finding what one is looking for.

A sophisticated PApp gives the administrator the ability not only to define fields at the screen level, but also to specify when they should be visible and/or accessible. For example, the administrator can define custom fields on the page through which users enter information about the requested items. Depending on the type of item being requested, different fields can be displayed. For instance, if a computer is being requested, a custom field can be defined as the preferred type of mouse. If on the other hand, the requisition is for a financial analyst, then the custom fields can be defined in relation to his or her area of expertise.

■ USER ROLES

Users can have designated security privileges for accessing various modules, or different rights within each module. In a typical organization, a majority of users are *end users,* or standard users, who can only initiate purchase requests. The remaining are typically managers, who have the privilege of approving purchase requests and submitting them to the purchasing department. The concept of *role* makes the association between a group of users and the rights that they have in accessing various components of the application.

> **Purchasing involves spending the organization's money — security must be strict.**

The common roles in an organization include the following:

➤ *End user (or standard user):* This type of user only has the right to make a requisition. They typically cannot approve a purchase request or initiate an order with a vendor. In PApp, they are usually the people who create requisitions.

➤ *Manager:* The manager usually has the privilege to approve requisitions. Usually, there are limits on the dollar amounts that any manager can approve. When any purchase request exceeds the manager's approval limits, the request must be automatically routed to the next level of management. In addition, there is the possibility of auto-approval for the preapproved budget amounts. This allows the new purchase request to proceed without the manager's intervention. Also, there are usually additional authorization rules for certain types of purchases (such as extra restrictions on hiring consultants, engaging in contracts, buying computer hardware, etc.). In PApp, the manager receives requests that are assigned after end users have submitted them.

➤ *Chief financial officer, chief operating officer, president, and chief executive officer:* These are the senior executives that approve requisitions that are above the highest predefined limits. After the purchase requests are created and approved by lower management levels, they will be automatically routed for additional approvals. In PApp, the proper management level automatically receives the purchase request as an assignment after it has been approved by first-level managers.[2]

➤ *Purchasing manager:* This person deals with vendors and often has good negotiation skills. In most cases, this person is the final contact to receive the multitude of requests. The purchasing manager is responsible for grouping the POs together, detecting patterns in repeat orders, making and suggesting improvements to the purchasing process, and ordering the goods.

➤ *Human resources manager:* This is the person who receives requests for hiring new staff, initiates a job posting, carries out preliminary interviews, and recommends candidates to the manager requesting the resource(s).

➤ *Receiving agent:* In some organizations, the receiving department is different from the purchasing department. The responsibility of this person is to ensure the goods received match what was requested.

---

2. The highest level of approval is usually the board of directors, and major expenditures and deviations from the budget would have to be presented at this level at some point before the approvals are granted.

■ SECURITY

Although it is desirable to have a fully automated system that eliminates manual labor, it is essential that the system ensures that users do not take advantage of the automation by bypassing the system's control mechanisms and potentially making unauthorized project purchases, or by corrupting crucial data. Operating simply based on trust is not feasible; rigorous security measures have to be put in place.

Requiring users to log on using passwords, applying standard database security, and applying audit trails are basic features that any nontrivial PApp should support.

Typically, the approval of a purchase request is a central feature that should be incorporated in a robust PApp. This feature should allow the administrator to enforce the necessary approval process relevant to the purchase order type. Furthermore, the application should ensure that the necessary security requirements are in place to prevent any possible *backdoor* entry points. For example, users should not have the ability to modify purchase requests that have been approved, so that quantities or dollar amounts cannot be changed.

Component-based security allows the administrator to provide specific access rights to users, allowing access to certain areas in the application while being blocked from others. The access can be further defined in terms of read-only versus modification and deletion rights.

Automatic e-mail or pager notification is another feature that can also be viewed as a security measure. The automatic sending of an e-mail to be triggered at a certain threshold set by the administrator can be utilized to inform the appropriate staff of, for example, an over-budget purchase.

Another control factor is implementing limits per item, as well as a total dollar limit for a given purchase request. The quantity can also be controlled by restricting the number of items that can be purchased at a given time.

■ ACCESSIBILITY

Given the tremendous efficiencies and cost savings of web-based solutions, PApp must be fully web-based. Another important aspect of using web-based software to track purchases from the beginning to end is access to structured data (i.e., data in a database, as opposed to free text in e-mails or documents). Web-based purchasing software allows one to run reports, analyze purchasing patterns, view business intelligence charts and graphs, and integrate with other applications, such as accounting systems, for further automation.

> Modern PApps must be web-enabled— this ensures ubiquitous access and reduces the total cost of ownership.

In the case of purchasing, especially in certain industries such as construction or traveling sales personnel, in which there are no permanent offices, it is also advantageous to be able to make requests through wireless devices. For example, a project manager at a construction site notices that there is an immediate need for certain material. By accessing the corporate servers through a hand-held wireless device, the project manager can easily select the items required and submit the request. Instantaneously, the manager can have the purchase request processed in accordance to a predefined workflow, and quickly have the request expedited with a full audit trail. The efficiency of an automated purchasing system is evident in this process.

It may also be desirable to have the capability to make an offline request without being connected to the corporate network; this is typically the case with traveling employees. Such a solution can be provided by a PApp that supports structured e-mail-based requests, or a fat client[3] that uses a local database, which then synchronizes with the main PApp server after a connection is available. For example, let us consider a representative of medical supplies who visits many hospitals and clinics and who regularly takes orders from each of the clients that he or she visits. The agent can take orders and save them on his or her own computer, and at the end of the day submit all the orders to the corporate database.

---

3. Technology issues are further discussed in following chapters; however, a *fat client* refers to application software that must be physically loaded onto a person's computer. This installation and later support tends to increase the total cost of ownership of fat client applications.

■ INTEGRATION WITH ACCOUNTING APPLICATIONS

After a purchase requisition is turned into a purchase order, an accounts payable (AP) entry should be made in the accounting system to track payments due for this purchase. All the information required for the AP entry is already contained in the purchase order. This information includes description of the goods purchased, the price, quantity, taxes, shipping costs, and vendor information.

Another inefficiency that often arises from using a paper-based system is that duplicate information is entered repeatedly at each step. By using a PApp that integrates with the corporate accounting system, the information can be easily imported into the accounting system without manual intervention. This results in the elimination of unnecessary manual steps and errors due to rekeying of data.

■ DOCUMENT ATTACHMENTS

Often, describing an item is much more difficult than simply providing images of it. It may be required to attach these images, drawings, brochures, and so on, to the actual detailed specifications in the purchase request. In addition, receipt attachments from the vendor are often required to be kept and tracked. A PApp should allow additional information to be attached to purchase requests, purchase orders, and receipts.

■ INFORMATION ANALYSIS

Over time, priceless information is accumulated in a PApp that allows managers to analyze patterns in purchasing, ordering, and approval. This information can be analyzed and used to optimize operations.

For instance, consider a large consulting organization in which many independent groups work on customer projects and members of each group routinely order similar equipment; analysis from a global perspective may determine that certain resources can be shared across various groups, hence reducing the cost of purchases. Furthermore, some items could be ordered in larger quantities for better pricing and lower shipping costs.

Part of the costs of a project are the equipment, material, consulting, training, and other items that are purchased. By having data on purchases as part of the tools

> Over time, priceless information is accumulated in a PApp that allows managers to analyze patterns in purchasing, ordering, and approval. This information can be analyzed and used to optimize operations.

used for tracking projects, a manager will be able to report on such costs. Project-oriented purchase tracking can be used to monitor the following:

➤ Purchases used for R&D activities

➤ Measures of project, team, group profitability

➤ Tracking of order turnaround and response times in various projects, teams, and groups

■ RETURN ON INVESTMENT

Although the time wasted on a single purchase may not be evident and does not seem to impact the productivity of employees, when repeated many times throughout the year (as is typical in most organizations) it adds up to a significant amount of unproductive time and unnecessary cost to the organization (see Figure 6.3).

The cost savings of using a purchasing application that eliminates most of the overhead is significant when calculated for an entire year. The following table illustrates this savings for different numbers of purchases made in one year:

Number of purchase orders processed	20	50	100	200	1,000	10,000
Cost of traditional purchasing process[a]	$2,800	$7,000	$14,000	$28,000	$140,000	$1,400,000
Maverick buying savings[b]	$350	$878	$1,755	$3,510	$17,550	$175,500

continued

Savings from direct purchases[c]	$1,600	$4,000	$8,000	$16,000	$80,000	$800,000
Total annual savings	$1,950	$4,878	$9,755	$19,510	$97,550	$975,500

[a]VISA U.S.A. estimates that transaction costs associated with traditional purchasing processes range from $130 to $150. *Source:* [mandtbank.com/commercial/card.html]

[b]According to Gartner, 33% of spending for indirect goods and services takes place outside authorized buying agreements in most organizations, and according to McKinsey & Company, a 38% reduction can be achieved in such purchases when a streamlined and online system is available to users in the organization. *Source:* [computingsa.co.za/2001/06/18/News/new04.htm]; McKinsey Source: [purchasesoft.com/eprocurementinfo.html]

[c]According to McKinsey & Company, 85% cost savings can be achieved by making direct purchases online. In this table, this saving is applied after the reduction in number of purchases because of reducing maverick purchasing. *Source:* McKinsey Source: [purchasesoft.com/eprocurementinfo.html]

Calculate your own ROIs online on purchasing by visiting the psabook.com/roi/pr.htm web site.

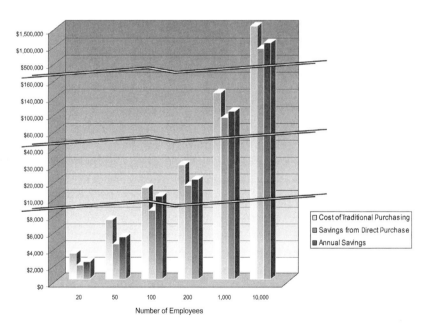

Figure 6.3 Annual Cost Savings

■ SUMMARY

A purchasing system should be flexible enough to automate the process of making a wide variety of purchases such as requests for staff, training, equipment, and material; at the same time, it should have the restrictions and approval policies in place to prevent misuse and misappropriation. The system should allow users to use a variety of access points, platforms, and in particular Web access that minimizes the overhead of installed software on users' PCs, thus significantly reducing the total cost of ownership and maintenance costs. It should also allow the users automatically to track requests and perform self-service status inquiries. With powerful reports, managers can gain insight into purchasing patterns to identify inefficiencies and redundancies across the organization.

Modern PSA solutions incorporate a staff purchasing system that can be linked to partner networks such as staffing agencies. Since PSA solutions are designed to automate the process of delivering services and carrying out projects, it is only natural that the same purchasing system and workflow engine be used also to track project-related training, equipment, and material purchases.

Chapter 7

Revenue and Cost Accounting

■ INTRODUCTION

The ability to convert billable time and expense information into detailed invoices can be a nuisance or a competitive advantage. If the required information is easily acceptable by the billing process, customers can be provided with the right level of detail that they need to quickly validate and issue payment, while the service organization benefits from improved cash flow and a low-cost, yet highly automated internal billing system. Billing is a complicated process in which there can be numerous settings, calculations, and options that are working simultaneously in order to ensure effective invoicing. Can multiple billing and cost rules be applied to the same project, client, team, or consultant? Certain features that should be present are a flexible cost and billing rate engine, support for dependencies, history, customizable rules, fixed/hourly/daily/custom rates, split billing settings, multicurrency support, tax categories and jurisdictions, various adjustment types, inclusion of notes within invoices, maintenance of invoice history, invoicing and payroll wizards, payment processing, provision of detailed information for works in progress (WIPs), and seamless integration with enterprise accounting systems.

■ RATE ENGINES

Rate engines are used to calculate the cost and revenue of work performed. The rate information is used to generate the following:

> A sophisticated rating engine is an important component of PSA.

- ➤ Cost, revenue, profit-loss reports

- ➤ Invoices, payroll, and accounts payable data

- ➤ Graphs, such as pie and bar charts

- ➤ Business intelligence reports, so that one can drill up and drill down to pinpoint strengths, problem spots, and inefficiencies

Rate engines should support multiple cost-revenue types such as hourly, daily, fixed, and custom rates defined at various WBS and OBS levels.

■ RATING MODELS

➤ Work Breakdown Structure and Organizational Breakdown Structure Rate Allocation

Cost and billing information can be defined within an organization's WBS as well as its OBS. This type of rate allocation gives organizations with various types of costing and billing models the flexibility to associate rate information to their WBS level (which consists of clients, projects, tasks, and activities), as well as at the OBS level (which consists of groups and resources or users).

➤ Hourly

Specify hourly rates for a group, resource (user), client, project, activity, or task. Rates should be effective for a defined date interval.

➤ Fixed

Fixed rates can be specified for projects, activities, groups, and resources. Fixed rates are effective for a defined date interval.

➤ Daily

Daily rates can be specified for resources working on a client, project, activity, or task. These rates are effective for a defined time interval. Daily charge applies for each day of work done, no matter how many hours of work are actually performed.

➤ Custom

Rate type can be daily or hourly. Rate type can be specified for workdays, weekends, and holidays. Custom rates are effective for a defined date interval.

■ APPLICATION REQUIREMENTS

In addition to supporting various rating models, project accounting applications must support the following features.

➤ Variance

Consultants, lawyers, accountants, and other professionals often have minimum time charges. Alternatively, time charges may vary depending on the type of service provided. For example, a consultant may speak to a client ABC on the telephone for five minutes, but the agreement is that every phone conversation will be billable for 60 minutes. These agreements may vary on a client basis, or even on an incident basis.

To support variance time entry, users would need to be able enter information as shown in the following table.

Activity	Time	Billable Time	Costed Time
Client ABC phone consulting	5 minutes	60 minutes	5 minutes

➤ Rate Precedence

Most resources may have standard billing rates. However, rating could vary depending on the specific client, project, or activity. *Rate precedence* would allow an organization to define default rates for resources, clients, projects, activities, and tasks, and then override them on a case-by-case basis. Consider the following example: Charge Client Acme $75 per hour for all consulting services. However, if Joe works on Acme Project XYZ, then charge $100 per hour.

■ MAINTAINING HISTORY

Keeping track of rate changes is critical. Without maintaining rate history, cost, revenue, and profit-loss reports that span rate changes (such as multimonth/year reports) will produce inaccurate results. Rate history can be maintained by ensuring that every rate rule has a specific start and end date. Consider the example in the following table:

Jeff Jones' Rate History

Date Interval	Rate rule
January 1999 to March 2000	$65 per hour
April 2000 to December 2000	$70 per hour
December 2000 to open-ended*	$75 per hour

*This rate will remain in effect until a new rate entry is created.

➤ Marking Entries

Services performed (timesheet data), expenses incurred, and miscellaneous charges (project overhead and other charges) can be marked as billable and/or costed. If an entry is marked as billable, then its amount is considered as revenue. A billable entry would eventually be invoiced. If an entry is marked as costed, then its amount is considered as cost. A costed entry could eventually be part of payroll or the accounts payable batch.

Cost and revenue accounting feeds the payroll, accounts payable (AP), and invoicing subsystems of an enterprise system. It is essential that the aforementioned subsystems have a mechanism for marking time and expense entries as billed and/or posted (i.e., posted to the payroll or AP system). Marked entries should not appear in subsequent payroll, AP, or invoice batches. This feature prevents double charging and double counting of critical financial data.

➤ Project Overhead

In addition to tracking cost and revenue of work done for a specific project, the project accounting system should support in some way the tracking of project overhead. Project overhead can be in monetary or hourly units. For example, it could account for 200 hours of administrative overhead for every three months of project-related work or $10,000 of administrative charges for each month of project work. The charges can be one time, periodic, or based on criteria determined by the organization.

➤ Off-Project Overhead

In addition to project-specific overhead, an organization may wish to track off-project overhead. Off-project overhead can be administrative-related activities and charges. The rate engine should be used to track off-project resources, whereas a different mechanism has to be employed to track fixed off-project overhead.

➤ Nonrecurring Charges

The system should also allow tracking of nonrecurring charges such as equipment and material purchases and penalties for late projects, discounts, and bonuses.

➤ Taxes

Various levels of taxes have to be taken into consideration—state sales taxes and value added taxes (VAT in Europe and GST/PST in Canada) to mention a few. Services performed should always be considered as taxable (taxes should be optionally overridden or ignored when creating an invoice). Expenses and other charges can be marked as taxable or nontaxable.

➤ Negative Entries (Reversed Transactions)

Negative time, expenses, and charges should also be supported so that one can track discounts, penalties, and other project-related or administrative negative charges and adjustments.

➤ Tracking On-Call Time

Employees and consultants who carry pagers or are on call during their off hours may be compensated in some form. For example, an employee may be allowed to enter two hours of extra time per week just by agreeing to carry a pager. A project accounting system should have a way of tracking, distinguishing, and reporting hours when employees are on call.

➤ Multicurrency

A project accounting system should define the system's functional currency. This is the organization's main currency.

- ➤ The main currency can be overridden per site (ability to define sites is a requirement for larger organizations with offices in various geographic locations).

- ➤ Expenses can be incurred in different currencies. The system must automatically convert these expenses to the main currency.

- ➤ Every rate rule definition must also have its own currency.

- ➤ Employees and consultants may have a preferred currency (for payroll and reimbursing expense reports).

- ➤ Customers have a preferred currency. Invoices issued to a client should default to the customer's preferred currency, but one should be able to override this default and issue the invoice in a different currency.

■ BILLING METHODS

➤ Work Completed

Many organizations create invoices for a given date interval based on work completed. For example, client ABC would be invoiced for services and expenses on a monthly basis. The rate engine as previously defined will be able to compute total revenues and generate an invoice for the requested date interval.

> PSA solutions must support various billing options such as work completed, up-to billing, milestone or progressive billing, flat charging, and split billing.

➤ Up-to Billing

Let's assume that after negotiating with a customer, the agreement is that the budget for Project XYZ is $10,000. Whenever an invoice is created, the total amount to be invoiced is compared to the specific maximum billing. If the total billable amount exceeds the fixed charge, the system will automatically provide the user who is generating the invoice with a list of user-activity pairs. The user can then decide which activities should not be invoiced. Consider the following example:

Project XYZ should be billed for $10,000, assuming project is charged at $100 per hour.

Work Performed

Activity	Time (hours)	Charge ($)
XYZ: Analysis	30	3,000
XYZ: Support	40	4,000
XYZ: Consulting	50	5,000
Total billable work		12,000

When generating an invoice, you can see that total billable charges are $12,000. However, because the maximum billing cannot exceed $10,000, there is a variance between the total agreed upon by the customer and the totals being generated. Therefore, the user must select which activities and what amounts to invoice. For example, consider the following table.

Activity	Time (hours)	Billable Time (hours)	Charge ($)
XYZ: Analysis	30	30	3,000
XYZ: Support	40	20	2,000
XYZ: Consulting	50	50	5,000
Total billable work			10,000

Using this variance concept, the invoicing engine reduced the billable time for XYZ support from 40 to 20 hours (note that users should be able to select which activities and what amounts can be invoiced).

➤ Milestone or Progressive Billing

With the milestone billing method, the client is charged based on the following criteria: the completion of a specific phase of a project (phases are defined as date intervals) and/or predefined project milestones. To support milestone billing, the project accounting system should handle the concept of project phases (such as analysis, development, maintenance); every project phase must have a specific start and end date. The system must also support the definition of project milestones. Billing amounts must be associated to every project milestone or phase depending on how the client is billed.

After a specific milestone is reached (whether it is specific date or a phase change initiated by the project manager), the system must automatically create billable system entries and notify those responsible to ensure that the client is billed for services.

The following table shows an example of phase-based progressive billing.

Phase	Date Interval	Billing Method
Analysis	5/1/2000 to 9/3/2000	Flat fee: $10,000 on end date
Prototyping	10/1/2000 to 10/31/2000	All billable time and expenses for this date interval on end date
Development	11/1/2000 to 5/1/2001	Flat fee: $100,000 on end date
Final delivery	5/2/2001 to 6/1/2001	All billable time and expense for this date interval on end date

The following table shows an example of milestone billing with fixed charges.

Milestone	Date Interval	Billing Method
Specification	5/1/2000 to TBD	Flat fee: $10,000 upon reaching milestone
Completion of phase 1	TBD (user should be able to provide estimated start and end dates)	All billable time and expenses for this date interval upon reaching milestone
Completion of phase 2	TBD (user should be able to provide estimated start and end dates)	Flat fee: $100,000 upon reaching milestone
Final delivery	TBD (user should be able to provide estimated start and end dates)	All billable time and expenses for this date interval upon reaching milestone

Note: TBD = to be defined; date is determined when project manager indicates that milestone has been reached.

➤ Flat Charging

With this billing method, the client is charged X number of hours at a specific hourly rate. As soon as even one hour of work is completed, the full amount can be invoiced. Content providers that manage video and multimedia productions often use flat charging.

➤ Flat Charging by Cost Center

Flat charging can also occur by cost center or group. In this case, every cost center that works on the project can flat-charge the customer. A cost center is considered to have worked on a project as soon as a single hour of work is completed by any resource from that cost center.

➤ Split Billing

Split billing means that the same project is charged to multiple clients. Total charges can exceed 100 percent (there should be no restrictions on the split). Split billing can occur in the following two instances:

1. Project has specific billing information based on the rates of the users who worked on the project or other rate rules defined for that project. Every client is charged a percentage of this rate based on the split percentage.

2. Every client that is billed has a specific billing rate. Project is billed based on the split client's hourly billing rate, whereby the appropriate percentage of the time entry is billed at that split client's billing rate.

■ BILLING ISSUES

➤ Preventing Double Charges

As discussed previously, the system must allow the marking of entries as billed and posted. Therefore invoicing, payroll, and accounts payable batches must all support the concept of submitting or issuing an invoice or batch. After an invoice is issued, all entries (time, expenses, and other charges) that are included in the invoice must be automatically marked as billed. After a batch is issued, all entries included must be automatically marked as posted.

➤ Work In Progress

An important concept in project management is that of work in progress (WIP). A project accounting system should include reports that, for a given date interval, display the following items:

- ➤ Total billable time

- ➤ Total amounts of billable services, expenses, and charges

- ➤ Total nonbillable time

- ➤ Total billed services, expenses, and charges

- ➤ Total unbilled services, expenses, and charges

The WIP report can be on a client, project, and user basis, or it can be for the entire organization. A WIP report provides a quick snapshot of a project or the organization's current billing status.

➤ Revenue Recognition

Revenue recognition is an important subject that is not addressed by a majority of project accounting systems. There is a constant demand from financial stakeholders for prompt and accurate revenue reporting. Having flexible PSA tools allows the reporting to be cost effective, mechanized to a high degree, and accurate to easily support mandatory reporting on monthly and quarterly cycles. A powerful PSA system also allows flexible real-time access and reporting of the information. It is essential that the project accounting system that is selected allow the organization to define its revenue recognition policy and then report accurately on the amount of revenue that must be recognized.

> PSA solutions automate revenue recognition so that PSORGs can quickly and accurately report revenue on monthly and quarterly cycles.

For example, company ABC may define its revenue recognition policy to be based on any billable time, expenses, and charges, because it has a reliable client list and it has signed contracts to that effect. However, company XYZ may define its revenue recognition policy in such a way that only approved invoices should be recognized as revenue. For XYZ, customers may or may not agree to all of the charges detailed in the initial invoice.

Therefore, a revenue recognition policy can specify revenue as recognized in any of the following situations:

➤ Entries are marked as billable.

➤ An invoice is created.

➤ An invoice is approved or marked as "recognize revenue."

➤ Payments are received (for very conservative companies or for certain customers or projects).

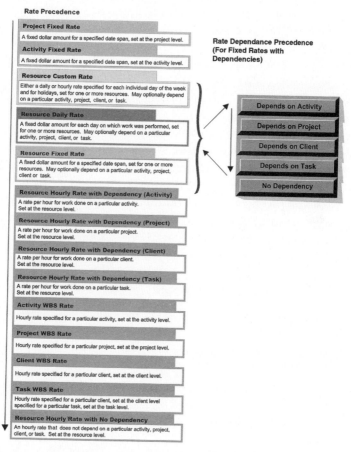

Figure 7.1 Rate Rule Precedence

One should be able to define a global revenue recognition policy and override the policy on a client-by-client basis. Revenue recognition reports can be used to accurately report on revenue that needs to be recognized and WIP (for accounting purposes: WIP = total billable amount minus recognized revenue) for financial reporting. As Figure 7.1 shows, there are many different rates and rating rules.

■ SUMMARY

As this section has described, project accounting is a powerful and critical feature that must be part of any time and billing, professional services, or project management application. Moreover, general-purpose billing is a complex area that can quickly suffer from its own design. Most large organizations are sufficiently broad in their services, and in their customer bases, that they should seriously consider a best-of-breed billing solution tailored to their type of business.[1] It is not difficult to uncover (or even develop) primitive systems that multiply hours worked by an hourly rate. However, those considering an enterprise-wide project accounting solution must ensure that the issues of precedence, maintenance of rate history, prevention of double charges, fixed billing, and other complexities are addressed by the solution that is under consideration. Customers and projects today demand this flexibility. A flexible, intuitive, and comprehensive project accounting system can provide an invaluable competitive advantage.[2]

---

1. Historically, telecom and utility companies have been heavy consumers of specialized billing systems costing tens or hundreds of millions of dollars to meet their sophisticated, high-volume billing needs. Often, their billing departments are comprised of hundreds of specialized billing-systems personnel.

2. Purchasing a best-of-breed PSA system with sophisticated billing capacity could be a significant competitive advantage by reducing costs and decreasing turnaround time.

Chapter 8

Timesheet Management

■ INTRODUCTION

One of the most crucial, yet neglected areas within PSA solutions is that of timesheet and expense management. Most PSA solutions simply offer generic or basic functionality within this category—they offer primitive and simple workflows for time or expense entry and approval. However, it will be those vendors that have developed sophisticated functionality within this area that will ensure greater ROIs for their customers. Professional Services Automation solutions that offer sophisticated functionality for timesheet management will not only significantly streamline these processes for immediate efficiencies, but also enable enhanced analysis, improved financial liquidity, and compliance with business rules. The submission of timesheet and expense reports for work accomplished or costs and billable time provide the necessary information for effective project analysis. Functionality should include the following:

> One of the most crucial and neglected areas in a PSA is that of time sheet and expense management.

➤ Validation and approvals

➤ Compliance reporting

➤ Multiple timesheet and expense views

➤ Supervisory controls

➤ Multiple notes

➤ Document attachments and work assignment

➤ Regional holidays

➤ Multicurrency capabilities

➤ Overtime and administrative task processing

➤ Constraints

➤ Adjustments

➤ Status indicators

➤ Mass updates

➤ Auto time entry

➤ Compliance for regulation settings for governmental and re-gional guidelines

➤ Expense markups and document/receipt attachments

➤ Thresholds

➤ Foreign currency conversions

➤ Comparisons of actual to planned time

➤ Multiple sites and scoping

➤ Seamless integration with payroll

➤ Accounting and project management applications

Project-oriented time management (PTM) goes beyond simple traditional time capture that is typically used to feed attendance and payroll systems. When applied properly and facilitated by an appropriate mechanized system, it provides the means to ensure that projects are accurately tracked, costed, and delivered on time and within budget. Project-oriented organizations can therefore experience tremendous benefits by capturing accurate and relevant information in a timely and efficient manner using the latest user interface (UI) and input devices. This will drastically reduce dreadful administrative tasks and paper-intensive procedures, as well as avoid the heavy training costs of using antiquated systems designed a generation ago, providing all the necessary information for crisp and accurate billing. Project-oriented time management is a best-of-breed alternative to single-vendor software applications whose expertise lies elsewhere; it also avoids the limited functionality usually found in custom-built in-house systems (which few enterprises actually have!).

Project-oriented time management requires more information than simple time and attendance management (TAM) systems can provide; however, TAM systems are necessary first steps. They serve to decrease data entry errors using poorly designed systems, inaccurate charges, and excessive payroll and billing times. In short, they are a necessary part of the solution.

Project-oriented organizations traditionally face challenges managing worker productivity—for example, minimizing *bench time,*[1] as well as actually managing the revenue-generating projects to which they are assigned. Many of the difficulties are caused by situations in which necessary information for making decisions is not collected, collected but available at the wrong level of detail,[2] poorly catalogued in the database(s), out-of-date—or all of the above. Managers for each department need direct and real-time access to their group's timesheets and expense reports in order to track internal costs

> **Project-oriented organizations traditionally face challenges managing worker productivity such as minimizing bench time, as well as actually managing the revenue-generating projects to which they are assigned.**

---

1. *Bench time* is the amount of time that professional resources are not assigned to revenue-producing activities (i.e., time billable to customers), and instead are sitting on the bench, so to speak (not bringing money into the organization). When this happens, they are not covering their own salaries; consequently, the organization can quickly find itself in a loss situation.

2. Data is often captured at a good detailed level, but is summarized into the ERP or accounting system at too high a level to be useful to the project managers.

and calculate client billing information. It is for these reasons that the management team often requires functionality well beyond what a general time and attendance solution can provide.

PSORGs need to track their work at two main levels. First, they must define who does the work—in other words, they must define the hierarchical view of the enterprise, a term also referred to as the OBS (organizational breakdown structure). Second, and of equal importance, PSORGs must be able to define what is the work being done, and for whom it is being done; this relates to the concept known as the WBS (work breakdown structure).

In essence, PSORGs need to identify, track, analyze, and manage all their internal information using the OBS and WBS. Any PTM must be capable of addressing these issues, as well as have the ability to provide a means of incorporating other important best practices detailed here.

Figure 8.1 shows the different levels of complexity that can occur in organizational breakdown structures, and the work breakdown structures they control.

■ BEST PRACTICES

A PTM should be designed and include templates based on *best practices*. Best practices[3] are practical techniques gained from experience that have been shown to produce best results.

➤ Activity-Based Costing

Activity-based costing (ABC) is really the essence of a PTM solution; ABC tracks work at the activity level, providing the lowest level of detail necessary to capture all the required information about the work being performed. A PTM solution should allow simple association of generic work (also known as tasks) to projects (also known as accounts) to created unique activities (also known as jobs).

The major challenge in using this functionality is to balance the excellent details that such a setup can provide with the admin-

---

3. A great source for such information is "A Guide to the Project Management Body of Knowledge" provided from the Project Management Institute (pmi.org), which details sound management practices for projects.

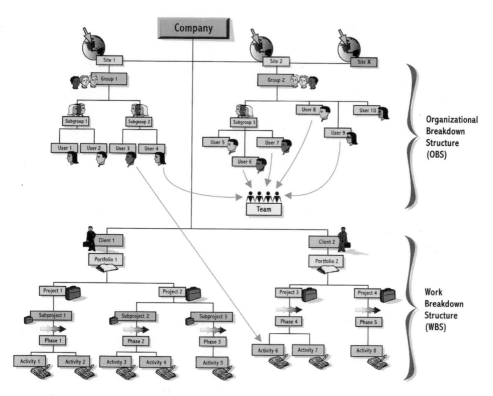

Figure 8.1 Sample Organization

istrative overhead that it entails. Too many levels of detail will create an administrative nightmare far outweighing ABC benefits, whereas depending on the organizational requirements, not enough detail will mean that important information is not being captured and will be lost forever.

A good design should allow organizations to use a tree structure to define their entire hierarchical organization (OBS) and work structure (WBS) while having the flexibility to adjust the level of detail necessary for each project so that necessary changes can be made along the way.

The work must also be tracked at the activity level, but reporting has to be possible on both the generic task and detailed work levels. The ability to roll up this information across various tasks and activities is also powerful and necessary.

➤ Customizable Workflows

A workflow is defined as a series of tasks within an organization to produce a final outcome. Sophisticated work-group computing ap-plications allow you to define different workflows for different types of jobs. For example, in a PSORG, a timesheet might be automatically routed from an employee to his or her project manager for approval prior to being posted to pay-roll, billed to a client, or updated in the project schedule. At each stage in the workflow, one individual or group is responsible for a specific task. After the task is complete, the workflow software ensures that the individuals responsible for the next tasks are notified and receive the data re-

> Sophisticated work-group computing applications allow you to define different work flows for different types of jobs.

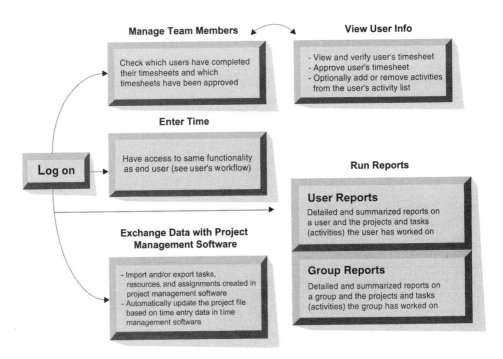

Figure 8.2 User Interaction Model

quired to execute their stage of the process. A PTM with a customizable workflow approach for each user type (e.g., administrator, manager, standard user) offers the flexibility to set up the necessary processes for any PSORG. A component-based security system should also be available to limit and define the access type (read, create, modify, or delete) for the various states and functions.

User Interaction Model with a PTM Solution

Figure 8.2 shows the typical type of user interaction seen in a project-oriented time management solution. Time can be charged, activities can be assigned, and reports can be generated for the individual's timesheet.

Manager Interaction Model with a PTM Solution

Figure 8.3 shows the typical interaction a manager would have with a PTM solution. In this case, the manager can assign activities to the team members, as well as view team members details, run project reports, and exchange data into other project management software.

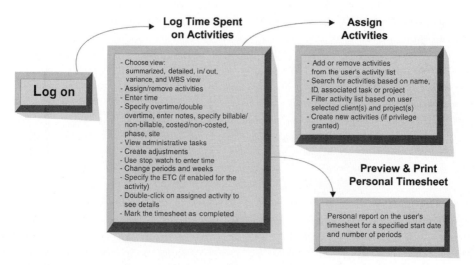

Figure 8.3 Manager Interaction Model

Work Submission and Approval

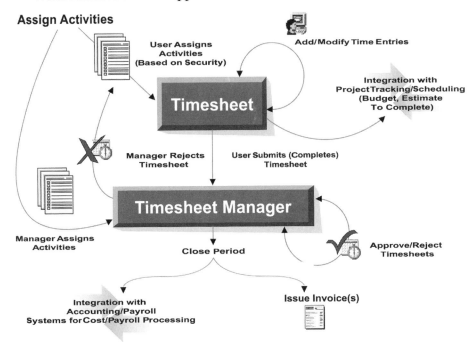

Figure 8.4 Work Submission Approval Model

Administration Interaction Model with a PTM Solution

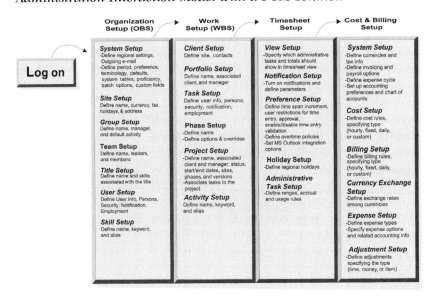

Figure 8.5 Administration Interaction Model

■ THE IDEAL PTM SOLUTION

Implementing a complete best-of-breed workforce optimization and project accounting solution is an important business activity that is often overlooked and underestimated. A complete PTM solution must include most or all of the features listed in the accompanying table to deliver a good return on investment.

Feature	Description
Resource time tracking	Multiple timesheet views with validation at the time entry level. Timesheet approval with multiple levels, including line item, client, and alternate with automatic routing. Regional holiday, overtime, and administrative task processing, constraints, validations and usage rules with full compliance for various government regulations such as DCAA (Defense Contract Audit Agency) time-keeping guidelines.
Expense reporting	Multiple expense sheet views. Expense sheet approval with multiple levels, including line item, client, and alternate with automatic routing. Managing travel and entertainment (T&E) expenses. Support for various expense categories, mileage reimbursements, markups, and business rules for expense entry with foreign currency conversion and automatic tax considerations.
Cost and revenue accounting	Support for rate dependencies and history (defined for general conditions and overridden for special cases). Rate rules for fixed, hourly, daily, and custom rates defined at various WBS and OBS levels.
Budgets and ETC	Budgets and ETC (estimates to complete) to be set at various levels (project, activity, or assignment) and in various amounts (time, cost, or billing) with automatic suspension based on set thresholds and notification.
Invoicing	For professional services organizations who need to charge for their time and expenses. Include user notes, select currency, and apply tax jurisdiction and billing information. Issue invoice and maintain invoicing history. Export to accounting system.
R&D tracking and claim management	Identify, track, and process all R&D-related work by specifying the projects, phases, activities, time, expenses, and adjustment entries that qualify.

continued

Feature	Description
OLAP	Advanced and sophisticated multidimensional enterprise reporting. Adds business intelligence to your data for enterprise optimization, change, and project management, as well as customer and decision support. Anyone with the proper access rights can drill up or down and gain significant insight about the organization's operational efficiencies and weaknesses.
Adjustments entries	Making positive or negative changes to users' data. These modifications should be in time, cost, or billing amount with the ability to flag these entries.
Site and scoping	Maintain a central database and track work by location, but allow users, managers, and administrators of each site (or within a virtual site) to only have access to site-specific information.
Project phases	Tracking of projects based on a stage. For example, a project can be in research, analysis, development, or maintenance phase.
Mass update	Make massive changes to data for past periods, changing the status of the submission over time.
Note entries	Various types of notes to be used for reporting and included in R&D claims, client invoices, project status updates, etc.
Document attachment	Attach to clients, projects, activities, users, timesheets, time entries, expense reports, and expense entries with keyword-based search capabilities.
Status indicators	Mark any time or expense entries status, such as R&D funded, as costed and billable.
E-mail notifications	Event-triggered notifications such as incomplete and rejected timesheets, expense reports, budget overruns, and evaluation dates.
Tree format	Set up hierarchies and better represent the organizational and work breakdown structures. Support for search-find and drag-drop.
Suspend/ decommission	Manage users, projects, and activities temporarily not being used or deactivated permanently.

Feature	Description
Adapt default terminology	Modify and adapt the existing terminology on any window or report to match your organization's requirements.
Software development kit (SDK)	Develop enhancements and extensions or extract and manipulate data from a local or remote database.
Import/export	Built-in wizard to export data to leading project management software, as well as leading payroll and accounting systems.
General ledger (GL) numbers	Associated to various items within the PTM with complete history being kept in case of GL changes.
Audit trails	A complete log of users' access to the system and any entry modifications.

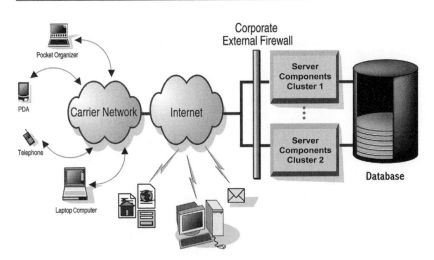

Figure 8.6 Data Access Graph

■ DATA ACCESS OPTIONS TO CONSIDER

Access to data via Internet, wireless communication, e-mail, Windows, and other devices delivers a far more flexible solution to cater to various types of users who need to interact with the PTM database (see Figure 8.6).

Figure 8.7 Project-Oriented Time Management Data Access Graph

■ PROJECT-ORIENTED TIME MANAGEMENT AND OTHER ENTERPRISE SYSTEMS

Live bidirectional data synchronization with other ERP, CRM, project management (PM), payroll, and accounting systems is vital for a best-of-breed solution (see Figure 8.7).

> Modern PTM must be web-enabled—this ensures ubiquitous access and reduces the total cost of ownership.

■ SUMMARY

A PTM solution must deliver a comprehensive web and wireless solution that streamlines timesheets, expense reports, cost and revenue accounting, and billing and client invoicing. Project-oriented time management is ideal for PSORGs that wish to automate these aspects of their operational processes while allowing the information collected to be seamlessly integrated to their accounting, payroll, and project management applications.

Chapter 9

Labor Management

■ INTRODUCTION

Labor management is an ongoing activity critical to any organization and an important part of the payroll cycle. Typically, time and attendance data is collected using paper and spreadsheets, and no automated mechanism gets this information into the payroll system. The accuracy of information is also difficult to control, as there are no built-in mechanisms to validate, inform, and report on data. A solution that seamlessly ties into the payroll software can greatly streamline the process, reduce human errors, facilitate reporting, and lead to a quick and tangible return on investment.[1]

Time is money. In today's economy, this statement has never been truer. Efficient time and labor management is vital to any organization's success. Most companies do not really appreciate the losses they incur due to their lack of proper time and attendance accounting. Generally, time and attendance systems are primitive paper- or in-house–based systems, often one per department, incompatible with each other as well as with most of the enterprise systems in place. There is a very low penetration rate of these types of mechanized systems, whether simple time and attendance management (TAM) systems or full-blown PSAs. Considering that the United States is the leader in most mechanization and modern

---

1. Based on studies from American Payroll Association and Robert Half Associates. Information is available at [http://www.majoraccounts.adp.com/time/etcalc.htm]. Retrieved on 11/05/2001.

management techniques, we assume that the penetration is even lower in most other countries.

■ TIME AND ATTENDANCE DATA CAPTURE

Employees do not like filling out timesheets; this is a fact that is hard to overcome. However, because the lifeblood of a PSORG is billable services or budgeted time, accurate timesheets that can also be used to bill customers are imperative. Often employees rush to fill and submit a timesheet without considering the consequences in time-consuming administrative corrections.

■ TIME MISAPPROPRIATION

Time loss, which is the time misappropriation for longer-than-appropriate lunches and breaks, late arrivals, and early departures is equal to 4.08 hours on average each week.[2] If there is no system that can accurately track the arrival, departure, and break times systematically, then abuse and carelessness add up to a significant weekly, monthly, and yearly loss, especially when amortized over the total number of employees. Because at some point all these costs must be burdened by employers and customers, more efficient organizations will either be more profitable, lower-cost producers, or both.

■ DATA VALIDATION

Receiving the data is only part of the challenge. Usually the time entries need to be manually validated, and then the work really begins. The person who has to check the timesheets will notice discrepancies, from wrong codes to missing time entries and violations of the organization's time and attendance policies. The inaccuracies caused by human error are estimated to be up to three percent.[3]

---

2. From a joint study including the American Payroll Association and Robert Half Associates. Available at [http://www.majoraccounts.adp.com/time/etcalc.htm]. Retrieved on 11/05/2001.

3. Based on studies from American Payroll Association and Robert Half Associates. Available at [http://www.majoraccounts.adp.com/time/etcalc.htm]. Retrieved on 11/05/2001.

■ PAYROLL PREPARATION TIME

Payroll preparation time, which is intimately tied into the time and attendance process, is always delayed by late time cards, wrong job codes, and after-the-fact administrative adjustments. This preparation process can be reduced by 80% through the use of an automated solution. The seven minutes that it takes to audit each card can be reduced to one minute using an automated solution, a saving of six minutes, or over 85%. This *single* small incremental savings per employee and per pay cycle represents, in a 1,000-person organization, about 100 hours per pay cycle, and assuming two pay cycles per month, represents a savings of 2600 hours over the full year, or 325 eight-hour work days. As can be seen from this example, a *very small* insignificant savings—*per* employee, per payroll cycle—translates into significant savings over the year, and in this case can support an extra employee on the payroll or can flow directly to the bottom line.

> **Large yearly savings to the enterprise come from small savings in payroll preparation time per employee.**

■ BENEFITS OF A TIMESHEET SOFTWARE SOLUTION

➤ Eliminating Paperwork

An automated solution drastically reduces and in certain cases eliminates any need to use paper in your time and attendance cycle. This will result in savings directly associated with printing, distributing, and handling the heaps of paper that need to be processed every week

> **An automated solution drastically reduces and in certain cases eliminates any need to use paper in the time and attendance cycle.**

➤ Online Access to Information and Policies

Some of the common questions of employees are the following:

➤ How much vacation or sick leave do they have remaining?

➤ To whom should they submit their timesheets?

➤ How should they deal with various exceptions?

➤ What is the company's time and attendance policy?

Or they may just want to see their timesheets from previous periods.

A best-of-breed time and attendance software will give employees online access to this information and allow them to make automated requests for vacations, personal days, and so on.

➤ Streamlining the Process

The manual process of users receiving their timesheets from the HR department and submitting the timesheets involves a lot of excessively wasted time, including walking around, printing faxes, and then routing the information to the appropriate parties for approval until it finally discovers its way to the payroll department. Also consider that at any time, the manager or payroll department may need to send back the timesheet to a user who is required to modify and then resubmit the timesheet to the appropriate parties throughout the approval process. This lengthy and cumbersome process can be significantly streamlined using an automated system that sets up a clear workflow and simplifies the process of prevalidating and correcting timesheets.

➤ E-Mail Notification and Online Status

There is always room for increased efficiency when a task involves a workflow including several parties with potential transitions going back and forth. Timesheets can be halted due to one or any combination of the following parties:

➤ The users who forgot to submit their timesheets

➤ The manager who did not approve the employee timesheets

➤ One of the managers who is out of the office

➤ The payroll department or manager who recognizes an error that the user had to correct but did not

A system that provides e-mail notification and online status of timesheet workflows allows organizations to manage these points of failure, which can cause the process to break down. Using software, the payroll administrator can work proactively, be advised to review the workflow as to where a timesheet has been delayed, and quickly resolve the issues.

➤ Reducing Payroll Adjustments

Making adjustment entries to employee pay is yet another time-consuming activity. Having the right data flowing directly to the payroll system can alleviate errors and manual entry. Time and attendance management software that also manages pay adjustments can result in substantial time savings; this allows all parties involved—the employee, manager, and payroll administrator— to more easily input, track, and identify changes for previous pay periods.

> Using software, the payroll administrator can work proactively to resolve issues quickly and eliminate errors and delays.

➤ Avoiding Double Entry

Payroll is ongoing and for the majority of organizations one of the biggest (if not the biggest) costs, and with the use of modern PTM tools, this area can be better controlled. Timesheets are collected and validated manually, and are required to be entered into the payroll system for employee payroll. This type of double entry of data leads to human error. Employees can be overpaid or underpaid, which both have associated direct and indirect costs.

➤ Other Enterprise Systems

Time and attendance data certainly has to interface with the payroll system and in many cases, the organization will also need to share the same data with various other enterprise systems to avoid human error and time loss in rekeying of data.

Live bidirectional data synchronization with other ERP, CRM, PM, payroll, and accounting systems is vital for offering a best-of-breed solution.

> Live bidirectional data synchronization with other internal systems is vital.

➤ Return on Investment

In the following table, we see in more detail how small improvements in efficiency can translate into large dollar savings.

Number of employees	20	50	100	200	1,000	10,000
Department timesaving/week	$20	$50	$100	$200	$1,000	$10,000
Reduced human error savings/week	$113	$281	$563	$1,125	$5,625	$56,250
Total wages recaptured/week	$1,224	$3,060	$6,120	$12,240	$61,200	$612,000
Total annual savings	$65,136	$162,768	$325,584	$651,120	$3,255,600	$32,556,000

Note: Table assumes 37 1/2 average hours/employee/week, $15 average hourly rate, and $20/hour department head/auditor's hourly rate.

Based on studies from American Payroll Association and Robert Half Associates (majoraccounts.adp.com/time/etcalc.htm, 11/05/2001):

➤ Six minutes saved auditing each card

➤ One to three percent the estimated human error factor

➤ 4.08 hours was the average weekly *time theft*

Automated payroll can greatly decrease inaccuracies caused by human error, payroll preparation time, management of labor costs, and time misappropriation for lunches, breaks, arrival, and departure (see Figure 9.1). Calculate your own ROIs online on time reporting by visiting the psabook.com/roi/tm.htm web site.

■ THE IDEAL SOLUTION

Implementing a complete best-of-breed TAM solution is an important business decision that is often overlooked and underestimated. A complete TAM solution must include most or all of these features to maximize the return on investment.

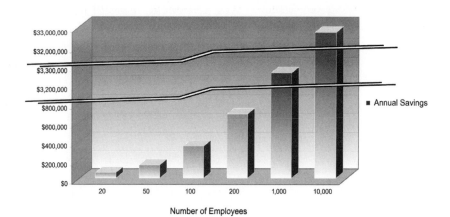

Figure 9.1 Return on Investment Bar Graph

Feature	Description
Various timesheet views	Offer several views to accommodate the different ways data needs to be entered and captured.
Shift management	Prefill and apply various rules based on employee type and work shift, with support for rotating shifts. Shift time is entered automatically without user intervention. Manual timesheet changes are flagged and require approval.
Exception reporting	Schedule the system to auto-create and submit a predefined timesheet for a specified date interval for various users. Users make changes to their timesheets only if there are exceptions such as time off for vacation, etc.
Approval	Timesheet approval with multiple levels, including alternate, line item, client, and alternate, with automatic routing.
Prefill holidays	Site-specific defined holidays; every user can be assigned a specific holiday set for which time is automatically entered.
Work-hour thresholds	Enforcing work minimums and maximums (daily, weekly, and period) before allowing users to submit their timesheets.
Request processing	Request processing (vacation, leave, travel, personal day, etc.).
Overtime policy system	Overtime accrual and usage rules to be specified for every weekday, on a daily, weekly, or per-period basis.
Labor management	Administrative tasks (e.g., vacation, sick leave, personal day, jury duty) processing, constraints, validations, and usage rules.

(continued)

Feature	Description
Compliance for various government regulations	Full support of government regulations such as DCAA time keeping guidelines. California Wage Laws, European Time directive, Family Medical Leave Act (FMLA), Fair Labor Standards Act (FLSA), United States' per diem (FAR) regulations.
E-mail notifications	Event-triggered notifications, such as incomplete and rejected timesheets.
Adjustments entries	Track special charges; make positive or negative changes to time data.
Note entries	Various types of notes to be used for reporting, R&D claims, client invoices, project status updates, etc.
Status indicators	To mark time entry status, such as R&D, as funded and costed.
Mass update	Make massive changes to data for past periods; for example, marking all time entries in a date range as posted.
Access	Access to data via punch devices, terminals, web, wireless communication, e-mail, Windows, and other devices delivers a far more flexible solution to cater to various user types that need to interact with the TAM server.
Site and scoping	Maintain a central database and track work by location; allow users, managers, and administrators of each site (or within a virtual site) to have access only to site-specific information.
R&D tracking and claim management	Identify, track, and process all R&D-related work by specifying the projects, activities, time, and adjustment entries that are eligible.
Business intelligence analysis	Advanced and sophisticated multidimensional enterprise reporting can add business intelligence to your T&A data. Anyone with the proper access rights can drill up or down and gain significant insight about the organization's operational efficiencies and weaknesses.
Document attachment	Attach documents to clients, projects, activities, users, timesheets, time entries with keyword-based search capabilities.
Tree format	Set up hierarchies and a better representation of the organizational and work breakdown structures. Support for search-find and drag-drop.
Suspend/ decommission	To manage users, projects, and activities temporarily not being used or being deactivated permanently.
Adapt default terminology	Modify and adapt the existing terminology on any window or report to match your organization's requirements.

Feature	Description
Software development kit (SDK)	Develop enhancements and extensions or extract and manipulate data from local or remote databases.
Import/export	Built-in wizard to export data to leading accounting systems. Live and seamless data integration is a preferred method because it is less error prone, quicker to use, and more efficient than simple text-file data exchange.
General ledger (GL) link	Associated to various items within the TAM.
Audit trails	A complete log of users' access to the system and any modifications.

■ SUMMARY

A time and attendance management solution will reduce the costs and errors associated with the collection, submission, approval, and administration process, greatly decreasing inaccuracies caused by human error, payroll preparation time, management of labor costs, and time misappropriation for lunches, breaks, late arrival, and early departure.

Chapter 10

Expense Management

■ INTRODUCTION

Project-oriented expense management (PEM) is vital to the success of most projects; however, most current control procedures are often extremely labor-intensive due to the lack of appropriate mechanized tools or their lack of sophistication. Project deliverables and associated costs can be severely impacted by the systems used to manage expenses. Streamlining expense reporting and control processes can bring about tangible benefits for an organization's bottom line by reducing the amount of administrative tasks and paperwork, as well as mechanizing the associated workflows. This section outlines the details of how PEM applications can greatly simplify and improve project management efforts by providing the tools necessary to streamline and automate the expense reporting process.

Expense reporting is an ongoing and labor-intensive reality for the majority of businesses today. Therefore, a small gain in the expense management process can have enormous benefits and a positive impact on an organization's bottom line.

The workplace continues to expand beyond its local geographic boundaries and the need to cope with multiple currencies, tax jurisdictions, and increasing amounts of trade regulations specific to these varying locations continues to place increasing amounts of restrictions on most enterprises. Nevertheless, most workers who perform project work in multiple locations around the world continue to rely on simple spreadsheets to capture the basic information and send them to rigid legacy systems, often by first printing the documents, and then sending them to clerks who attempt to manually apply corporate and legal guidelines in a consistent manner.

In PSORGs, the situation is aggravated further because expense reports are often an integral business component and can represent a major portion of the total project costs. These costs need to be properly tracked and in some cases must be accurately billed.

The collection and approval of expense reports is not the only difficulty. Trying to establish and implement thresholds of key metrics, tracking and reporting on the history of these expense reports, and sharing this data with other enterprise applications all present further challenges. In most cases, the proper gathering of this information is simply neglected, as the cost of compilation is often considered not worth the effort. Exchanging information with other applications is often accomplished by the manual rekeying of data, which is not only a resource-intensive task, but also greatly increases the probability of human error.

Various expense categories need to be set up and analyzed by PSORGs. Some examples include travel, client entertainment, mileage, hardware, software, office expenses, training, and cash advances. In each case, different types of information need to be collected and various business rules can often apply. For example, in the case of mileage, information such as destination and distance must be specified.

PSORGs desperately need to relate the right expense types and amounts to their projects to better estimate budgets and to be able to deliver them on time and within budget. In the case of PSORGs, who also bill clients for their project expenses and in certain cases mark up these costs, additional information and detail is required (such as timely client approval).

> **PSORGs that bill clients need to track expenses, in some cases mark up costs, and obtain client approval.**

In many cases, employees who have to submit their expense reports typically feel as though they are racing against time. This frustration is directly proportional to the report frequency and to the particular organizational expense-reporting policy and cycle.

■ AUTOMATION BENEFITS

When you consider the tremendous benefits associated with expense report automation, it is just incredible. Consider the following:

➤ The average cost to manually process an expense report is approximately $40 and can be as high as $80 for some organizations (Rusty Carpenter, David Marcus, and Alan Sandusky, ©2001 American Express Travel Related Services Co., Inc. All rights reserved, June 2001). An automated solution can reduce expense-processing costs by at least 40% and can be as high as 90%.

➤ The third-largest corporate expense today is travel and entertainment (T&E).

➤ The Hackett Group has found that on average a corporation processes 20,000 expense reports for every $1 billion in revenue (Hackett Benchmarking & Research; part of Answerthink).

➤ American Express Consulting Services revealed that the average expense report costs more than $36 and can take up to 18 days to process. This cost represents 3 to 15 percent over the total T&E budget (Rusty Carpenter, David Marcus, and Alan Sandusky, ©2001 American Express Travel Related Services Co., Inc. All rights reserved, June 2001).

➤ CFO magazine's annual SG&A (sales goods and administration) survey concluded that for most organizations, cutting just $1 of operational costs could have the same impact on the bottom line as increasing the revenue by $13 (Randy Myers, survey by Exult Process Intelligence Center, December 2000 issue, pages 66 to 80, CFO Publishing Corp.).

Indeed, the manual processing of expense reports is inefficient and results in redundant data entry and human error. Those who are susceptible range from the individuals who report expenses to the managers

> **Large savings are possible from automation of expense reports.**

who approve them to the administrative staff, who process this information.

Every expense-reporting process one streamlines can dramatically reduce the cost of administration, expense report submission, reimbursement, and approval (see Figure 10.1). Expense automation can provide strict control over the direct and indirect costs. Organizational expense policies can be seamlessly integrated into the submission and approval process.

➤ Actual Annual Cost Savings Calculation

The following table presents the typical savings that can be expected by mechanizing expense report creation for various organization sizes.

Calculate your own ROIs online on expense management by visiting the psabook.com/roi/er.htm web site.

Number of employees submitting expense reports	20	50	100	200	1,000	10,000
Number of expense reports annually (assuming one each month)	240	600	1,200	2,400	12,000	120,000
Total administrative cost savings[a]	$6,852	$17,130	$34,260	$68,520	$342,600	$3,426,000
Total productivity cost savings[b]	$4,000	$10,000	$20,000	$40,000	$200,000	$2,000,000
Total actual cost savings annually	$10,852	$27,130	$54,260	$108,520	$542,600	$5,426,000

[a] Based on a study conducted by the American Express Consulting Services Group, the average cost savings per expense report processed is $28.55, which is calculated as $36.46 (the average cost per expense report processed without automation) subtracted from $7.91 (the best-in-class cost per expense report processed with automation; Rusty Carpenter, David Marcus, and Alan Sandusky, Copyright 2001 American Express Travel Related Services Co., Inc. All rights reserved, June 2001).

[b] Based on a study conducted by the American Express Consulting Services Group, the average productivity savings per expense report is 40 minutes, which is calculated as 55 minutes (the average processing time per expense report) subtracted from 15 minutes (best-in-class processing time per expense report). Every employee saves 40 minutes × 12/60 = 8 hours per employee/year. Assuming an annual average salary of $50,000/50 weeks/40 hours = $25/hour (Rusty Carpenter, David Marcus, and Alan Sandusky, Copyright 2001 American Express Travel Related Services Co., Inc. All rights reserved, June 2001).

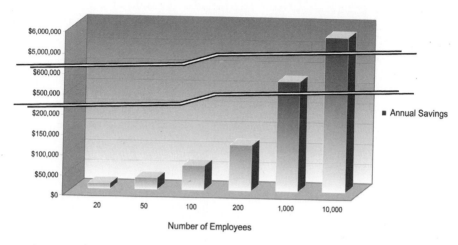

Figure 10.1 Cost Savings Bar Graph

➤ Workflows, User Types, and Roles

Users of the expense reporting system will have security access rights based on their profiles. Their interactions will be limited to the roles they play within the organization. Typical roles include standard users who need to submit their expense reports, managers who need to approve their subordinates' expenses, and the administrators who need to set up and manage the entire process. Each organization may have many other resources that need to access or work with expense-related data. Furthermore, different workflows may be required, depending on the respective organization's approach to managing its operational processes.

■ THE IDEAL PROJECT-ORIENTED EXPENSE MANAGEMENT SOLUTION

Implementing a complete best-of-breed expense-reporting solution is an important business decision that is often overlooked and underestimated. A complete PEM solution must include most or all of the features listed in the following table to deliver a better return on investment. Some of these features deserve further descriptions, which are discussed in the following paragraphs.

Feature	Description
Expense reporting	Multiple expense report views. Manage travel and entertainment (T&E) expenses. Support for various expense categories, mileage reimbursements. Business rules and validation at expense entry level.
Approval	Expense report approval with multiple levels, including line item, client, and alternate with automatic routing.
Multiple currency and tax jurisdictions	Support for foreign currency entry and conversion, as well as automatic tax jurisdictions and category considerations.
Invoicing	For professional services organizations who need to charge for their expenses. Include user notes, select currency, and apply tax jurisdiction and billing information. Issue invoice and maintain invoicing history. Export to accounting system.
R&D tracking and claim management	Identify, track, and process all R&D-related expenditures by specifying the projects, phases, activities, expenses, and adjustment entries that are marked as R&D.
Business intelligence analysis	Advanced and sophisticated multidimensional enterprise reporting can add business intelligence to your expense data. Anyone with the proper access rights can drill up or down and gain significant insight about the organization's operational efficiencies and weaknesses.
Adjustments entries	Track special charges; make positive or negative changes to expense data.
Site and scoping	Maintain a central database and track work by location, but allow users, managers, and administrators of each site (or within a virtual site) to only have access to site-specific information.
Offline expense reports	Fill in expense reports offline and synchronize data with central database after a connection is available.
Limits and auto-approval for certain thresholds	Budgets and limits to be set at various levels (project, activity, or assignment) with automatic suspension and notification, as well as approvals based on set thresholds.
Markup field	Mark up billable expenses.
Automatic credit card update	Ability to automatically upload credit card expenses into expense reports and apply business rules and validations to avoid double entry and after-the-fact administrative adjustments.
Mass update	Make massive changes to data for past periods; for example, marking all expenses in a date range as billable.
Note entries	Various types of notes to be used for reporting and included in reports, R&D claims, client invoices, project status updates, etc.

Feature	Description
Document attachment	Attach documents or web links to clients, projects, activities, users, expense reports, and expense entries with keyword-based search capabilities.
Status indicators	Mark any expense entries' status, such as costed, billable, R&D, and funded.
E-mail notifications	Event-triggered notifications; for example, for incomplete and rejected expenses reports.
Tree format	Set up hierarchies and give a better representation of the organizational and work breakdown structures. Support for search-find and drag-drop.
Suspend/ decommission	Manage users, projects, and activities temporarily not being used or deactivated permanently.
Adapt default terminology	Modify and adapt the existing terminology on any window or report to match your organization's requirements.
Software development kit (SDK)	Develop enhancements and extensions or extract and manipulate data from a local or remote database.
Import-export	Built-in wizard to export data to leading accounting systems. Live and seamless data integration is a preferred method because it is less error prone, quicker to use, and more efficient than simple text-file data exchange.
General ledger (GL) numbers	Associated to various items within the PEM.
Audit trails	A complete log of users' access to the system and any entry modifications.
Access	Access to data via Internet, wireless communication, e-mail, Windows, and other devices delivers a far more flexible solution to cater to various user types that need to interact with the PEM server.

➤ Approval

The following are several aspects to approving expense reports:

➤ Several levels for expense approval, depending on expense type and amount

➤ Automatic routing of approvals to the next appropriate manager

➤ Client's approval in some cases in which typically they are billed

➤ Automatic approval of certain preallocated expenses

The application should allow the administrator to associate approval levels required to different expense types and amounts; for example, for hardware purchases, the first-level IT manager may be authorized to approve relatively large amounts, but for entertainment-related expenses, for example, a much lower threshold may be set for the same manager.

When it comes to billing customers for expenses, actions are taken in reverse order: The billing party sends the customer the bill, and the customer rejects the bill as unacceptable, which then results in discussions and possibly an adjustment to the expense and resubmission of the bill. In contrast, if the expense-tracking software provides a feature for the customer to log into the vendor's system to approve the expense reports that are to be billed, it will simplify the process and eliminate a considerable number of after-the-fact corrections.

Sometimes approval for certain expenses is obtained in advance; in such cases, it would be convenient for the manager or the accounting department to preapprove an expense and not have to approve it again after the expense is incurred.

Just as with any other application that tracks approval workflows, the manager should receive an e-mail that is sent automatically when an expense approval is required. An even nicer feature is to have the URL correspond to the employee's expense report that needs to be approved embedded in the body of the e-mail, so that a simple click takes the approver to a specific web page to allow the customer to view and approve the expense report. This is a convenience and ease of use that managers would appreciate, especially when compared to the arduous task of sifting through employees' paper slips and trying to make sense of it all.

➤ Multiple Currency and Tax Jurisdictions

The requirement to support multiple currencies in an automated expense reporting system goes beyond the selection of the currency for amounts spent.

In some situations, an employee lives in one country (currency A), the organization for which he or she works is in another country (currency B), and he or she travels to the customer's site abroad (currency C) and incurs some expenses. In this scenario, the person typically wants to be reimbursed in his or her own currency (A), the customer company wants to be billed in its local currency (C), and the organization doing the accounting needs to keep track of all expenses in its main currency (B). sophisticated expense-tracking system with powerful reporting is required that makes all these conversions seamless and provides the option to the employee and the corporation to indicate conversion rates.

Furthermore, a large corporation can be multinational, which underscores the need to support multiple currencies. The concept of site or location can be used to identify each division of the corporation and to associate a base currency with each site; if needed, expenses related to each site can be processed based on the preferences set for the site independent of the rest of the organization.

As for taxes, by capturing the tax information at data entry time (automatically reverse calculated when user enters the gross amount), the corporation can easily calculate and reimburse taxes corresponding to the location where the expense was incurred.

➤ Corporate Policy Compliance

Combined with a business intelligence engine, managers can identify patterns in purchased items, preferred suppliers, and other spending trends; this helps in forecasting future trends, identifying and establishing agreements with preferred suppliers for better pricing, and ensuring that employees comply with policies set by the organization.

For example, by running reports on regions and routes where employees travel, it is discovered that the best prices can be obtained by negotiating a deal with a certain airline that already services these routes heavily; this reduces the overall cost of travel and saves the time of having to shop for the best deals.

The ability to quickly define queries by using guided user interface dialogues (also known as wizards), as opposed to manually writing queries, can save managers a considerable amount of time. Using queries, managers can identify expenses, projects, and users that require closer scrutiny. For example, one can run a query against all subordinates' entertainment expenses to see which ones exceed certain acceptable amounts. Therefore, expense approval or verifying reasons for a budget overrun can take the form of checking for exceptions rather than examining every expense item, hence expediting the approval and verification process.

➤ Integration with Accounting Systems

Providing easy-to-use expense data collection for end users is an important aspect of overall expense report automation; however, processing of this data at the back end is also critical for total elimination of data rekeying. After data is saved in the application database, it should be possible to export that data by a click of a button to the associated accounting system for further processing, be it for accounts payable or accounts receivable purposes.

When expense entries are made, each expense type should already be defined in the system corresponding to a GL (general ledger) set up in the accounting system, without end user intervention. This association eliminates the need for the user or the accounting staff to manually classify each expense item.

A smart expense tracking application can even detect what expenses can possibly be categorized as expensed; hence, these items can be marked as tax deductible when exported to the accounting system.

➤ Offline Expense Reports

It is common for a road warrior to return to the office, especially after having been on the road for a long time, with numerous expense slips and the obligation to submit the expense report on time. What typically happens is that some slips are lost, others do not have the date or the amounts written on them (typical of taxi receipts), and the employee has to spend additional time trying to make sense out of the large pile of paper and do his or her best to report the expense accurately. Needless to say, this is tremendous amount of unproductive time wasted—not to mention the frustration caused by tedious paperwork.

Those travelers who are out of the office for extended periods of time often wait until they come back to the office to submit their expense reports; the impact that this delay has the following disadvantages:

> ➤ Expenses that need to be billed to the customer are submitted late, hence postponing the collection of such amounts.

➤ The number of expense reports to be approved by the manager becomes large; hence, the manager spends less time per report to scrutinize the validity of each item, therefore increasing the chances that illegitimate expenses will go unnoticed.

➤ Credit card payments become due, and in absence of corresponding expense reports, typically are paid off without being checked; also, when the expense report does become available, it creates a backlog of data entry for the accounting department.

Contrast the previously described scenario with one in which the expense automation system supports offline expense entry, which the employee can use to enter expenses on a daily basis without having to have a connection to the head office. An offline expense entry solution eliminates all the problems mentioned above. If this solution is coupled with e-mail support and automatic entry of expenses into the system, it becomes the ideal method both for the traveling employees as well as for the in-house staff.

Also by supporting PDAs (personal digital assistants), employees can enter expenses in such devices when even laptops are not practical or not available, and later upload the expense reports to the corporate servers. Using a WAP phone, on the other hand, provides the user the means to submit expenses when other methods of connectivity are not available.

■ SUMMARY

A project-oriented expense management solution streamlines the expense reporting process by dramatically reducing the costs and errors associated with the administration, expense report submission, reimbursement, and approval process. A PEM is ideal for PSORGs that wish to automate these aspects of their operational processes while allowing for the information collected to be seamlessly integrated to their accounting and project management applications.

Chapter 11

Invoicing

■ INTRODUCTION

Processing invoices is generally a paper-intensive and disconnected process that is often tedious and typically involves great human intervention. Invoicing is a core business activity that is critical to the health of the organization; it can be neither delayed, nor can it be allowed to be error prone. It goes beyond the accounting or finance department and is of central importance to the survival of the enterprise. Project- and service-based organizations need to be able to depend on a complete end-to-end system that can manage the complex invoicing work flow directly from the project accounting system and feed the data directly to the billing system. These sections outline the details of how invoicing automation solutions can greatly simplify and improve project management efforts by providing the tools necessary to streamline and automate the invoicing process.

> Invoicing is a core business activity — the enterprise depends on it.

An *invoice* is defined simply as a detailed list of goods shipped or services rendered, with an account of all invoiced items. Organizations depend heavily on their invoicing process. Any deficiencies, oversights, and delays can result in significant losses. Naturally, the accuracy and efficiency of invoicing is very much dependent on the systems implemented to streamline the process and to make it error-free. The invoicing process is usually designed around the organization's products or services, is complex, and causes quite a few complications within management for accounts receivable.

Typically, organizations rely on an extensive error-prone paper trail to collect and process their invoices, and to enter the data into their accounting systems. In some cases, organizations attempt to manage their invoices by using expensive accounting systems. The problem in both cases is that the invoicing process is too disconnected from the actual accounting system. It would be simpler and more effective (especially for PSORGs) to manage an integrated invoice generation and project tracking system, which can then seamlessly feed the invoicing information directly to the accounting system.

> Organizations often rely on an error-prone paper trail to invoice properly.

Although laborious, issuing the invoice is at least a process that can be controlled and optimized. Any means found to streamline the invoicing process can represent considerable gains in productivity for PSORGs.[1] Invoicing is a core business process that involves gathering, preparing, entering, authorizing, exception handling, approving, issuing, reporting, filing, and updating. It is our objective to describe the process, explain what can be streamlined, and recommend software system requirements.

■ COMPONENTS

Several options should be specified in order to determine what charges are considered in the process of generating an invoice.

➤ Services

The invoice generation process should allow for the selection of billable time. Users should have the option to include all time entries for billable activities belonging to projects related to a client.

---

1. Productivity gains can be achieved by reducing the time taken to invoice and reducing errors, as well as by containing the growth of the actual accounting, clerical and professional staff involved in heavily manual or poorly mechanized environments.

Users should be able to do the following:

➤ Specify which projects are being invoiced to the client.

➤ Select all or some of users that have worked on the selected projects.

➤ Select line items to include or exclude specific activities.

It should be possible to optionally (based on security level) adjust the number of hours of each activity and the charge amount (determined by the billing rule applied to each user) to be included on the invoice.

➤ Expenses and Materials

In addition to accounting for work performed, invoices may also include billable expenses and materials. Users should have the option to include any expenses and materials that are entered against selected billable activities.

Users should be able to do the following:

➤ Specify which projects are being invoiced to the client.

➤ Select all or some of the users who have entered expenses on the selected projects.

➤ Select line items to include or exclude specific expenses.

It should be possible to optionally (based on security level) adjust the expense amounts to be included on the invoice.

➤ Charges

Invoices may also include billable charges, including time and money charges that are entered against billable activities. These charges may be positive (e.g., bonuses for early project delivery) or negative (penalties for late delivery and special discounts). Project-oriented time management (PTM) software with a customizable work flow approach for each user type (e.g., administrator, manager, standard user) offers the flexibility to set up the necessary processes for any PSORG. A component-based security system should also be available to limit and define the access type (read, create, modify, or delete) for the various data collection, approval, and invoicing states and functions.

■ INVOICING WORK FLOW

A system designed for PSORGs should include the invoicing work flows to support project-based billing and professional services, similar to that shown in Figure 11.1.

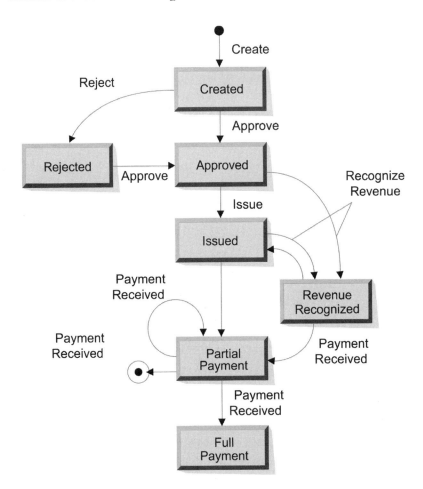

Figure 11.1 Invoicing Workflow

■ GENERATION

➤ Data Collection

When preparing an invoice, the first challenge is to ensure that the collection of pertinent data is achieved in a timely fashion. This section is covered in depth in the following sections:

- ➤ Project-oriented time management
- ➤ Project-oriented expense management
- ➤ Revenue and cost accounting

These sections detail the data that need to be captured, such as time entries, expenses, charges, markups and markdowns, materials, billing rates, notes, currency, tax jurisdiction, and all associated general ledger and accounting information.

➤ Entry

After the data is collected, select the following:

- ➤ Client to be invoiced
- ➤ Invoice number and date interval
- ➤ Information to include (e.g., time, expenses, materials, charges)
- ➤ Projects, users, and work to include in the invoice

■ APPROVAL AND SUBMISSION

➤ Initial Invoice Data Approval

Typically, the first stage in the approval process is approval of the initial data that were collected. Here, customers should sign off on this information via an Internet log-in option to review data remotely. In this manner, clients can review, approve, or reject all associated time sheets, expenses, materials, charges, and billing rates. Invoice approval may also be just an internal process in which a designated manager or project leader approves the proposed invoice.

➤ Issuance

After invoice data is approved, the following must be done

- ➤ Apply client discount rate (if any), which is based on the preferred customer terms that have been negotiated.

- ➤ Choose how to display work details and note types entered by those who did work for this customer.

  - *Work done:* The number of hours or days. When days are displayed, the number of hours per day should be specified so that the number of days can be accurately calculated. Average rate by user can be calculated by dividing the chargeable amount by the number of hours entered and displayed on the invoice. Total bill-per-invoice entry will be the total of all the expenses on the invoice.

  - *Group:* Allow entries to be sorted by user, project, or activity.

  - *Detail level:* It is important to include the level of detail shown on the invoice (e.g., summarized, detailed, or one line per item).

  - *Notes:* Notes entered for time entries by users should be included in the invoice. Also specify which note types to include and (optionally) specify to include the notes entered for the line item.

- ➤ Add billing information, including details such as company and invoice payment contact(s), associated purchase order number (if any), and complete billing address.

- ➤ Taxable amount should appear with the specified currency and exchange conversion rate, including tax jurisdiction (country, state and method) and tax rates.

- ➤ Include potential interest and finance charges.

- ➤ Select the notes to include in detail, all the terms and conditions, and where they should appear on the invoice. This should include payment terms, return policies, warranties, limitations on liability, service and support conditions, and dispute resolutions.

➤ Choose an invoice template that displays the data and information based on customer type.

➤ Select the accounting system to export invoices.

➤ Final Invoice Approval

The second phase is for the customer to approve the actual invoice being issued, which also includes the customer's discount rate (if any), taxes, and all supporting documentation, including all related invoicing descriptive notes, terms, and conditions.

➤ Maintenance

After an invoice is approved and has been issued, all associated time, expense, material, and adjustment entries should be marked as billed to prevent double billing. The system should allow a lot of flexibility in the maintenance of the invoice to keep track of invoice status. For example, the invoicing system should track partial or full payments and maintain detailed payment history.

■ AUTOMATION BENEFITS

An automated and best-in-class invoicing system can reduce the invoicing collection and processing dramatically in the following ways

➤ The expected gain in productivity and reduction in administrative tasks is approximately one hour per invoice.

➤ An automated solution can reduce one to three percent of the total invoicing imprecision caused by human error.

■ RETURN ON INVESTMENT

The following table shows the savings for various sized organizations from mechanizing invoice processing.

Number of invoices processed annually	20	50	100	200	1,000	10,000
Savings from imprecision caused by human error[a]	$4,000	$10,000	$20,000	$40,000	$200,000	$2,000,000

continued

Number of resources involved in the invoicing process	1	1	1	1	3	10
Savings from gained productivity and administrative tasks reduction[b]	$2,500	$2,500	$2,500	$2,500	$7,500	$25,000
Total actual cost savings annually	$6,500	$12,500	$22,500	$42,500	$207,500	$2,025,000

[a] Based on savings from improvements in human error imprecision (1%) in the invoicing cycle and an average amount of $20,000 per invoice.

[b] The productivity gain per invoice is one hour, which represents a savings per invoice of $25, assuming an average salary of $25/hour.

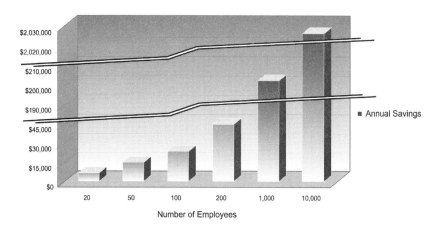

Figure 11.2 Invoicing Return on Investment Bar Graph

Calculate your own ROIs online on invoicing by visiting the psabook.com/roi/iv.htm web site. Figure 11.2 graphs the savings and ROIs from mechanizing invoicing using the above assumptions.

■ APPLICATION REQUIREMENTS

Implementing a best-of-breed invoicing solution is an important business decision that is often overlooked and underestimated. A complete solution must include most or all of these features to

Feature	Description
Invoice wizard	Guide the user step by step through the entire process to ensure that no important steps are omitted.
Security	Assign certain users the right to create and issue invoices and allow them to change times, expenses, adjustment data, and invoice numbers.
Charges	Track special charges; make positive or negative changes to expense material and time-related data.
Note entries	Support various types of notes to be included in the client invoice.
Markup and discount field	Be able to mark up and discount time-, adjustment-, expense-, and material-related information.
Mass update	Make massive changes to data for past periods; for example, marking all expenses in a date range as billable and approved.
Day locking	Should allow for day locking of user data, so that invoices can be issued at preset intervals or by exception, and not necessarily corresponding to the payroll cycle.
Multiple currency	Support foreign currency entry and conversion.
Taxes	Automatic tax calculations with support for various tax jurisdictions and category considerations.
Payment tracking	Track the invoice status (e.g., approved, rejected, issued, partially paid, fully paid), payments, and detailed payment history.
General ledger (GL) numbers	Associated to various items within the invoicing system (users, activities, expenses, and charges).
Templates and reports	Include several invoice templates and allow the customization of existing invoice reports or create new ones and add them to the system.
E-mail notifications	Event-triggered notifications to work proactively to manage the invoicing process.
Audit trails	A complete log of users' access and modifications to the system.
Software development kit (SDK)	Develop enhancements and extensions or extract and manipulate data from a local or remote database.
Data exchange to accounting systems	Built-in wizard to export data to leading accounting systems. Live and seamless data integration is a preferred method because it is less error prone, quicker to use, and more efficient than is simple file-based data exchange.

deliver a better return on investment. Most important is that the invoicing system be integrated with a powerful revenue and cost accounting system.

■ SUMMARY

An automated solution must streamline invoice creation, approval, issuance, and maintenance by reducing the human intervention and paper-based administration associated with the entire process.

To avoid manual intervention and data rekeying, an invoicing system must be an intimate component of any complete project cost and revenue accounting system. PSORGs must automate these aspects of their operational processes while allowing for the information collected to be seamlessly integrated to their accounting and ERP systems.

Chapter 12

Request and Issue Tracking

■ INTRODUCTION

Another underappreciated component within PSA solutions is the concept of *workflow*. A workflow helps manage and streamline the flow of business processes.

Key workflow features include priority setting, alert-triggered notifications, approval process, escalation, classification, notes, document attachments, and assignment, as well as tracking and reporting on various issues. Such issues include client issues, change requests, feature tracking issues, bug tracking issues, tasks, milestones, reporting and search capabilities, a customizable workflow engine, advanced queries, and support for role-based transitions. Workflows can help organizations mechanize and standardize internal activities.

The purpose of this chapter is to define a workflow and present various types of workflows that can be used to automate and track many aspects of running a business. It highlights the issues associated with the haphazard tracking of processes in an organization that may be poorly managed. Furthermore, the benefits of using a Workflow and change management (WF&CM) software application to streamline and define structure to otherwise chaotic processes are also discussed.

A WF&CM system completely defines, manages, and executes workflows using software. The sequence and progression of the workflow is driven by the computer representation of the workflow logic.

In an organization in which all staff is experienced and accustomed to commonly used processes and workflow, problems may be *invisible*. As long as the procedures don't change and the staff remembers them, this flow may continue without a glitch. However, in the ever-changing business environment of today, even companies with well-established business models and processes need to examine, redefine, and re-engineer themselves regularly to remain efficient—this means doing things differently.

Traditional processes of documentation and staff training run the risk of having newly defined rules, policies, and methods that are not well understood or followed. Resistance to change might emerge because the staff is used to doing things the old way. On the other hand, if an application is used to guide the employees through the proper steps, and the application includes online help, tips, and reminders, the outcome of the process will be much more predictable and the quality and efficiency of operations of the organization will tangibly improve.

■ WHAT IS A WORKFLOW?

A workflow is a structured way of defining and automating procedures and processes within an organization. When a workflow is implemented using a software application (versus defining it in a document or using e-mail to send information back and forth), it guides all the individuals that participate in the process and enables them to record their activities at every phase of their involvement.

A workflow can consist of two or more states; it usually has a well-defined initial state and one or more final states. The process can flow from one state to another; this is called a transition. Different individuals are assigned at each state with certain privileges to take the process to the next step (i.e., change the state) or assign it to other individuals. A state may make a transition into one or more states, depending on the conditions that have been set.

Figure 12.1 illustrates a simple workflow that includes a few steps that are common to many processes.

At each state, one or more of the following resources and objects are associated to the state.

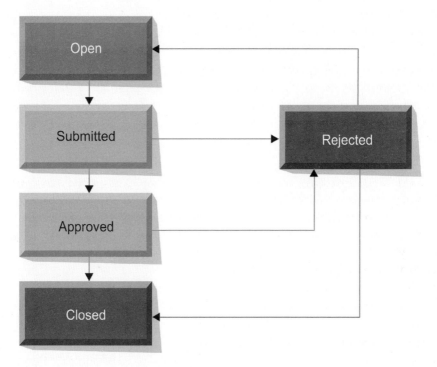

Figure 12.1 Issue Workflow Diagram

User: This person carries out a portion of the process. For example, when a new project needs to be executed, the steps may involve planning, analysis, design, implementation, testing, and delivery. In each of these phases, certain users are assigned to be responsible for completion of that portion of the project.

Task: For each state, a different set of tasks may be involved. For example, in a project in the initial phase, the tasks are planning and analysis, whereas in later stages they are implementation and quality assurance.

Time: Whenever any work is done, one of the immediate required pieces of information is the amount of time spent on that phase. More specifically, project managers need to know how much time and resources were spent at each phase of a project so that they can better budget for the next project. Users must be able to record their time while using the WF&CM application; this calls for a tight integration between the WF&CM and time-tracking applications.

Documents: Customer specs, guidelines, regulations, rules, drawings, and test cases are some of many types of documents that need to be associated with different stages of a workflow. The WF&CM system should allow users to attach documents to each state in which they are working.

Custom fields: The ability to define custom fields in an application makes the software more flexible. If the user can specify custom fields specific to certain workflows and limited to certain states within the workflow, it gives even broader capability to the user to fully fine tune the application.

■ THE CURRENT SITUATION

It may seem that casual conversations or use of e-mail are efficient ways to initiate and execute a process in an organization. However, in a company with more than just a handful of employees, the number of times requests are forwarded and escalated, the number of assignments and reassignments made, and the redundant questions that are asked are very high and time consuming. In addition to the time wasted and resulting delays, this lack of a well-defined structure for guiding people to complete the right processes results in a lot of imprecision and a high error rate.

E-mails and conversations cannot be classified, sorted, and analyzed for tracking and reporting purposes. Following and completing a process requires that various people follow the (official) proper sequence to do their work, allocate and track their time and budgets, and capture all the generated information for their mechanized systems. These goals cannot be achieved cost effectively without using a mechanized software solution that is tailored to the organization's needs.

Change management (whether it is built into the project management solution itself or simply integrates with it) is a concept that is often forgotten in standard project management practices, even though change is an obvious occurrence in the life cycle of a project. If changes that occur in the midst of an ongoing project are not well managed, how will managers keep the project on track while respecting budgets and delivery times? Serious consequences may arise if the aspect of change is overlooked.

Changes in a project can be difficult to manage because of their frequency and unpredictability. It is important to have a software solution that helps managers deal with change by automating the process of identifying, analyzing, resolving, or proposing solutions and approving or rejecting the proposed solutions to issues that have been encountered.

> One of the essential features for any project management application is change management and issue control software.

■ WHICH PROCESSES NEED WORKFLOWS?

The answer is all the nontrivial processes in an organization! Here are but a few of the processes that are common to many organizations:

Tracking internal issues: Any organization with more than four or five people has sufficiently complex processes to warrant the use of a software application to track issues. For example, in any office there will always be users who have problems with their computers and someone, such as a network administrator, who needs to fix the problem. Reporting issues using a WF&CM solution instead of calling or e-mailing the administrator (which is disruptive and hence nonproductive) allows for the recording and prioritizing of each issue according to its importance and urgency. This data can then be used for identifying the type of problems the organization is encountering, whether they are hardware-related, software-related, or results of training deficiencies, as well as how often they repeat and how effective the remedial action was that was taken to correct the situation.

Defect tracking: Also known as bug tracking in the software industry, this is one of the essential tools in any engineering, R&D, construction, and (in general) any project-oriented organization. Data accumulated as a result of tracking defects can be used much as previously discussed for tracking internal issues. Tracking defects and issues in a mechanized system not only helps in ensuring that a

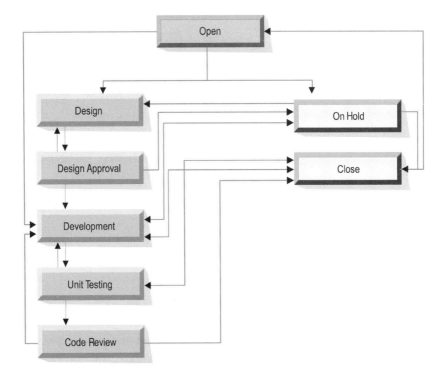

Figure 12.2 Feature Development Workflow

particular defect is followed up and corrected, but it also provides a valuable database of information that can be analyzed for organization-wide corrective action. This can help in scientifically based re-engineering efforts.[1] Figure 12.2 illustrates a simple process of defect tracking.

Request tracking: Many actions that need to be taken in organizations are not necessarily an issue or a problem, but rather are simply ordinary business processes that have to be executed. For example, an employee may need to obtain a corporate credit card prior to a business trip or ask for additional insurance coverage. The employee may not know the proper procedure for this task, or for the multi-

---

1. *Scientific* here is used in the sense that the re-engineering efforts are based on actually analyzing real data that have been collected from the actual running of the enterprise.

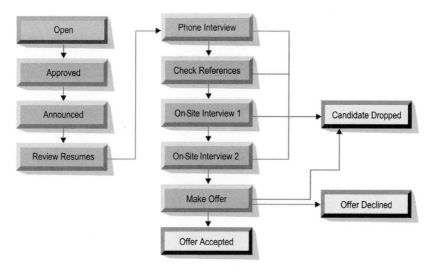

Figure 12.3 Hiring Workflow

tude of other day-to-day ordinary corporate activities. In these situations, open-ended queries, paper, or mechanized handbook lookups or some other unstructured process usually takes place. On the other hand, if the HR department maintains a list of commonly asked requests and defines the rules and requirements in the WF&CM software, the system will help guide the users through the right process. In the credit card example, the requirements can be defined in the system so that an employee, for example, must have been employed at the company for at least six months, and a credit check must have been performed on that individual.

Human resources: Hiring new staff is traditionally a well-defined process involving several steps that need to take place consecutively before the new employee is hired (see Figure 12.3). These steps may include receiving requests from managers for additional staff, getting budgets approved, posting and announcing positions, gathering and classifying resumes, conducting interviews, checking with references, making offers, sending information and documentation, notifying other departments upon hiring, organizing welcome events, and training the new employees. At each of these steps, the HR personnel use the WF&CM to move the process forward.

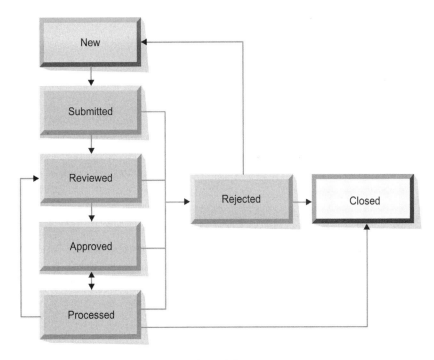

Figure 12.4 Document Approval Workflow

Document management: Documents that are used by more than a few people usually go through a cycle of being drafted, reviewed, edited, finalized, distributed, and so forth. When sophisticated routing, approving, and editing of documents take place, specialized routing software is of great benefit. On many occasions, however, a WF&CM application that is capable of maintaining various versions of a document, storing the comments of various people involved in the cycle, and maintaining access rights by users accessing the documents, will be sufficient to meet most of an organization's needs. Figure 12.4 shows an example of a document approval workflow.

Internal Organization for Standardization (ISO) certification: One of the fundamental purposes of ISO certification is to document procedures and meetings that are attended and decisions that are made. A user-friendly WF&CM application can serve as the structured repository of many of the procedures that need to be followed.

Also captured are the actual instances of such procedures that have been executed. A WF&CM application can ensure that the project manager follows each procedure properly, without taking any steps out of order or skipping. When the mechanized solution is used for each project and the details are captured, it allows a seamless method of auditing the entire project in the future.

Process re-engineering: Process re-engineering involves defining new efficient processes to replace older inefficient ones. Purchasing a WF&CM application and starting to use it is not equivalent to re-engineering an organization. Analysis must be done and plans have to be put in place to initiate a re-engineering process. The WF&CM will improve the efficiency of executing such a plan.

Customer service: It is almost impossible to have clients and not receive questions from them or have them report problems. A WF&CM will be of great use to record the clients' requests and assign them to the appropriate individuals in the organization to service, resolve, and eventually communicate with the client. See Figure 12.5 for an illustration of the flow involved in supporting customers.

Field service: This activity may be part of the overall customer service process, but it deserves a workflow definition of its own. It often involves steps that need to be prioritized either during or after a visit to a customer. For example, prior to visiting customers, an engineer may need to contact them in order to obtain information about the tasks that will be carried out during visits and the requirements that the customers must provision prior to encounters. During a visit, information such as specs may be obtained that will need to be stored as part of this process; after the visit, activities such as a customer satisfaction survey may be required. It is common in such a multistep process that the people involved forget one or more steps. Use of the WF&CM will ensure such procedures become mechanical and the quality of the work done will not be dependent on the knowledge or memory of the people involved.

Travel requests: Because of the apparent simple nature of this activity, many organizations use e-mail and spreadsheets as the means by which employees make travel requests. However, when considering all the various conditions and events that are associated with

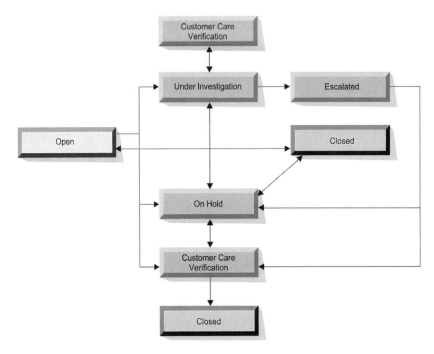

Figure 12.5 Support Workflow

a travel request, one realizes that a structured and automated means of making such requests is needed to ensure accuracy and efficiency.

For example, typically approval is required prior to making any travel arrangements. Following this step, the user should specify the itinerary and other details. Software can help guide the user to specify the following

➤ *The airline:* Many companies have preferred airlines. The software can suggest or enforce a specific carrier; otherwise, this rule will have to be repeated to every newly hired employee (or buried in a manual describing many other rules and regulations).

➤ *The class:* Using business class or first class may be reserved only for executives or altogether banned for all employees. The software can ensure that unauthorized employees do not make such a request.

➤ *The destination:* Due to lack of proper communication or knowledge, it is common for an agent or assistant to book a flight to the wrong city or the wrong airport. By using predefined cities and airports in the software, it can be ensured that the proper city and airport are selected.

➤ *User preferences:* The software can store user's preferences and whenever a new request is made, those preferences are loaded automatically. For example, an employee may prefer an aisle seat, a special type of food on the plane, a nonsmoking hotel room, and a certain type of vehicle when renting a car. Other information, such as frequent flier miles and hotel and car rental membership numbers, can all be stored to avoid repetition of such information for every single request.

Product development/improvement: Most companies offering products and services to their clients often receive requests for new features and enhancements. These requests are forwarded through conversations, e-mails, and meetings, and are often (at least) partially lost because they were not recorded and tracked properly. Using online software through which clients can directly enter their requests themselves can greatly improve this process and ensure that a well-documented trail is created. The software can be customized to allow clients to choose from many predefined fields, such as product name and version, and allow clients to input their feedback and requests.

Figure 12.6 illustrates the complete cycle of processing such a request, from the time it is made by the customer, including the steps of approval and acceptance, to the final stage of delivering it.

Request for information (RFI) processing: Organizations routinely need to evaluate products when making purchases, or when responding to RFIs if they are the vendors. Standard steps need to be taken for completing each of these processes, and a WF&CM software can eliminate the problems associated to enforcing a standard process, as well as streamline the whole process itself. Figure 12.7 depicts the steps a vendor typically takes to process an RFI.

Knowledge management: Knowledge management is the systematic process of collecting, sharing, and transferring information. This knowledge is used to leverage lessons learned from past decisions

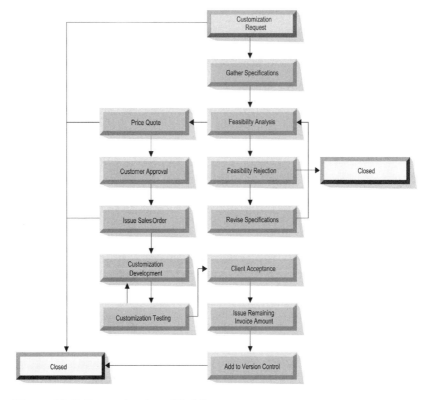

Figure 12.6 Customizations Workflow

and experiences, to share best practices, and to develop consistent processes. A WF&CM tool streamlines the creation, approval, classification, and ultimately the use of such information.

Other processes, such as time and expense tracking, purchase requisitions, project management, lead tracking, opportunity management, and CRM require specific functionality and have unique characteristics to warrant an application specifically designed for these purposes. However, a very powerful and generic WF&CM application that allows definition of user-defined fields, as well as customization of screens and reports, can address the needs of a diverse set of processes such as the ones mentioned above.

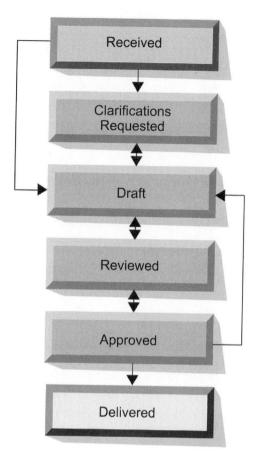

Figure 12.7 Request for Information Workflow

■ SOME CHARACTERISTICS OF WF&CM APPLICATIONS

A usable and powerful WF&CM system must have the following features and functionality.

➤ Issue or Ticket Types

To be able to classify the issue or ticket type is a very powerful basic characteristic that is extremely important for the WF&CM Application to provide. A generic WF&CM application should allow creation of many different types of classifications of potential issues or tickets.

➤ Priorities

Another necessary attribute of any issue is its associated priority. An issue's priority is usually determined by the person creating the issue and is usually approved by the manager or a third party, such as the customer. This attribute enables the person assigned to the issue to realize the importance of the issue and act accordingly.

➤ Assignment

At any stage of the workflow, someone (usually the manager) should be able to assign a user to any state. It should also be possible to associate certain roles or users to a given state or a component of a workflow, so that when it enters into that state or the component selected, that user automatically receives the assignment.

➤ Changing of States

After completion of the task, the user who is assigned to a given state must be able to change states from one to the next without manager involvement in every state change.

➤ Roles

Different users of a WF&CM application need specific security privileges for using the application. For example, managers might need the ability to assign issues to subordinates, or the CFO might need to be able to approve certain purchase requisitions. Roles can also be used by the application to send certain notifications to specific types of users rather than just individuals. For example, an organization may want to notify critical issues reported after hours to users with the role of supporting such clients.

➤ Client Access

Not only do the employees within an organization need to exchange information in the form of a WF&CM application, but also the interaction is often initiated by the client. This interaction may extend inside the organization and even back to the client. Allowing customers access to the WF&CM application in a controlled manner so that they see only issues related to themselves creates a valuable opportunity for customers to follow a predefined (and probably mutually agreed upon) process. This self-service facility avoids clients' asking repetitive questions of the vendor (and avoids the vendor staff's having to answer repetitive questions) and allows them to report issues at their convenience online without having to wait for an answer by a live person, as well as update the reported issue later.

➤ Tracking the Status

Because a workflow can be in any state at any given time, the initiator of the process and the managers involved in the process may need to know the status in terms of what stage it has reached. An application that allows the manager to keep track of each state of the process helps to maintain control and report on the time and duration a state is open, in progress, or closed.

➤ Creating Advanced Queries

One should be able to create queries to search the database with issues that match certain criteria. The following are some of these criteria:

- ➤ Has priority equal to, less than, or greater than (or any combination thereof) a certain priority level
- ➤ Is of a certain type, such as software bug, network issues, customer care, and so on
- ➤ Is created or originated by certain individuals or customers
- ➤ Is in a certain state, such as open, deferred, or rejected
- ➤ Is assigned to certain users, roles, or teams
- ➤ Is associated with a certain client or project
- ➤ Was created within certain dates
- ➤ Contains certain keywords in their descriptions
- ➤ Has attachment (and more specifically, has attachments that are certain types of documents)
- ➤ Is a query based on user-defined fields

➤ Statistics

Information on a number of issues with certain priorities, the date span in which they were created, the time it took to be resolved, the time spent on each issue, the number of issues resolved by certain individuals, and so on are crucial for making plans for future projects, as well as for quantifying performance and work done. The WF&CM application must provide a powerful reporting system to answer these questions seamlessly.

➤ Visualizing the Flow

For complex workflows, it is essential for users to view the relationship between states, the transitions, and the overall flow of the process in a graphic manner. It is even more powerful for the WF&CM to give the user the capability to define the flow graphically to begin with, which will provide the user with intuitive ways to define the process. Additionally, the graphic representation of a workflow helps users identify inconsistencies and missing or repeated steps, as well as intricate redirections; this therefore streamlines the entire process.

➤ Handling Exceptions

When users carry out a process, the focus is usually on events that occur or must take place. However, sometimes parties need to be notified if certain actions are not taken. The following are some of these cases:

➤ If a critical issue is created and not resolved within a certain threshold period defined by the administrator, a reminder may need to be sent out alarming the people who need to take action regarding this matter.

➤ If a deadline is reached and the issue has not been resolved or is not in the closed stages, alarms need to be sent to the assigned person(s) as well as to the manager(s) prior to the deadline.

➤ When a budget is exceeded for a workflow, the assigned user and the manager need to receive notification.

➤ Assignment and Notification

Assigning an issue to a user without having a mechanism for informing him or her of the assignment can lead to unserviced issues.

Depending on the severity or urgency of the matter, different methods of notification should be used. For example, for a blocking type of issue (such as a web server down), the cellular phone of the person assigned to work on the issue should be called; in other cases, a simple e-mail may well be sufficient.

➤ Templates for Various Issue Reports

Customers in general should be encouraged to use online tools that create efficiency both for themselves and for their vendors. Unless the tool is user friendly and functional, this goal cannot be achieved. One of the ways to create efficiency for both parties is to make prefilled online forms available to customers so that they do not need to create new issues every time from scratch. For example, when customers need to report product bugs, the form should have a list of all supported products and the associated information (version, platforms supported, and other characteristics) so that the customer does not need to search for such information and enter it manually.

➤ Triggers

One of the common issues that occur in an organization is the lack of communication when certain events occur and a dependency exists between two or more systems. For example, in a client-server environment, when the database on the server is updated, the client software also needs to be updated. An administrator who is unaware of such dependency may proceed with updating the server without upgrading the client work stations at the same time. This obviously can create dissatisfaction and loss of productivity with end users, or it may even result in a massive network failure. A seemingly minor change that unknowingly impacts others can have devastating consequences.

The solution to such problems is to define and embed the events and notifications that need to be triggered when certain conditions are met or a series of states are reached. In the example mentioned, if the person initiating the changes uses a WF&CM that has all the steps involved for such a task and the state is reached that has an impact on others, the application can pop up a reminder, as well as notify the parties of other requirements.

➤ Achieving Parallelism

In the real world, not everything is sequential. Often, many processes need to start at or nearly at the same time. A sophisticated WF&CM system should allow the user to define multiple substates as the next steps of a given state, and specify one or more conditions for moving forward in the flow. The following are some examples of such conditions:

- ➤ When the first subflow completes, the next state can be reached.

- ➤ Specific subflows must be completed before the next state can be reached.

- ➤ If one or more of the subsequent states fail, an alternate state is reached.

- ➤ All the subflows should complete successfully before the next state is reached.

➤ Customizable Workflow

No matter how diverse and extensive an application may be, unless the WF&CM allows users to define and completely customize their workflows and not be bound by predefined workflows, the application will not be useful for long.

Customization includes creating an unlimited number of distinct workflows, states, and transitions within other workflows, and defining custom fields for various screens and states.

➤ Linked Flows

Again, in the real world, the boundaries between processes are often not clear cut, especially when one needs to be performed in sequential order for successful completion. For example, when a service is rendered to a client, the process of communicating with the client should take place first, then the planning and scheduling of resources, then the actual rendering of the service, followed by an action such as invoicing the client. Each of these processes can have several states and secondary workflows. In order to ensure that each process is well defined, simple, independent and reusable, all processes should be briefly and simply defined individually in the

WF&CM software.[2] Each process needs to be tied to the other to ensure that the next process is initiated upon the completion of the previous one. The WF&CM must be able to automatically initiate the new process from the completed one, with the appropriate parameters and transfer of pertinent data. In this example, after the service is rendered, the system should create an accounting workflow so that the invoice is prepared and sent to the customer.

➤ Customizable Application

No matter how rich the WF&CM application is in terms of functionality and fields/attributes, companies often have unique needs that cannot be addressed by a generic application. Furthermore, a deeply specialized application for each one of the domains of usage makes the product too restricted. Therefore, it is essential to adopt a WF&CM application that supports an open architecture, customizable user interface, configurable business logic, and a fully documented software development kit.

➤ Other

Like other corporate software, WF&CM applications must allow for Internet access, PDAs, wireless devices, and e-mails, as well as the desktop. It should also have comprehensive sets of reports, and business intelligence (OLAP) capabilities, in order to allow detailed analysis of the data stored in the database. Integration with other applications, such as time tracking, telephone system, and billing applications is another requirement in order to ensure a seamless flow of data from one system to another. Finally, security at the system and data access levels and component-based security are required to prevent unauthorized access to data.

■ BENEFITS

➤ Centralized and Structured Knowledge

When issues are reported verbally or through e-mail, important information such as problem descriptions, causes, and possible solutions often do not get stored in a medium that facilitates analysis.

---

2. The definitions should be defined briefly and simply to allow the processes to be reused.

In a bug-tracking application, for example, the more available data is, the more valuable it becomes for identifying the weaknesses of the products or services offered, creating frequently asked question (FAQ) and known bug lists, as well as forecasting resource requirements in the future.

Measuring performance and productivity of individuals involved in a process is another key benefit of using an application for tracking issues. Information such as the time (and other resources) used to resolve issues, number of issues closed, escalations, reassignments, failures, and retries are critical indicators that can be used to assess product quality and identify areas for improvement.

Knowledge bases and FAQ lists can be built automatically by extracting and processing the information gathered in a WF&CM application; this can save tremendous amounts of research and documentation for achieving the same goal manually.

➤ Integration with Other Applications

Different departments within a corporation always need to share data stored in one system with other applications. Integration of WF&CM software with other systems eliminates the need to rekey data, as well as reduces the inaccuracies arising from manual entry. At various steps of a workflow, data usually needs to be posted to other applications, such as time tracking, purchasing, or accounting. The WF&CM software should allow a controlled exchange of such data with other applications at intermediate stages of a process.

Attributes such as budget, deadline, and estimates are key to being cost efficient and ensuring timely completion of processes. These fields are typically defined in other project management software applications.

➤ Reduced Training

Procedures can be documented and enforced, but it is not guaranteed that employees will always remember to follow the steps. Furthermore, with each new employee, the same training needs to be repeated. In contrast, a WF&CM application allows the system to walk the user through the process.

■ RETURN ON INVESTMENT

Using a WF&CM application that meets or exceeds most of the requirements mentioned here will result in significant savings (see Figure 12.8). The following annual ROI calculation is based on conservative estimates that can easily be exceeded in a typical organization.

Number of employees	20	50	100	200	1,000	10,000
Hourly salary[a]	$15	$15	$15	$15	$15	$15
Total actual work weeks annually[b]	47	47	47	47	47	47
Minimum productivity projected gain per week[c]	2 hours	2 hours	2 hours	2 hours	2 hours	2 hours
Total annual savings	$28,200	$70,500	$141,100	$282,000	$1,410,000	$14,000,000

[a] Assume 37.5 average hours/employee/week and $15 average hourly rate.

[b] 47 weeks is calculated based on 52 weeks per year subtracted from 5 weeks of administrative weeks, including vacation, sick time, and holidays.

[c] Based on a total 37.5 hours of work per week, the expected hours gain in productivity and reduction in administrative tasks is about 2 hours. The workflow business process automation will streamline and optimize employee task time, helping companies realize significant productivity and efficiency gains both from internal interactions and across external relationships.

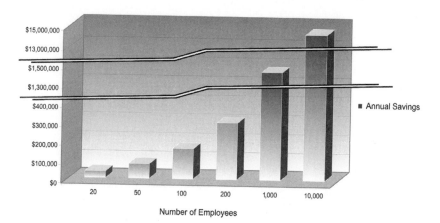

Figure 12.8 Issue Return on Investment Bar Graph

Calculate your own ROIs online on workflows by visiting the psabook.com/roi/wf.htm web site.

■ SUMMARY

Using a WF&CM application simplifies the task of defining processes and enforcing them, and it reduces the need for written procedures and practices. Use of such a product also greatly reduces the training required for new staff and leads to significant reduction of omissions and mistakes.

Chapter 13

Knowledge Management

Knowledge management (KM) is a streamlined approach to improving knowledge sharing across the entire organization.[1] This component improves the accessibility of information, documents, best practice methodologies, templates, libraries, and other pertinent information, result-

> **Lack of information and information starvation have been replaced by information overload and information glut.**

ing in improved performance and productivity. Some features include hierarchical views of the entire organization, knowledge repositories, document management, full text search, best practice templates, keyword searches, advanced queries, company policies, organization and indexing of documents, security features to document knowledge, and collaboration areas to share ideas.

Just a decade ago terms such as *lack of information* and *information starvation* were still common terms. Widespread acceptance and use of the Internet have led to terms such as *information overload* and *information glut*. With the continued explosion of data, complex business processes, increased interaction with colleagues, clients, and partners, and higher turnover rates, KM has become extremely important for organizations.

Knowledge management is the systematic process of collecting, sharing, and transferring information and knowledge that is used

---

1. Portions of the knowledge database may also be made available to outside customers as a self-service feature.

to leverage lessons learned from past experiences and decisions, to share best practices, and to develop consistent processes.

Knowledge management promises to enable collaboration, increase knowledge sharing across multiple teams, accelerate learning, improve decision making, and reduce time wasted on solving repetitive problems and issues.

Paradoxes of Knowledge[2]

➤ Using knowledge does not consume it.

➤ Transferring knowledge does not lose it.

➤ Knowledge is abundant, but the ability to use it is scarce.

➤ Producing knowledge resists organization.

➤ Much of it walks out the door at the end of the day.

This section describes KM systems for PSORGs, what they should include, what to do in order to maximize benefits, and how to measure the ROI of using a KM system.

■ INTRODUCTION

Knowledge management involves the accumulation, classification, and sharing of knowledge.

➤ Current Situation

➤ Tough economic times and high turnover are leading to a severe knowledge drain and leakage in many organizations.

➤ The accelerating pace of change is due to global competition, wide availability of information, and the Internet.

➤ Growth in organizational scope and geographic dispersion associated with globalization of markets lead to a serious knowledge management challenge for any organization.

➤ People create a lot of valuable data and ideas. However, this

---

2. Australian Center for Innovation and International Competitiveness. Available at [http://www.aciic.org.au/knowledge/index.htm].

data is lost in a massive wasteland of e-mails and local documents, or is made available only to a limited group of people.

➤ Employees spend a substantial amount of their time looking for information; such as repeatedly solving a problem that has already been solved by another coworker in the same team or a different group.

➤ Although organizations create an enormous amount of data, management still does not have an accurate snapshot of the organization's current status.

➤ Research has indicated the following:

•After one day, we forget 46% of what we've heard.

•After seven days, we forget 65%.

•After 14 days, we forget 79%.

➤ Organizing information and providing cataloging and search capabilities for quick and efficient access are vital for preserving acquired knowledge.

Knowledge management systems offer the opportunity to do the following

➤ Organize and classify information seamlessly and with minimal effort.

➤ Reduce administrative, unproductive, and repetitive work, and allow employees to focus on their primary responsibilities.

➤ Identify and understand critical issues and what works within the organization.

➤ Share knowledge and best practices throughout the organization.

➤ Gain a high-level perspective of the organization's current status.

➤ Dramatically reduce dependency of the organization on single individuals. The KM system incorporates a body of knowledge that is quickly available to current and future employees.

The four stages[3] of cause and effect are shown in Figure 13.1, which presents the process by which business process reimproved and lead to enhancing financial results.

Rudy Ruggles,[4] a leading KM thinker/practitioner, has identified the following items as integral components of KM:

➤ Generating new knowledge

➤ Accessing valuable knowledge from outside sources

➤ Using accessible knowledge in decision making

➤ Embedding knowledge in processes, products, and/or services

➤ Representing knowledge in documents, databases, and software

➤ Facilitating knowledge growth through culture and incentives

➤ Transferring existing knowledge into other parts of the organization

➤ Measuring the value of knowledge assets and/or impact of knowledge management

This section describes how KM relates to strategic activities of an organization, it describes the KM cycle and recommended components of a KM system for PSORGs.

■ LINK BETWEEN CAUSES AND BENEFITS

Knowledge management is a strategic activity. Most of the benefits of implementing a KM system are qualitative. It is very difficult to

---

3. Balanced scorecard approach, Kaplan and Norton present a chain of cause and effect that leads to success .Robert S. Kaplan and David P. Norton, The Balanced Scorecard: Translating Strategy into Action, 1996, Harvard Business School Press.

4. http://www.sims.berkeley.edu/courses/is213/s99/Projects/P9/web_site/about_km. html Copyright and disclaimer © 1999, Gotcha. Last updated on April 27, 1999.

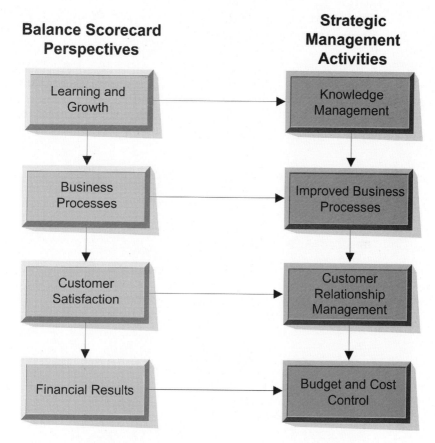

Figure 13.1 Knowledge Management Link Graph

quantitatively measure benefits. For example, how does one measure the amount of new revenue gained because employees have time to pursue new opportunities and the amount of time employees save because information is already available? Many other factors can directly or indirectly impact revenue and productivity. Measuring ROI is discussed in more detail in a later section.

Figure 13.2 maps Kaplan and Norton's cause and effect to strategic activities of the organization and the resulting benefits.

The process of KM is circular and unending (see Figure 13.3). Participants in the KM process may enter it at any point and traverse it repeatedly. The diagram shows the most common pattern of

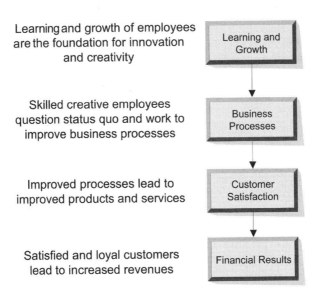

Figure 13.2 Knowledge Management Cause and Effect

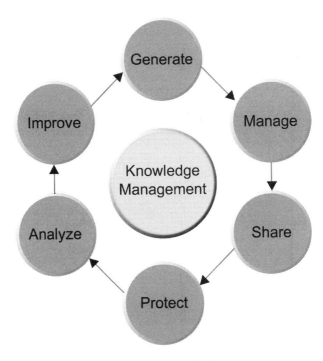

Figure 13.3 The Knowledge Management Cycle

traversal; however, the steps presented are not necessarily followed in sequence. Different types of users will enter and exit the cycle according to their own needs and priorities.

The KM cycle consists of the components listed in the following table.

State	Software Process	Human Process
Generate	Data mining	Learn, interact, brainstorm, solve problems.
Manage	Review/approve entries, revise as needed, organize, store in data store	Manage knowledge articles and documents, approve/reject, discuss, reach consensus (e.g., through voting).
Share	Classification, web-based architecture, centralized database, access using wireless devices	Organize knowledge into hierarchies, classify, add keywords and metatags, publish, and recommend.
Protect	Application and data security (filtering based on user roles)	Define user profiles and determine access rights by user role, as well as what specific classes of knowledge a user can view.
Analyze	Reporting and business intelligence (OLAP)	Create and share 2D and 3D reports, graphs, and charts; analyze the data to identify problem areas, bottlenecks, points of conflict, patterns of success and failure.
Improve	Search/filtering capabilities, business intelligence (OLAP)	Using the data, reports, and search tools, determine how a process or an element of knowledge can be improved. Make the improvement and share findings.

■ COMPONENTS

The following section discusses some of the key components that a KM system must include for PSORGs.

For a KM system to be effective, information must be captured and organized into a well-defined, natural, and clear hierarchy. Organizational breakdown structure (see Figure 13.4) defines the

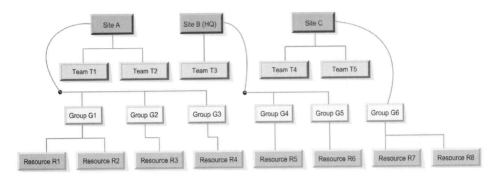

Figure 13.4 Organizational Breakdown Structure

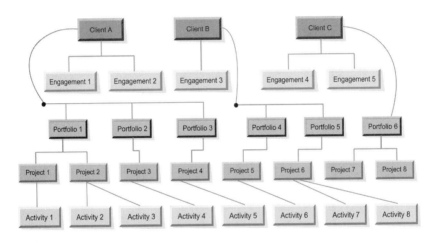

Figure 13.5 Work Breakdown Structure

structure of an organization broken down into sites, business units (cost centers), groups, teams, and resources (employees, consultants, and equipment). Employees should be able to associate documents, keywords, and web/LAN links to various OBS elements. Later, one should be able to perform keyword queries and text queries, or navigate the OBS hierarchy in search of specific documents or information.

➤ Work Breakdown Structure (WBS)

In a PSORG, work is classified and tracked using OBS and WBS structures. Work breakdown structure (see Figure 13.5) defines the hierarchy of work. Employees should be able to associate documents, keywords, and Web/LAN links to various WBS elements. Later, one should be able to perform keyword search, text queries or navigate the WBS hierarchy in search of specific information.

➤ Engagement Management

PSORGs often have to deal with hundreds and thousands of engagements. These engagements can consist of multiple projects and can have associated budgets, milestones, deadlines, cost/revenue rules (rates), associated documents, and notes. The KM system should track engagements and all associated information for future analysis, audit, and review.

➤ Proposal Development

For every engagement, there are one or more proposals. Proposals are processed using a predefined workflow (see Figure 13.6). The PSORG's KM system can include a few canned workflows, but must allow the organization to totally customize this workflow to suit its own requirements or create new ones.

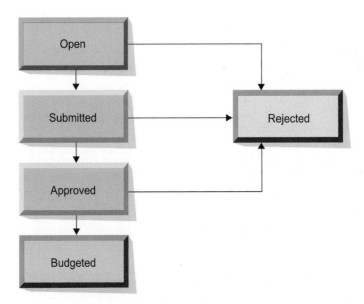

Figure 13.6 Project Proposal Workflow

➤ Resource Planning

Planning for resources, deciding what priorities and factors need to be taken into account, and reserving and assigning resources to projects are the domains of resource planning (RP). Resource planning queries should be associated to engagements and stored for future access, analysis, and review.

➤ Document Management

Document management (see Figure 13.7 for a document approval workflow) in the context of PSORGs consists of the following:

- ➤ Document approval: A KM system should not assume that all documents could be automatically approved and posted. A document approval workflow ensures that only approved and reviewed documents are made available to the parties concerned.

- ➤ Attachments: As discussed in the section on OBS/WBS, users should be able to attach documents, links, and notes to OBS, WBS elements, as well as to corporate documents such as timesheets, time entries, expense reports, expense entries,

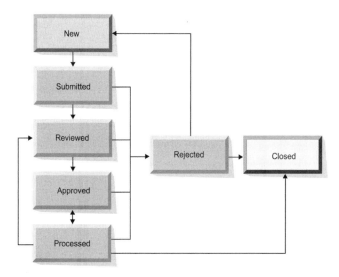

Figure 13.7 Document Approval Workflow

purchase orders, purchase entries, and invoices. The information should be managed and stored in a central location and can be queried later.

➤ Document classification: Documents may be classified as public, shared within one or more groups, or private.

➤ Organizational policy and guidelines: In addition to a document management system, KM systems should provide the infrastructure for a centralized portal that maintains the organization's policies and guidelines. Some examples include online employee handbooks, holidays and events calendars, timesheets, expense reports, help desk policies, guidelines for proposing a budget, and other such information.

➤ Business Intelligence

Business intelligence, also known as OLAP, is a key component of any KM system. Using BI, executives and managers can look at the acquired knowledge graphically and at a very high level (such as in Figure 13.8). The user can then *drill* into and out of the details of specific sites, projects, customers, and other such items in order to get a better picture of what is going on.

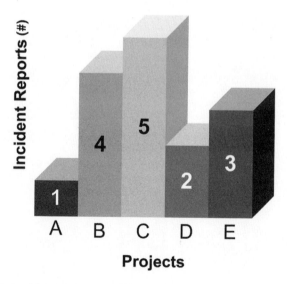

Figure 13.8 Incident Reports Bar Graph

■ KNOWLEDGE SEARCH

One should be able to perform powerful queries and statistical analysis on information that is associated to issues, corporate documents such as timesheets/expense reports/invoices, and OBS/WBS elements. The queries can be part of a report (as in the case of BI), ad hoc, or preconfigured. One should be able to perform queries based on keywords, classification, OBS/WBS elements, and association between OBS/WBS elements.

➤ Classification

Corporate documents such as timesheets, expense reports, purchase orders, and service requests are inherently associated to various OBS and WBS elements (e.g., an invoice is created for a client, a timesheet belongs to a specific user). The ability to associate such corporate documents into one or more classes is called classification, which allows an organization to reclassify documents into completely new hierarchies based on classes (see Figure 13.9). This feature is very useful for KM. For example, one can create a hierarchy of best practices for timesheet management, expense management, resource planning, and other similar concepts. The best

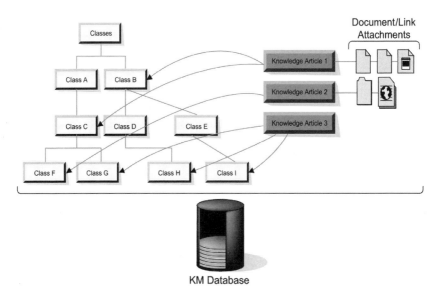

Figure 13.9 Sample Classification

practices tree would be used to collect all documents, links, and files that collectively explain and promote the specified best practice.

➤ Trees

As discussed previously, KM knowledge is classified in OBS, WBS, and classification trees. The KM system should show this information in a tree format and allow users to quickly navigate the tree and view associated documents, files, and links.

➤ Natural Language Queries

The ability to ask questions from a KM system through either text or through interactive voice response (IVR, a speech recognition system) systems is highly desirable. Current technologies in both natural language queries and IVR are a work in progress; few commercial implementations meet the demands of a KM system. Although both systems are capable of handling simple requests, accuracy and processing are not acceptable for inquiries that are more complex.

■ INCENTIVES FOR SHARING

A KM system must be designed to encourage knowledge acquisition throughout the normal daily course of doing business. However, many organizations also implement incentives to further encourage knowledge sharing.

➤ Point System

One way to encourage knowledge sharing is to implement a point system. Each time a user creates a knowledge article, comments on an article, or provides additional information, that user would receive a number of points. The user is then rewarded on a monthly, quarterly, or periodic basis by receiving a gift such as cash rewards, airline tickets, or a personal digital assistant.

➤ Recognition Awards

Organizations can go even further and establish official knowledge player of the month/year awards, or implement other similar award programs that further encourage and emphasize knowledge sharing.

➤ Employee Evaluation Process

The information from the point system and awards can be used as a basis for recognizing those who excel in knowledge acquisition and sharing. Those who exceed expectations can receive favorable reviews, evaluations, and recommendations by their immediate managers.

■ MEASURING THE BENEFITS OF A KNOWLEDGE MANAGEMENT SYSTEM

➤ Reasons for Implementing

Information technology managers direct funding to KM to improve corporate communications and facilitate a culture focused on information sharing through collaboration. International Data Corporation (IDC) conducted a survey with *Knowledge Management* magazine to understand the reasons that IT professionals are adopting knowledge management, and to examine the concerns those professionals have with implementing KM solutions.

The following table shows that the key driver behind the implementation of a KM solution is a chance to improve profit and grow revenue, while other drivers include employee retention and increased customer satisfaction. The table shows that although profit is the major driver behind KM implementation, over 50% of the re-

Most Important Reasons for Adopting a Knowledge Management Program

Reason	% of Respondents
Improving profit/growing revenue	67
Retaining key talent/expertise	54
Increasing customer retention and/or satisfaction	52
Defending market share against new entrants	44
Gaining faster time to market with products	39
Penetrating new market segments	39
Reducing costs	38
Developing new products/services	35

Challenges Companies Face in Implementing Knowledge Management Initiatives

Challenge	% of Respondents
Lack of understanding of KM and its benefits	55
Lack of employee time for KM	45
Lack of skill in KM techniques	40
Lack of encouragement in the current culture for sharing	35
Lack of incentives/rewards to share	30
Lack of funding for KM initiatives	24
Lack of appropriate technology	18
Lack of commitment from senior management	15

Source: Greg Dyer, *Knowledge Management: Hitting its Stride.* IDC Bulletin no. W21834, March 2000. Available at [http://www.idc.com/ITAdvisor/press/IT000605.htm].
Note: Multiple responses were allowed.

spondents cite a lack of understanding of KM as a major challenge. Other obstacles to KM are so ingrained in corporate culture, such as knowledge sharing, that realization of ROI becomes a long-term goal; consequently, the cost of a KM solution rises above the initial sticker price.

➤ The Brain Drain

Figure 13.10 emphasizes an important reason for KM. Forty-two percent of an organization's knowledge is within the minds of its employees. Capturing and preserving that knowledge and reducing this percentage and dependency as much as possible must be a primary objective of any KM project.

➤ Measuring Benefits

Measuring the benefits of knowledge management (see Figure 13.11) is difficult because the task requires placing a value on an intangible return on investment. The following metrics can be used to measure benefits: enterprise, team, and work effectiveness. The organization should try not to create new metrics just to measure KM benefits because it is important to select metrics that the KM program will impact and that are already accepted within the enterprise.

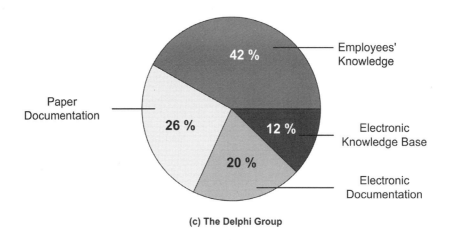

Figure 13.10 Breakdown of Organization's Knowledge

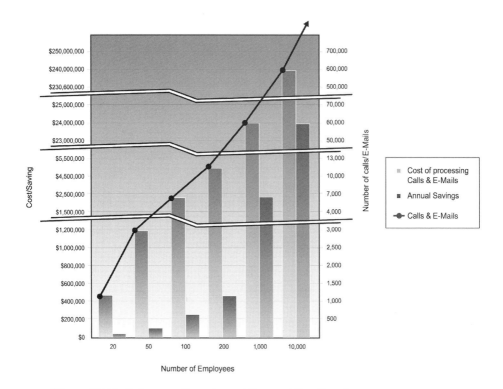

Figure 13.11 Return on Investment Support Bar Graph

Enterprise effectiveness: The organization should define a set of ratios and other measures that define enterprise effectiveness prior to the implementation of a KM system. Some examples include proposal development time, project success rate, profit margin, key new customers per quarter, and other such measures. The performance of the organization prior to the implementation of KM versus performance at various points in time after launch can be used as a form of ROI calculation.

Return on Investment in the Context of External Client Support

	Number of Call Center Representatives					
	20	50	100	200	1,000	10,000
Number of calls per month	800	2,000	4,000	8,000	40,000	400,000
Number of e-mails per month	400	1,000	2,000	4,000	20,000	200,000
Estimated annual cost of call processing per employee[a]	$16,000	$16,000	$16,000	$16,000	$16,000	$16,000
Estimated annual cost of e-mail support per employee[a]	$8,000	$8,000	$8,000	$8,000	$8,000	$8,000
Estimated total cost per employee	$24,000	$24,000	$24,000	$24,000	$24,000	$24,000
Total cost	$480,000	$1,200,000	$2,400,000	$4,800,000	$24,000,000	$240,000,000
Annual savings for the entire organization	$48,000	$120,000	$240,000	$480,000	$2,400,000	$24,000,000

[a]Assume each call center representative has an average salary of $40,000. Also assume 40 hours per work week.

[b]The ROI assumes that 40% of a call center representative's time is spent on responding to external client phone requests (percentages are based on a cursory survey of several organizations with in-house call centers).

[c]The ROI assumes that 20% of a call center representative's time is spent on responding to external client e-mails (percentages are based on a cursory survey of several organizations with in-house call centers).

Team effectiveness: A KM system encourages collaboration and sharing across teams, especially in non-R&D groups. An ROI system should track sharing of best practices, employee satisfaction, process/product/service improvements or innovations, and customer satisfaction that result from using a KM system.

Feature	Description
Access	
Web	Be accessible via the Internet with any client operating system that is used by the organization. Pure web-based solutions offer the most flexible and cost effective solutions (specially with regards to maintenance).
Wireless	Support wireless access from any e-mail or browser-enabled wireless device.
Audit trails	Allow for a complete log of users' access to the system and any entry modifications.
Decision tools	Support decision tools such as polling or custom decision workflows that are used to solve problems or address project- or client-related issues.
Document management	Attach documents to clients, projects, activities, users, timesheets, time entries, expense reports, expense entries, purchase orders, and issues with keyword-based search capabilities. Certain documents need to be submitted and approved with a predefined workflow.
Home view	Allow user to configure home view and run custom queries to display various issue types.
Incentive management	Let organization define a reward policy using a point system and user knowledge participation report cards that track and encourage KM use.
Notification	Provide event-triggered notifications such as new knowledge articles, articles, or documents that are ready for approval or that have been rejected.
OLAP	Allow for advanced and sophisticated multidimensional enterprise reporting. Adds business intelligence to your data for enterprise optimization, change, and project management, as well as customer and decision support. Anyone with the proper access rights can drill up or down and gain significant insight into the organization's operational efficiencies and weaknesses.
Strategic Sourcing	Associate skills and proficiencies to users, associate skills and experience requirements to projects and tasks. This information can be used to provide KM functionality such as expert profiling (the KM system finds the most appropriate expert based on search keywords/information and other criterion) and "find an expert" where one can quickly browse user profiles based on search parameters
Security	Define user roles such as knowledge manager and standard user that define what screens and function (create/modify/query) to which a user has access rights.
Setup *OBS*	Let administrators set up and maintain OBS.

continued

Feature	Description
WBS	Let administrators set up and maintain WBS.
Classification	Create and manage a classification tree.
User	User management is part of OBS, but we wish to stress that user log-ins, profiles, skills, and associated documents must be managed by the KM system.
Site and scoping	Maintain a central database and track work by location, but allow users, managers, and administrators of each site (or within a virtual site) to have access only to site-specific information.
Software development kit (SDK)	Develop enhancements and extensions or extract and manipulate data from a local or remote database.
Tree format	Set up hierarchies and form a better representation of the organizational and work breakdown structures. Support for search-find and drag-drop.
Version control	Maintain a history of document changes.
Workflows	Allow administrators to define new or customize existing workflows to map business processes into the KM system.

Work effectiveness: A KM system must empower individuals of an organization with access to knowledge, experiences, and accumulated expertise so that they can do their jobs efficiently and quickly, and so that they can make the right decisions. Work effectiveness measures how well a KM system addresses the knowledge needs of the individual. Some examples include number of times a knowledge base article is accessed and the activity level related to KM activities.

Management will expect ROI to be based on the previously outlined measures. Because KM is a strategic tool that streamlines critical business processes, it is important to focus on factors that affect the time or rate to achieve an objective in a business process.

Calculate your own ROIs online on knowledge management by visiting the psabook.com/roi/km.htm web site.

■ RECOMMENDED SYSTEM FEATURES

A KM system must include the features listed in the following table in order to be an instrument of real change. Knowledge management systems for PSORGs map into the organization's OBS, WBS, and daily business activities (such as engagements, service requests, timesheets, and expense reports).

■ SUMMARY

Knowledge yields value when employees, clients, and partners have easy and simple access to it. Knowledge management systems are most effective when they also participate in keeping the information up-to-date and useful. Management experts agree that learning and growth are keys to strategic success and the building blocks for any organization. A growing enterprise understands the importance of knowledge management activities. Thus, a growing business must incorporate this process as part of everyday business by leveraging the experiences, knowledge, and wisdom of everyone who is associated to its organization.

Chapter 14

Performance Analysis

■ INTRODUCTION

This component provides the ability to generate real-time access to business metrics pertaining to project status, activities, utilization, clients, requests, revenues, costs, profits, and other such information. Some features would include numerous predefined reports, customizable reports, OLAP-based multidimensional data analysis, support for or integration with other business intelligence tools, import/export features, and customizable home views or portals (also known as digital dashboards) for executives, managers, or users. Online analytical processing, also known as business intelligence (BI) and analytics, is a powerful means of data visualization. Using BI software, project- and service-oriented organizations can gain clear, real-time insight into their operational efficiency and status.

By providing real-time visual project and service delivery status, BI technology significantly enhances the decision-making process. Managers and executives are no longer forced to make decisions based on insufficient results, incomplete information, or nothing more than their judgment, memory, and experience.

This chapter explains the needs and problems addressed by a BI solution and the latter's value to PSORGs. It also describes what features to look for in a BI tool as part of an overall PSA strategy.

Online analytical processing is one of the most critical techniques that an organization can use to improve and streamline the decision-making process. In a rapidly changing world with global competition, managers and executives are under pressure to make major decisions quickly and on a regular basis. BI software lets decision makers view the status of current engagements visually, concisely, and with the ability to drill through live data in order to identify trouble spots and recognize best practices.

Many organizations use a diverse set of information systems, each having its own central repository of information (database). The data from all such heterogeneous systems are merged into a single database (centralized data); this process is known as *data warehousing*. BI tools are then used to perform detailed visual and real-time analysis on the data.

What is BI? Business intelligence allows organizations to access, analyze, and share information across the enterprise and in extranet environments, using both tools and analytic applications. In an enterprise network, BI provides employees with information to make better business decisions. In an extranet environment, BI is deployed as part of applications that allow organizations to deliver new services and build stronger relationships with customers, partners, and suppliers via the Internet. In customer relationship management, the prerequisite for acquiring, developing, and caring for customers is understanding existing customers' purchasing patterns and satisfaction level. Similarly, the foundation of good HR and project management is the ability to understand the availability, skills, interests, and accomplishments of an organization's resources. Providing this customer, resource, and project intelligence is one of the unique strengths of BI.

This chapter describes how organizations make decisions with insufficient knowledge on a daily basis, presents BI as a solution to this vital need, explains the substantial benefits of using BI, and describes the features to look for in a BI solution for PSORGs.

■ THE INFORMATION NEED

How are decisions made in any organization? Hundreds of decisions are made daily, such as the following:

➤ Assign this project to the same team as last time.

➤ Delay this project because the expertise is unavailable.

➤ Accept this engagement because we can allocate or hire the resources we need.

➤ Site A is our most efficient site, so assign this critical engagement to that site.

These decisions are based mostly on experience; gut feeling and rule of thumb are used more often than facts. How can managers improve the quality of decisions?

➤ By performing the critical tasks themselves—and becoming the bottleneck

➤ By hiring more skilled staff—and raising costs dramatically

➤ By setting a policy for each decision—and leading to much bureaucracy and many exceptions

The most cost-effective approach is to give workers the means to make better decisions by providing them with access to strategic information. Access to information and the ability to analyze it mean better decisions. What is a good decision? One that is made in a timely manner and helps an organization move closer to its goal. What helps a manager make a good decision? Problem-related facts and information on the organization's objectives.

For example, a project manager plans the project, creates schedules, assigns tasks, and performs follow-ups to ensure the project is progressing as planned. Analytical information on the entire project will help the manager ensure that objectives are met and milestones are reached as planned. Strategic information is a powerful motivator and empowers project managers to get their job done effectively and efficiently.

■ THE INFORMATION PROBLEM

The problem with the decision-making process is the "fact gap." Organizations often maintain vast and growing quantities of dispersed data while a growing number of decisions require these data. However, the management team is unable to absorb the flood of information and makes decisions based on instinct, experience, and memory, a tendency that leads to the fact gap.

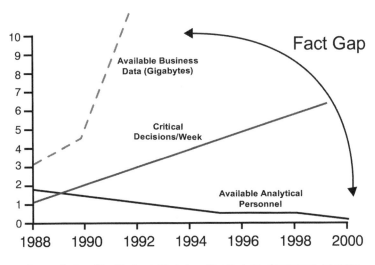

Source: Gartner,"The Electronic Workplace: The Evolution Continues," July 1998

Figure 14.1 Fact Gap

Organizations are rich in data but poor in knowledge. Vast quantities of data are stored in legacy systems, diverse and disconnected relational databases, ERPs, data warehouses, spreadsheets, web sites, and a large number of dispersed documents. These data must be transformed into knowledge.

Data in context = Information

Information in context = Knowledge

Organizations are in a data jailhouse:

➤ It takes hours, days, and sometimes much more time to get answers to questions:

• Project details are maintained in the project management system.

• Customer order and payment records are in the accounting system.

• Proposals and sales call histories are tracked by contact management software.

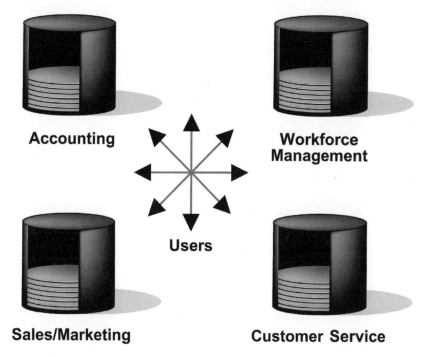

Figure 14.2 The Data Jailhouse

- Installation and support information are in the customer service database.

➤ There is no simple way for a nontechnical user to get answers.

➤ Answers lead to new questions.

■ THE SOLUTION: UNLOCKING THE INFORMATION

BI provides the key that unlocks the knowledge. BI provides simple access to multiple data sources and the tools to explore the data and share the knowledge with coworkers, other departments, customers, partners, and suppliers.

Here are some of the questions BI can answer for various departments:

Project Management

➤ Which projects were late?

➤ Which team handled the most projects?

➤ Which projects were the most profitable?

➤ Which projects and activities were over budget?

Human Resources

➤ What factors affect employee retention?

➤ Which resources are underutilized?

➤ Which departments are overloaded?

➤ Work Management

How many requests were processed per quarter?

➤ What is the support team issue close rate?

➤ Finance

Which department has the highest travel costs per head?

➤ What activities have delivered the highest profit margins?

➤ Sales and Marketing

Which products generate the most revenue?

➤ Where is the greatest sales opportunity?

➤ Which customer segment responded best to the recent promotion?

➤ What percentage of partners brings in the majority of the new leads?

One can unlock the information available in a variety of corporate databases with BI by giving users a single point of entry to all data:

➤ BI portal

➤ Easy access to and analysis and sharing of corporate information

Figure 14.3 Accessing, Analyzing, and Sharing Information

➤ Query, reporting, and analysis functions

➤ Quick answers to business questions

➤ Drill down to underlying detail

➤ Leveraging the use of the Internet throughout the value chain

➤ Extranets for customers, partners, and suppliers

BI enables people to access, analyze, and share information in Intranet, extranet, or Internet environments.

■ THE BUSINESS VALUE OF BI

When BI is used, projects and services are delivered on time, within budget, and profitably. Access to real-time information, decision-making tools, and analysis has the following advantages:

➤ It leads to less wasted time, higher yields, improved processes, and more employee, partner, and customer satisfaction.

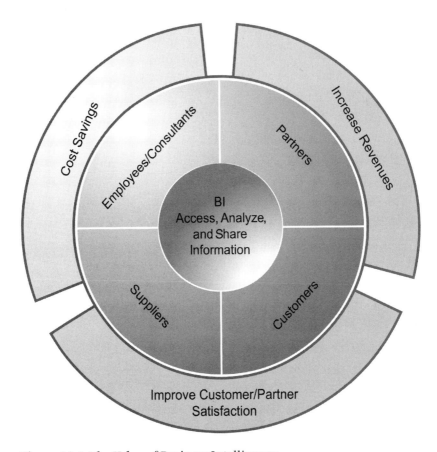

Figure 14.4 The Value of Business Intelligence

➤ Highest-cost projects are reviewed or eliminated.

➤ Unprofitable business units are restructured.

Using BI software reduces costs by improving operational efficiency through self-service access to information, eliminating reporting backlog and delays, enabling employees to negotiate better contracts with customers and suppliers, and finding root causes to problems and bottlenecks and taking action.

Business intelligence tools can generate new revenue opportunities by differentiating offerings and by sharing information over the Internet with customers, suppliers, and partners. Business in-

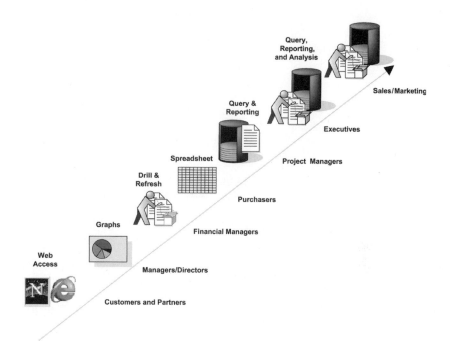

Figure 14.5 Functionality Tailored to Users

telligence tools can also improve strategies with better marketing analysis and empower the sales force by providing them with insight into previous successes and failures.

Business intelligence tools lead to improved customer satisfaction by giving employees, customers, and partners the means to make better decisions (self-service data access), provide quick answers to questions (answers on demand), and challenge assumptions with factual information.

■ JUSTIFYING THE INVESTMENT

Four benefits must be considered when building the business case to use a BI system.

➤ Quantifiable benefits: man-hours saved in producing reports; savings from not hiring staff

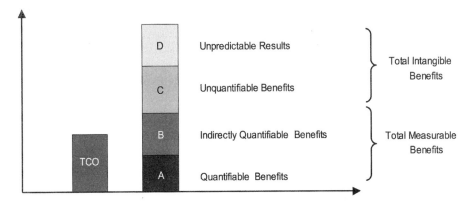

Figure 14.6 Business Intelligence Benefits

> ➤ Indirectly quantifiable benefits: a differentiated service that creates new sales opportunities

> ➤ Unquantifiable benefits: improved employee morale; more effective management of corporate knowledge

> ➤ Unpredictable benefits: discovering unexpected project management and process patterns

If measurable benefits outweigh total cost of ownership, then a BI solution will yield a positive return. Any software and IT project of such complexity should have clear and measurable objectives defined from the outset. By defining the objectives, reaching a consensus with the management team, having the full support of all decision makers, and reviewing project status at every milestone, the organization ensures that the BI project will become a powerful, essential tool that results in substantial efficiencies.

Feature	Description
Completely embedded leading BI tool	BI software has significant functionality and breadth. Therefore, most sophisticated enterprise software applications choose to embed such functionality from one of the leading BI vendors.
	It is important to select enterprise software (ES) that has this kind of functionality fully embedded. Loose integration will not do justice to this critical enabling technology.

Feature	Description
Pure web Internet interface, zero client install	BI features should be accessible in as many ways as possible. A pure interface with zero client install ensures rapid deployment and reduced maintenance costs. Installing BI on every client computer will lead to significant administrative, upgrade, and network management costs.
Support for multiple databases	The BI software must support many databases, such as Microsoft SQL server, Oracle, and IBM DB2 A BI that supports only a singe database management system could be a risky investment in the long run, limiting the organization's choices as needs, prices, technology, and market conditions change.
Security features	Access to BI features and BI-related security must be an integral part of the ES application security services. For example, if the ES defines a project manager as a role that has access to BI, then users with this role should immediately gain access to this functionality.
Home views	BI documents must become an integrated part of the tools, interfaces, and web pages used every day. For example, managers could customize their home views to dedicate the right side of the page to a BI document that displays the project status including requests per user, status of each activity, and summary of current progress by each team member.
Digital dashboard	Using digital dashboard technology, home-view web pages can be customized to incorporate an e-mail component, BI documents, lists of timesheets, expense reports, requisitions that require approval, lists of critical outstanding issues, and other features.
Create/modify/share BI documents	Based on their security profile, users should be allowed to create, edit, delete, and share BI documents. Documents can be defined as personal, sent to specific users, or made public for all to access.
Ad hoc reporting	The ability to quickly create various charts, bar graphs, and tables makes BI accessible and user-friendly to many users in the organization.

■ SOFTWARE REQUIREMENTS

➤ Analysis

The sections that follow present some graphs and reports that can be quickly created using BI software. Unlike static two- or three-dimensional reports, BI documents are live and dynamic reports. Users can drill up or down and slice or dice through the graphs and tables to identify trouble spots and key efficiencies.

WBS/OBS Cost/Revenue Analytics

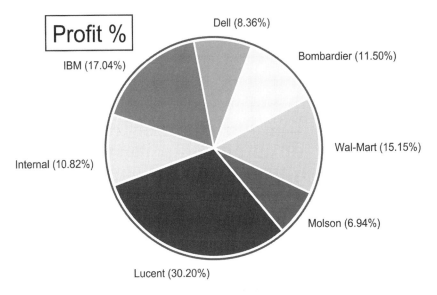

Figure 14.7 Business Intelligence Clients

Client Table

Client	Project	Cost Amount	Revenue Amount
Bombardier	Bombardier Project 1	20,111,800.00	60,398,000.00
Bombardier	Bombardier Project 2	10,062,400.00	28,624,000.00
Dell	Dell Project 1	1,492,250.00	–2,037,500.00
IBM	IBM Project 1	2,265,000.00	12,730,000.00
Internal	General	2,900.00	--11,000.00
Lucent	Lucent Project 1	367,500.00	1,680,000.00
Lucent	Lucent Project 2	1,880,000.00	5,280,000.00
Molson	Molson Promotion	817, 600.00	5,406,000.00
Wal-Mart	Wal-Mart Project 1	129, 075.00	390,750.00
Wal-Mart	Wal-Mart Project 2	62,300.00	193,000.00

WBS/OBS Time/Expense Analytics

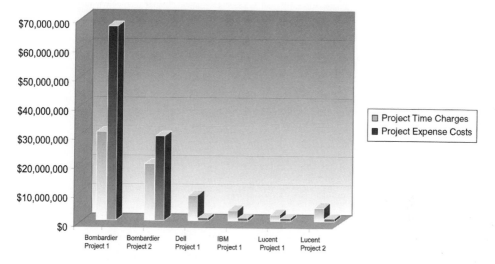

Figure 14.8 Project Time and Expenses

WBS/OBS Purchasing Analytics

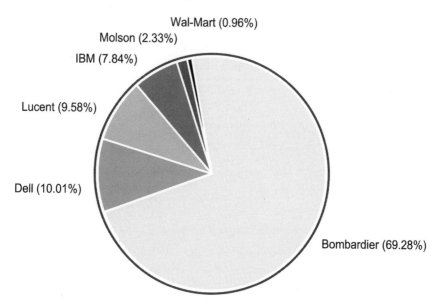

Figure 14.9 Purchasing

WBS/OBS Workflow Analytics

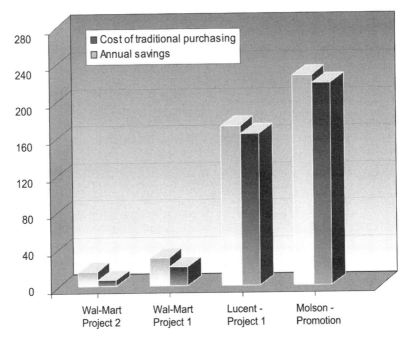

Figure 14.10 Workflow

Resources	Open Issues	Closed Issues
Adam West	88.00	78.00
Andy Bogart	390.00	380.00
Ashley Moore	390.00	380.00
Bill Turin	390.00	380.00
Burt Bixby	30.00	20.00
Chris Redmond	390.00	380.00
Dan Loomis	390.00	380.00
Edward Asner	30.00	20.00
Edward Gierrek	131.00	121.00
Eric Diaz	95.00	85.00
Frank Ramsey	390.00	380.00
Gail Ranford	390.00	380.00
Glenda Gates	390.00	380.00
Horace Yates	390.00	380.00

■ SUMMARY

Organizations are data-rich but information-poor. BI closes the fact gap, lowers costs, increases employee and customer satisfaction, and results in new revenue opportunities. Using BI, decisions that were previously based on incomplete information, intuition, and experience can be made more quickly, become more systematic, and are supported by real facts. Defining a clear and goal-oriented BI strategy should be an important priority for any PSORG.

Part 2

Section B.
Extended Components

Chapter 15

Customer / Partner Relationship Management

The main purpose of customer and partner relationship management software is to automate and improve front-office business processes by providing the means to track the organization's customers and partners as well as the results, effectiveness, and efficiency of the internal sales force. Customer relationship management (CRM) software is a customer and partner business strategy that encompasses all channels and media—from the Internet to field sales—and sales partners across the entire service supply chain. This accords directly with the requirements of PSORGs that need to maintain close synchronization with their solutions for project management, cost and revenue accounting, invoicing, and integration with accounting, payroll, and ERP systems.

Until recently, CRM and PRM (partner relationship management) software have been treated as two distinct applications. It is evident that CRM and PRM have unique features and benefits. This section takes a broader view, in which the CRM software is assumed to include substantial PRM functionality.

■ INTRODUCTION

Customer relationship management encompasses all aspects of an organization's interaction with its customers, whether sales- or service-related. Its main function is to optimize the customer contact

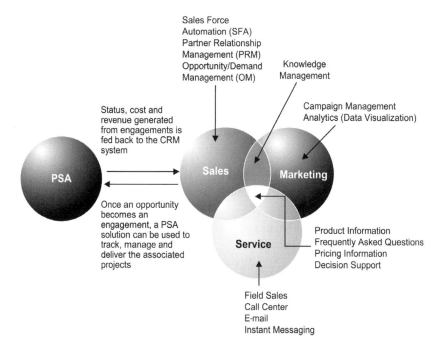

Figure 15.1 Components of a Customer Relationship Management System

business processes. Computerization has changed the way companies approach their CRM strategies because it has also changed customer behavior. With each new advance in technology, especially the proliferation of self-service channels like the ubiquitous web and emerging interfaces like WAP phones, more and more relationships are being managed electronically. Therefore, organizations are looking for ways to personalize online experiences (a process also referred to as mass customization), through more integrated voice help-desk functionality, client e-mail organizers, and the coupling of increasingly advanced web interfaces to knowledge databases, real-time chat, and more. The proliferation of ways in which the *same* customer may contact the service provider requires that all such mechanisms have access to the same consistent and common customer records, customer history, and so forth.

Partner relationship management is an extended business function of CRM dedicated to managing the interactions specific to partners, for example, their training, productivity, reselling activities, and channel-specific marketing campaigns.

Customer and partner management have evolved radically from the introduction of mechanized call centers. These systems have continued to improve and have come to be referred to by various acronyms, such as customer asset management systems (CAMS) and customer interaction systems (CIS), in addition to the ones used here.

The justification for buying hardware for upgrades or maintenance seems obvious; however, organizations do not immediately see the real need to upgrade their CRM and PRM software (for the purpose of this chapter, CRM and PRM will be collectively referred to as CRM). In contrast with other traditional software solutions such as General Ledgers, many of which have been used for decades, CRM systems are a new generation of solutions that are in the process of evolution. This poses several problems in terms of best practices and return on investment (ROI). Customer relationship management is still a work in progress in terms of functionality and the components it incorporates. Return on investment is particularly hard to measure. The improvements can be quite visible; however, they may appear to be more qualitative in nature, since there are typically no real historical foundation and statistics with which to calculate gains.

Project- and service-oriented organizations rely on a complete CRM solution to better accommodate customer requests, to channel opportunities and demand efficiently, and to avoid "bench time" for knowledge workers whose utilization rate is critical to the company's bottom line.

➤ Data Collected by Customer Relationship Management Software

A CRM solution allows for profile management, component-based security access rights, groupings, partner life-cycle management, contract management, sales training and planning, sales and partner proposal generation, lead management and consolidation, call center integration, automated lead assignment, event-triggered e-mail notification with escalation and routing, sales and marketing campaign reporting, and forecasting.

All the information related to customer presales and postsales, as well as channel partners, is available in the CRM. This includes

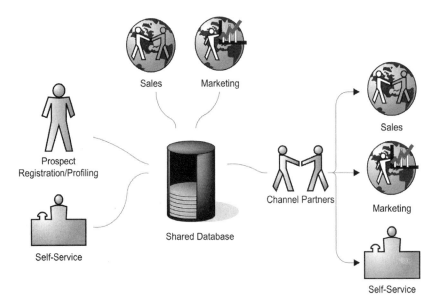

Figure 15.2 Customer Relationship Management Components

complete information on the organization, such as address and contacts, along with the ability to attach documents, e-mails, images, and so forth. This information is used to support customer and partner processes, including direct mail, conferences, meetings, and third-party activities.

This data can be categorized in countless ways to perform various kinds of analysis, such as determining sales campaign effectiveness, identifying key market segments, and analyzing primary accounts. Customer relationship management also provides support for strategic planning processes and facilitates customer, staff, and business partner communications.

Typically, an organization will attempt to motivate its channels and internal sales force by introducing exciting incentives in order to increase sales. Without a CRM solution, it is not easy to update, manage, and determine the effectiveness of such initiatives.

➤ Automation Benefits

A CRM system makes it much easier to implement and evaluate various marketing strategies and new initiatives.

Some important benefits (courtesy of META Group, CRM [http://www.metagroup.com/metaview/mv0485.html]) include the following abilities:

➤ Dropping call center phone time by 20 to 30 percent

➤ Slashing sales support charges by 25 to 40 percent

➤ Boosting customer retention 5 percent or more

➤ Paying for itself in six to twelve months

There are also some intangible benefits:

➤ Getting closer to the customer

➤ Finding out more about your buyers

➤ Being able to sell more to the same customers

Organizational Benefits

A CRM solution directly and indirectly results in revenue growth by allowing businesses to expand and gain new customers by

➤ Increasing cross-selling to the existing customer base and channel partners with the ability to market more high margin products and services

➤ Improving customer and partner loyalty and maintaining the relationship for a longer period

➤ Streamlining the sales process and reducing the time needed to close an account

➤ Helping to focus sales efforts on the right accounts and partners by clearly identifying and managing customers and partners in various stages of the sales pipeline (introduction, qualification, analysis, classification, etc.)

➤ Increasing channel and sales revenues

➤ Allowing partners and internal sales staff to better serve the end customer

➤ Improving the sales lead distribution and follow-up process

➤ Making it simpler to forecast revenues

➤ Leveraging the Internet with online tools to increase sales effectiveness

➤ Avoiding natural discords and "gray zones," which occur as various resellers or sales staff cross paths

➤ Reducing substantial costs associated with managing channel partners and an internal sales force

A good CRM solution allows the information loop to feed back to the organization so it can stay up to date with the latest products, services, promotions, and sales results.

Customer Benefits

Regardless of what sort of contact has taken place (sales, customer service, etc.), customers benefit when the service provider knows them well. The centralized, holistic view of the customer, which disregards the contact method or the branch of the service provider, is a significant benefit. In addition, the service provider can easily match customer requirements with products and services, thereby helping the customers find the solutions they need quickly. It also shortens the cycle required to satisfy the customer's demands for information, service requests, inquiry status, and so forth. Essentially, regardless of its size, a powerful CRM solution helps the enterprise present a single and consistent personal face to the customer.

Workflow Benefits

A CRM solution can help identify and manage the various states and transitions in the sales cycle from advertising, leads, visits or demonstrations, analysis, qualification, proposals, and closing, as well as the various states and transitions in the channel cycle—recruitment, certification, training, marketing campaign execution, lead management, opportunity reporting, and revenue forecasting.

Call Center Benefits

By automating more processes within the customer call center, the organization can benefit by using its staff more efficiently. The combination of automated support tools, consistent and complete customer data, consistent knowledge databases, and e-mail and chat integration leads to a richer and more efficient working environment.

Direct Mail Benefits

CRM solutions compile and classify large amounts of customer information. It is therefore much simpler to achieve more targeted, even completely personalized, direct mail campaigns, which can directly increase the response rate while reducing associated costs per contact.

Central Data Repository Benefits

Maintaining complete customer history in one central repository has countless advantages, which can include the following:

➤ If the salesperson or support contact happens to be absent or if the channel partner has left the organization, anyone can quickly take over and follow up by being able to review any notes and files before calling the customer. The salesperson can also verify what the customer has requested or already been sent, such as samples, demos, sales literature, and the like.

➤ Templates can be set up to quickly prepare and process proposals, frequently asked questions (FAQ), and quotations.

➤ It is easy to perform advanced analysis and gather statistics on sales forecasts, performance, and call reports.

➤ Sales staff and channel partners can quickly identify which leads to focus on and approach those contacts with much higher quality information, which can be accessed and grasped simply.

➤ The number of calls necessary to close a sale is reduced due to the capture of critical information at the point of sale, increased timeliness and usefulness of meetings, better conduct sales calls, and the ability to prepare the proposal in the presence of the customer.

➤ The business can more easily prepare and send proposals to customers, which helps avoid customer confusion and time wasted in resolving and overcoming complications and inconveniences.

➤ The ability to manage and provide information to customers using web-based presentations also greatly reduces travel costs.

➤ The business gains automated follow-up reminders and scheduled calls, organized prospect notes, sales qualification scoring methods, sales process and best practice templates, and industry knowledge guides.

➤ Sales goods and administration (SGA) costs are consequently reduced as the administration process is improved.

➤ Nonproductive time is decreased, as are the duration of training for new hires and travel-associated costs.

Increased Motivation and Reduced Turnover

Maintaining a motivated sales team is one of the biggest challenges any sales manager can face. Sales is a numbers game with many rejections that eventually lead to a close. A CRM solution can significantly affect the motivation level by allowing the staff or the channel to review and identify wins and losses in a much more objective fashion; it also allows the sales and channel manager to get involved and take corrective action to turn things around. More motivated sales force and resellers will directly translate into an increase in sales volume and reduced turnover, which allow the organization to save rather than having to constantly hire, retrain, and recruit new partners.

The results of the entire organization's personnel, including the administrative staff and channel partners, can be measured for increased efficiency. The META Group research indicates that resource utilization is on average 65 percent, indicating 35 percent resource underutilization, which includes other administrative and unproductive tasks that do not directly benefit the organization (SPEX 2000 PSA Market Analysis, META Group). Even a very small change in resource utilization can yield tremendous benefits.

Ability to Respond to Competition or Changes in the Marketplace

A CRM solution allows the organization not only to be more responsive to customers but also to adapt quickly to market changes

Figure 15.3 The Partnership Cycle

and technology shifts. As the wins and losses are recorded and analyzed, the organization can quickly introduce formal changes to the quality, pricing, and delivery of the product and service offering.

A PRM solution also allows partners with a complementary skill set to connect, collaborate, and communicate. This shared knowledge allows the customer to receive a complete solution, which leads to higher client satisfaction. This will ultimately have a positive impact an organization's revenues. Strong partnerships can also ward off competition and create additional barriers of entry for new players attempting to gain access to those markets.

➤ Other Enterprise Systems

Live bidirectional data synchronization with Enterprise Resource Planning (ERP), PSA, project management (PM), and payroll and accounting systems is vital for offering a complete solution.

■ SUMMARY

The amount of information and the ongoing process of maintaining all the data that must be prepared, communicated, sent, and understood by the direct sales and partner channels are massive. A

CRM solution allows a more harmonious and effective platform for sharing and updating all related information. With this solution, everyone can quickly access, understand, and benefit from the latest offerings and promotions.

Project- and service-oriented organizations focus on billable activities, whereas an internal IT department's focus is on budgets and charge backs. A CRM solution can help manage opportunities, engagements, campaigns, sales channels, and demand by seamlessly exchanging and integrating its data with other PSA components for resource management, project management, cost and revenue accounting, invoicing and charge back, and performance analysis.

A CRM solution can help an organization work proactively, process critical real-time information for its customers and partners, analyze trends, gauge marketing campaign effectiveness, and build more focused and grounded strategies. This will lead to an increase in customer and partner loyalty by enabling them to achieve their goals, hence directly affecting the bottom line.

Chapter 16

Human Resource Management

Human resource (HR) management is of particular importance to PSORGs. These organizations are very labor intensive and depend heavily on their human capital to deliver projects and services. Human resource management systems (HRMSs) are an enabling technology that can bring tremendous cost savings and benefits to this vital and everyday activity.

Human resource management systems must be fully web based. These systems automate the requesting of staff, approval of such requests, the recruitment process, and the resource management process once employees have been hired.

This section describes the HR process, the benefits of using software to automate and streamline these business processes, and important features in an HRMS.

■ INTRODUCTION

Human resource management is a sensitive and ongoing activity in any organization. It is of particular importance to PSORGs whose activities are highly human capital–intensive.

Human resource management systems automate and streamline all processes and activities that relate to recruiting, development, training, disciplinary action, evaluations, and reviews.

Consider the following situations:

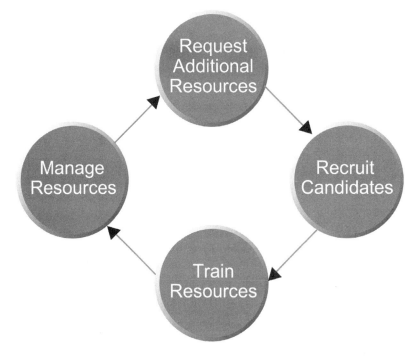

Figure 16.1 The Human Resource Management Process

> ➤ E-mail– and paper-based staffing requests and approvals are an administrative nightmare and very costly to process.

> ➤ Screening applicants and processing resumes and other job application forms requires substantial time and resources from the HR team.

> ➤ Even if an HRMS is installed to automate certain tasks, there is no web-based mechanism to request staff, recruit candidates, and manage hires.

> ➤ Turnovers and layoffs are processed using paper and without a formal process.

> ➤ E-mail or other inefficient means are used to communicate with staffing agencies.

Now, consider some of the benefits of an HRMS:

➤ It reduces general HR costs.

➤ It streamlines HR processes and reduces administrative over-head.

➤ It attracts and motivates the best employees.

➤ It improves retention by helping staff to focus on their responsibilities and offering a reward system.

➤ It aligns the objectives of employees with the organization's strategy.

➤ It maximizes collaboration and knowledge sharing between departments.

➤ It collects data and generates reports that comply with regulations, such as in the US: EEO-1, EEO-4, I-9 citizenship verification, Vets-100, and state new hire reports.

➤ It improves decision making through data visualization by using business intelligence products.

➤ It encourages self-service web sites through which employees can find answers to HR questions.

There are well-defined processes for various stages of an HR activity. This section describes the requirements of an HRMS for PSORGs, various HR processes, how an HRMS automates these processes, and other recommended features that should be part of any HRMS system employed by PSORGs.

■ STATISTICS ON HUMAN RESOURCE SELF-SERVICE

➤ Benefits of Human Resource Self-Service

Providing full web-based HR self-service results in tremendous cost savings and benefits. The following figure shows the results of a survey conducted on more than 340 companies that rolled out self-service HR systems within their organization. The figures clearly show the substantial streamlining, optimization, and cost savings that are achieved.

Quantitative Results Achieved[1]

	1999	2000	Comments
Employee satisfaction	Increase	Up to 50% increase	• Employees extremely satisfied; numerous requests to add more self-service functionality
Headcount changes	20 to 25% reduction	Up to 75% increase	• Able to control growth • Able to redirect/re-deploy staff to other tasks
Inquiries to service center	Not measured in 1999	Up to 50% increase	• Open enrollment inquiries: 75% call reduction
Cycle time		Average 50% reduction	• Time to fill new position: 50% reduction • Open enrollment: 94% reduction
Average cost per transaction	Average 30% reduction	Average 60% reduction	• Open enrollment: 90% reduction • Electronic paystubs: 50% reduction • W4 changes: $120,000 savings per year • Application acknowledgement letters 90% reduction
ROI/payback period	100% achieved within 18 months	100% achieved in one year	• $1.2 million required: $2.5 million achieved in one year

➤ Self-Service Objectives

Before implementing an HRMS or taking on a project to upgrade a legacy HR system, the project manager should determine clear and stated objectives for every phase of the implementation. The following figure depicts the objectives sought by other organizations that initiated an HR self-service project.

---

1. http://www.employeeconnect.co.uk/ecnet/assets/Published/General/2000_HR_ Self_Service_Survey.pdf, 2000 Human Resources Self Service Survey: The Hunter's Group Third Annual Survey, The Hunter Group, 2000, Page 5, 7, 8, 11, 14

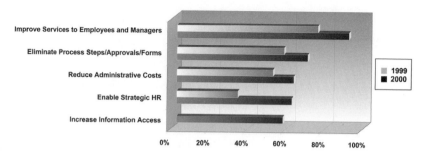

Figure 16.2 Self-Service Objectives
Source: The Hunter Group, 2000 Human Resources Self-Service Survey. Available at [http://www.employeeconnect.co.uk/ecnet/assets/Published/General/2000_HR_Self_Service_Survey.pdf].

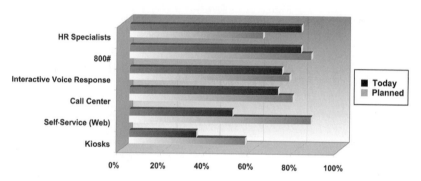

Figure 16.3 Service Delivery Methods
Source: The Hunter Group, 2000 Human Resources Self-Service Survey. Available at [http://www.employeeconnect.co.uk/ecnet/assets/Published/General/2000_HR_Self_Service_Survey.pdf].

➤ Self-Service Trends

Survey results indicate that most organizations have recognized the advantages of a self-service HR system. Most are planning to substantially increase self-service so that it becomes the primary method of service delivery.

➤ Knowledge Management

Survey results indicate primary objectives behind implementing a knowledge management (KM) system as part of the HRMS. The three primary needs to be addressed by a KM system are answering

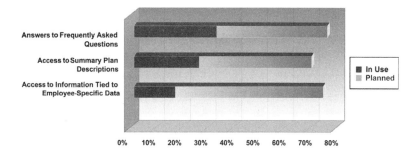

Figure 16.4 Needs Addressed by Knowledge Base Solutions
Source: The Hunter Group, 2000 Human Resources Self-Service Survey. Available at [http://www.employeeconnect.co.uk/ecnet/assets/Published/General/2000_HR_Self_Service_Survey.pdf].

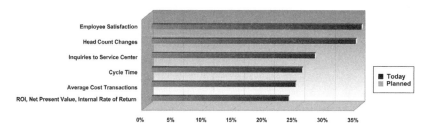

Figure 16.5 Metrics Collected
Source: The Hunter Group, 2000 Human Resources Self-Service Survey. Available at [http://www.employeeconnect.co.uk/ecnet/assets/Published/General/2000_HR_Self_Service_Survey.pdf].

frequently asked questions, accessing summary information on an HR plan, and accessing information related to specific employees.

➤ Building the Business Case

The success of any enterprise software project must be calculated using specific units of measure. The following diagram shows the metrics used by the survey participants and the measured percentage increase in that metric once the self-service system was used.

➤ Success Factors

As the following diagram indicates, the success of an IT project, especially one involving sensitive and vital issues such as HR, depends on some key factors: close cooperation between the HR and

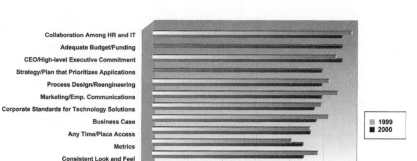

Notes: 1= not at all important; 2= somewhat important; 3- highly important.

Figure 16.6 Self-Service Success Factors
Source: The Hunter Group, 2000 Human Resources Self-Service Survey. Available at [http://www.employeeconnect.co.uk/ecnet/assets/Published/General/2000_HR_Self_Service_Survey.pdf].

IT teams, adequate budget, and commitment on the part of the organization's senior executives.

➤ Actual Annual Cost Savings of a Self-Service Human Resources System

The following table summarizes the actual annual cost savings that can be directly attributed to the use of a self-service HR system. The calculations are based on the results of the Hunter Group survey briefly presented in previous sections. Note that these are the tangible benefits of such a system and purely from an inquiry perspective. An HRMS significantly automates staff requisitioning, the recruitment process, and many administrative and repetitive tasks performed by the HR department. Cost savings related to the above are not reflected in the calculations that follow.

	Number of Employees					
Item	20	50	100	200	1,000	10,000
Total annual savings[a]	$2,658	$6,645	$13,291	$26,582	$132,910	$1,329,100

[a] Assuming only one transaction annually per employee.

Item	Manual	Self-Service	Savings	Savings
Open enrollment	$77.58	$31.25	$46.33	60%
Benefit inquiry	$10.91	$5.48	$5.43	50%
Request record	$9.91	$2.43	$7.48	75%
401k update	$23.64	$7.51	$16.13	68%
Dependent update	$15.53	$2.43	$13.10	84%
Beneficiary update	$15.38	$2.43	$12.95	84%
Address change	$20.82	$2.43	$18.39	88%
Emergency contact change	$15.53	$2.43	$13.10	84%
Total	$189.30	$56.39	$132.91	70%

Source: Hunter Group, 2000 Human Resources Self-Service Survey. Available at [http://www.employeeconnect.co.uk/ecnet/assets/Published/General/2000_HR_Self_Service_Survey.pdf].

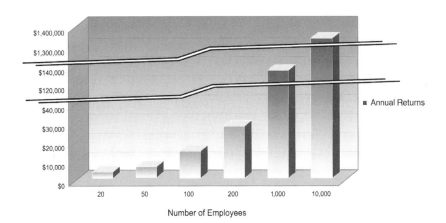

Figure 16.7 Human Resource Return on Investment

Calculate your own ROIs online on human resources by visiting the psabook.com/roi/hr.htm web site.

➤ Staffing Requisitions

Based on project or service delivery requirements and current staffing levels, various managers within the organization may require additional resources. Without a formal web-based process, these requests are issued in the form of paper, documents, spread-

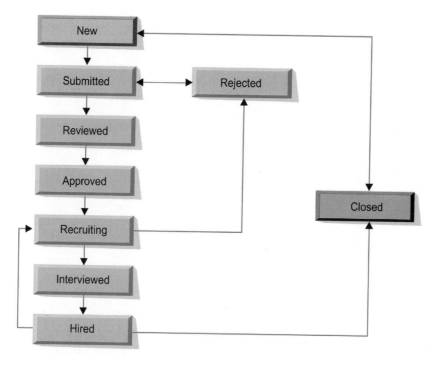

Figure 16.8 Sample Staff Purchasing Workflow

sheets, or e-mail to the HR department. The HR department then re-types the request into another system (possibly the HR component of an ERP system).

This task can be automated using a web-based HRMS that supports configurable workflows. The staff requisitioning workflow should be customizable in order to allow the notification of, and approval by, the required management and executives. Some organizations may have different staff requisitioning workflows for various positions or departments. Therefore, the system should allow administrators to create as many workflows as needed.

■ RECRUITING PROCESS MANAGEMENT

Once the staff requisition has been approved, the HR department has to prepare and place advertisements, conduct interviews, filter candidates, and make offers to potential hires. As one can see, just

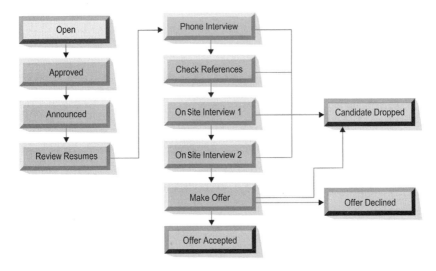

Figure 16.9 Hiring Workflow

like staff purchasing, recruiting is a process with a predefined workflow. Every organization has a specific recruiting workflow (a
sample workflow is shown previously). Any HR system selected
should have a few hiring workflows preconfigured out of the box, but
should be flexible enough to allow the organization to quickly customize system-provided prewritten workflows or build new ones.
The system should also maintain a dynamic log of hiring activities,
including interviews and prescreening conferences.

➤ Resume Processing

The HR team will receive resumes through fax, e-mail, online
forms, and mail. Processing resumes and maintaining files of potential candidates is a costly manual process that is repeated every
time additional staff is requested.

The HR system should perform the following functions:

➤ Process resumes: The system should be able to convert all resumes into searchable data. All the important fields and data
   within the resume should be automatically indexed and be
   made searchable and reportable. For example, basic information such as skill set, proficiency level, years of experi-

ence, educational background, and the like should be readily searchable to the user.

➤ Automate resume routing: As resumes are received from various channels, they should automatically be processed and forwarded to the appropriate HR personnel, screened by the HR team, and subsequently forwarded to the managers who requested those specific qualifications.

➤ Support search and retrieval: All candidate information should be stored in the HRMS database. HR personnel should be able to search for and retrieve this information using various search criteria as well as to generate reports on this information. The search system should also be flexible enough to understand different representations of the same basic information, for example, various representations of educational degrees that the user may consider equivalent—such as MBA, Masters of Business Administration, Masters of Administration, Masters of Business—by providing prebuilt cross-references, as well as allowing users to specify their own personal cross-references.

➤ Perform autoscreening: Once all the information is in the HR system, HR personnel should be able to consider various parameters and scenarios to screen applicants based on skills, interests, requirements, and salary and compensation expectations.

➤ Allow users to access HR information online: By providing a web-based central repository for all HR information, such as employee handbooks, corporate policies, employee contact information, official holidays, job openings, and organization events, the organization delivers a self-service system that allows employees to retrieve the information they need.

➤ Calendars and Schedules

The HR system should also incorporate shared calendars that are used by recruiters and managers. The calendars indicate the availability of recruiters and managers for various HR activities and are used for scheduling purposes.

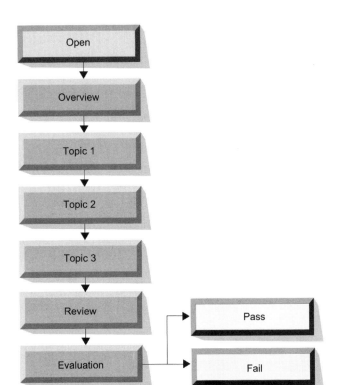

Figure 16.10 Sample Training Workflow

➤ Contact Management

The HRMS should provide services to keep information on staffing companies and future candidates, and should be able to query and retrieve this information using various search criteria. Basic contact information includes name, e-mail address, telephone number, cellular phone number, pager number, and full mailing address.

■ MANAGING RESOURCES

Once the candidate is hired, various HR-related issues emerge, such as training, disciplinary action (if necessary), review evaluations, and time tracking.

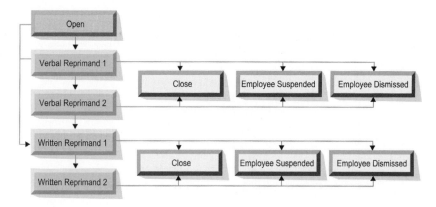

Figure 16.11 Sample Disciplinary Workflow

➤ Training

From the very first day, employees require various types of training. For example, there should be training sessions to orient the employees when they begin their new position with the company or another internal department.

A sample training workflow is shown in Figure 16.10. The HR system should allow the organization to create multiple training workflows, each catered to a specific training program, such as initiation, management, and leadership.

➤ Disciplinary Action

Some employees may be repeatedly late or disorganized or exhibit other unacceptable or questionable conduct that needs to be addressed. Every organization has specific documented policies to handle such issues. Human resource management systems can help automate and enforce a specific set of steps that ensure that employees are treated fairly and are provided sufficient warning and information regarding their conduct. It is important to follow the appropriate steps in order to avoid any legal consequences of HR mismanagement.

➤ Reviews and Evaluations

Year-end evaluations, scheduled performance reviews, probationary period completion, and other forms of evaluation need to be formally

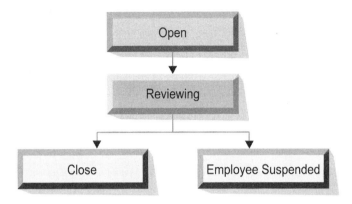

Figure 16.12 Sample Review Workflow

managed and documented. The HRMS should provide canned and customizable workflows for managing the review process.

➤ Time Tracking and Resource Management

An HRMS must be linked to a time and activity tracking system in order to perform the following functions:

➤ Processing timesheets for payroll

➤ Verifying employee attendance, workload, and work history

➤ Analyzing resource gaps and resource utilization levels and ensuring optimal resource utilization

➤ Tracking progress and following up on employees from an HR perspective

Recommended Features

Feature	Description
Staff-requisitioning workflows	Managers can use staff-requisitioning workflows to request hiring resources. This is a key HRMS component in the context of PSA solutions.
Recruiting workflows	Once the staffing requests are approved and budgeted, recruiting workflows helps the HR team search, filter, find, interview, and hire prospective candidates.
Disciplinary action workflows	These workflows reprimand and warn employees for being late or disorganized or for other questionable conduct.

Feature	Description
Review and evaluation	These workflows review and evaluate employees, as in performance reviews and year-end evaluations.
Customizable workflows	In addition to the workflows defined above, the HRMS should allow administrators to create new workflows as needed.
Resume collection	Resumes needs to be collected, processed, and automatically entered into the HRMS database.
Resume search and retrieval	Once the information is in the database, HR personnel should be able to quickly find resumes and candidates using various search criteria and filters.
HR calendar	Shared HR calendars are used to schedule and conduct interviews, conferences and other HR activities
Contact management	Contact information regarding staffing agencies, potential candidates, and current employees should be maintained online and accessible via the web.
Resource management	The system should have the ability to assign skills and calendars to users and projects, and then to find the most qualified users for a given project or activity based on skills, proficiency, experience, and availability.
Notifications	The system should be customizable to send notifications based on events (such as the arrival of a new resume or the need to interview a candidate).
Document management	The system should allow HR team and managers to attach various types of documents, including resumes, in mail to employees and candidates.
Knowledge management	Knowledge management is the process of collecting, documenting, and indexing various types of knowledge in the organization, using a web-based system. HR personnel can play a key role in promoting this vital and often ignored activity; by nature PSORGs need to retain their knowledge as much as possible, as workers are quite difficult to find and train and are costly to replace.
Screening	HR personnel should be able to specify various criteria for different positions and be able to screen applicants to find those most suitable.
Compensation and benefits	The HRMS should allow for the definition and management of various compensation and benefits packages; this information should be associated and tracked for every employee.
Employee reports	Information including resumes, contact information, and work history should be used to create detailed employee reports.
Compliance with reporting regulations	HRMS must comply with various regulations such as EEO-1, EEO-4, I-9 citizenship verification, Vets-100, and State New Hire reports.
Performance analysis (OLAP)	Advanced and sophisticated multidimensional enterprise reporting consists of adding business intelligence to HR, resource management, and decision support. Anyone with the proper access rights can drill up or down and gain significant insight about the organization's HR-related efficiencies and weaknesses.

continued

Feature	Description
Organization's online data center	A central web site that contains an employee handbook, policy documents, and sample documents for various HR- related activities, as well as other shared documents and information whose accessibility is based on various security roles.
Internal job postings	One of the most cost-effective ways of finding new candidates is to put out a request to current employees. The organization's online data center should also include a link to a list of the current job openings.
Time tracking	The HRMS should be integrated with a time tracking system so that the employee's work history, progress, resource gaps, and resource utilization can be reviewed, analyzed, and assessed from an HR perspective.

■ SUMMARY

This section described various HR processes, the cost savings and benefits of using software to automate HR activities, and the software requirements to automate them.

Human resource management is a vital and regular activity for PSORGs. A web-based online HRMS provides significant self-service functionality, allows HR personnel and management to communicate efficiently for staffing requests and recruitment, encourages knowledge capture and sharing throughout the organization, generates reports, and enforces policies. These features are essential in order for organizations to comply with required regulations; they enable sophisticated analysis and provide HR team and management with key insights related to the HR process.

Chapter 17

Complete Enterprise Accounting

Although most PSA solutions integrate with third-party accounting solutions, there are some that offer complete accounting functionality.

The accounting department is at the epicenter of any organization's operations. Hence, it is the department affected by almost all company decisions. The implementation of a PSA solution is no exception. Optimizing business processes will help ensure a company's efficiency. However, information entered in the PSA solution will eventually make its way into the accounting system. Automating the flow of information between these two systems will reduce administrative overhead and human error, as well as leading to significant savings, in any PSORG.

■ INTRODUCTION

Increasingly complex global markets, a service-oriented economy, changing regulatory environment, and the highly mobile and dispersed workforce of a PSORG has put new demands on enterprise software. From this situation emerges a new breed of software called PSA software.

Typically, the components of a PSA solution include the following:

➤ Opportunity or demand management

➤ Resource management

➤ Project management

➤ Timesheet and expense management

➤ Project accounting (billing and invoicing)

➤ Workflow requests

➤ Collaboration and knowledge management

➤ Purchasing management

Several of these components have either a direct or an indirect impact on the accounting department; therefore, the way some accounting issues are handled in a PSA solution is important. These issues can range from integration of these components with existing accounting software modules to internal tracking of projects for R&D purposes and to revenue recognition.

These sections focus on a number of these issues and how they relate back to the accounting system. In addition, this chapter highlights the benefits that can be derived from the seamless transfer of information between the PSA solution and the accounting system.

■ THE INTEGRATION PERSPECTIVE

The main objective of a PSA solution is to maximize the performance of a PSORG. This is achieved by automating and integrating core business processes to increase productivity and profitability.

With all the advantages most PSA solutions provide, one of the major weaknesses is their integration with accounting systems. Currently, very few PSA solutions provide seamless integration.

The updating of actuals in the accounting system can take place on many levels:

➤ Invoicing services

➤ Time for work in progress (WIP)

➤ Expense reports

➤ Purchase orders

➤ Payroll information

It is easy to understand why integration with an accounting system should be a major focus of a PSA solution. Automation of these tasks will reduce administrative overhead and decrease the risk of manual error. This adds up to considerable savings for the organization in the medium to long run.

➤ Invoicing services

Time tracking and invoicing is a critical component of any project management software in a PSORG. A good PSA solution must address the requirements for tracking and invoicing time and expenses spent on specific projects. A good PSA solution should handle billable time and expense entries to be reviewed by a project manager on a periodic basis so that quick and accurate decisions can be made as to the amount to invoice the client. In addition, invoiced time and expense entries are to be marked as billed, the dockets for these projects are to be cleaned up, and only unbilled entries should remain.

If all this is achieved, the integration with an accounting system will seamlessly exchange these invoiced amounts and once again reduce the manual overhead involved in re-entering all the information in a different system. An organization would be able to reduce the lead time necessary to invoice clients for work performed and actually improve the cash flows to a company.

➤ Time for Work in Progress

In most PSORGs, WIP is a critical component of their financial statements. Essentially, WIP is the difference between the work that has been performed and the work that has been invoiced. For example, if $1,000 of work has been performed on a project, but only $600 has been invoiced,

> **PSA solutions offer accurate Work In Progress (WIP) reports for the enterprise**

then management can expect an additional $400 in revenues. Essentially, WIP is a quick snapshot of a project's or an organization's current billing status.

Traditionally, an accounting department has to go through the individual projects in the organization and determine the WIP for each project manually. After this has been calculated, a journal entry is created and entered in the accounting system.

Most PSA solutions offer some form of WIP reporting that can provide management with an idea of the WIP at any given time. Some solutions even provide the organization the option to define their revenue recognition policies. If the PSA solution is performing the majority of the organization's work in determining the WIP at a given moment in time, then why not create a reversible journal entry to update the financial statements for a defined period? For example, most companies report monthly or quarterly results to either management or shareholders. An internal policy can be adopted to update the financial statements for the WIP at the end of each month. The reversible journal entry is created, entered in the accounting system at the end of the month, and reversed on the first day of the new month. This way, the snapshot of the company's operations taken at a defined moment is completely accurate and there is no need to go through a lengthy and tedious process of manually determining the WIP.

➤ Expense Reports

In any PSORG, consultants often incur expenses that will be charged back to the client. An expense report module in a PSA solution allows the consultant to enter these expenses in relation to the client, project, and activity, so that the organization can follow the cost of the project and invoice the incurred expenses.

This is at the very center of the T&E (time and expenses) world; tracking the costs and invoicing for incurred expenses is an absolute requirement for any T&E system, and a good PSA solution incorporates this functionality. Considering the volume of expense reports that employees of a PSORG generate, actually entering these reports manually in the accounting system can become a very frustrating and time-consuming activity.

By improving the transfer of information from the PSA solution to the accounting system, an organization can save a considerable amount of administrative overhead as well as reducing the time the organization takes to reimburse the employee for out-of-pocket costs. This, in turn, reduces the turnaround time to invoice the client.

By improving these aspects of the expense reporting process, the organization will lower costs related to administrative overhead and actually improve the cash flows of the organization by being able to invoice clients much faster than in the past.

➤ Purchase Orders

Requisitions are initiated by employees. Requisitions go through a series of approvals based on their size and type, a purchase order (PO) is generated, and the order is placed. It is inevitable that an automated purchase-ordering system reduces a great deal of administrative overhead.

However, once the invoice is received, if the accounting system does not get automatically updated with the proper information, the accounts payable clerk would have to match the invoice with the purchase order and manually re-enter all relevant information in the accounting system.

The information in the purchasing module can be used in many ways by the accounting department. First, it can be used in conjunction with the budget to determine if amounts being purchased are within the parameters set. With this information readily available in the accounting system, notifications can be sent out to various departments if they are close to their budgeted amounts. This system can enable a company to take a proactive approach to managing their budget issues as opposed to the common reactive or after-the-fact approach.

Second, the accounting department can calculate accruals more easily for items that have been ordered and received, but for which no invoice is available. By taking the amounts estimated on the individual POs, the company can estimate its liabilities at any given time and book this liability as an accrual in the accounting system. This would assist the company to close its books much more quickly and also provide the ability to report results of operations to management and shareholders in a much more timely and efficient manner.

Finally, when an invoice is received in the accounting department, there is no need to re-enter any information. If there is a strong integration between the PSA solution and the accounting system, all the relevant information will already be imported and the accounting department will only have to ensure that there are no differences between the original PO and the invoice. (The annual cost savings of a mechanized purchasing system for PSORGs has been previously discussed in the section outlining purchasing workflows.)

➤ Payroll Information

Time tracking modules help PSORGs track billable versus nonbillable time to be able to invoice clients and calculate WIP.

Approved time can also be exported to the payroll module, where the administrative overhead of processing payroll can be greatly reduced. With a seamless integration with the accounting system's payroll module, the simple click of a button results in a number of tasks' being performed.

Regular time for employees on an hourly wage can be entered automatically, as can any overtime or other payroll categories. With the export of the proper information into the payroll module, the system can automatically compute the employees' wages for that particular pay period. In addition, when only the approved time is entered in the payroll system, this creates an internal control, which ensures that the accounting department will pay only the approved time. The same applies for company overtime policies and administrative policies (such as vacation time). By using some of the built-in controls available in most PSA solutions, the accounting department ensures that employees are compensated only for time that they are entitled to, and not for unpaid work, such as an unpaid leave of absence.

The same reasoning also applies to companies that are using an outsourced payroll service, such as ADP. A strong integration with the third-party software for collecting payroll information greatly reduces the administrative work involved in processing payroll.

➤ Methods of Integration

The basic components of an accounting system are usually a system manager, general ledger (GL), accounts receivable (AR), and accounts payable (AP) modules. Of course, the more complex an organization's operations become, the more modules must be purchased.

There are essentially two choices when it comes to integrating a PSA solution with an accounting system: integrating directly to the GL, or integrating with the AR and AP modules. In general, when entries concern invoices or expenses, it is more effective to send that information to either the AR or the AP module. The reasoning behind this is that the information transferred to the accounting system is client- or vendor-specific and the organization needs to track this information on a client-by-client or vendor-by-vendor basis. In a system that sends information directly to the GL for invoices and expenses, the organization would not be able to track its AR from clients or AP from vendors.

Most accounting systems process entries in batches; therefore, the integration should allow the user to export invoicing or purchasing information to an open batch in the accounting system. To better achieve this type of integration, there must be a *live* connection between the accounting and PSA databases. That is, the accounting department should not have to export the information from the PSA solution to a file and then import that file into the accounting system. Rather, when exporting information, the user should be able to immediately select an open batch in the accounting system and export the entries directly.

When processing time entries for the payroll system, the information should be exported directly to the payroll module of the accounting system. Regular time, overtime, and any other relevant information should be exported to the proper fields in the payroll module, thereby decreasing manual intervention and the potential for error.

➤ The Internal Perspective

PSA solutions can be used to track projects not only for external clients but also for internal purposes. If we take the example of a company whose IT department develops a software application for internal use, it would be very important to track the opportunity cost involved in producing the software. In a company that tracks profitability on a departmental basis, they may want to transfer some of these costs over to the department for which the software is being developed.

These types of departmental charge backs help company management better track the performance of the company on a department-by-department basis. The accounting department would need a structured breakdown of the time, expenses, and purchases involved in the project so as to allocate the proper amounts to various departments. Therefore, the PSA solution can give the accounting department the breakdown of the work involved in developing the application. In addition, the department may want to determine the *direct cost* involved in the development as well as the *opportunity cost*. For the former, the company would look at the costing rules for the individuals on the project, whereas for the latter, the company would look at the billing rules for those individuals. With this information in hand, management can then make an informed decision on the amount of the charge back to be allocated.

➤ Research and Development

Under certain conditions, generally accepted accounting principles (GAAP) will allow for the capitalization of costs related to research and development (R&D). Similarly, government tax credits may be available in certain jurisdictions and can be claimed by the company for R&D costs or allocated to other government-subsidized programs. Tracking these costs on a paper-based system can be a time-consuming activity. A PSA solution aids in tracking the time and expenses spent on a project that qualifies for both R&D and other tax credits, as well as tracking those project costs that can be capitalized for accounting purposes. Once again, this helps to reduce the administrative overhead involved in determining R&D costs, thus improving the bottom line of the company.

➤ The 1998 Statement of Position

Since the release of the AICPA statement of position (SOP) 98-1 in 1998, *Accounting for the Costs of Computer Software Developed or Obtained for Internal Use,* tracking the cost involved in developing software has become more crucial from an accounting perspective. It requires that all costs related to developing computer software for internal use be capitalized and accounted for as long-term assets, exactly as would any other R&D costs the organization would want to capitalize on their balance sheet. Therefore, similarly to R&D, a PSA solution helps an organization determine the costs of capitalization to comply with this SOP.

Simply stated, this is the ability to track time and expenses related to a specific project. The process of actually capitalizing the project in the books of the organization is left to the accounting department, which will create a journal entry in the accounting system and start depreciating the asset based on the useful life of that particular asset.

➤ Revenue Recognition

For as long as companies have had to report earnings, revenue recognition principles have been at the center of discussions. This is true not only for public companies that use aggressive methods to enhance revenues so as to increase market capitalization, but also for private companies that understate revenues to defer tax liabilities.

Historically, revenue recognition has not presented itself as a major issue. Most companies are of the opinion that revenue should be recognized only when a transaction culminated in the exchange of a monetary asset.

Recently, however, the high-tech industry has been plagued with controversy regarding revenue recognition. In an effort to meet expectations, certain companies have used aggressive accounting policies and have recognized revenues earlier than in most traditional practices. As a result, the regulating bodies have found it necessary to address the problem by issuing special communiqués with regard to revenue recognition, as is evidenced by position papers such as the AICPA Statement of Position 97-2, *Software Revenue Recognition*, or Statement of Position 98-1, *Accounting for the Costs of Computer Software Developed or Obtained for Internal Use.*

Project- and service-related organizations have their share of revenue recognition issues, making it necessary to decide whether revenues should be recognized at the acceptance and signing of a contract or after final payment on the contract has been made.

The Generally Accepted Accounting Principles behind Revenue Recognition

Popular opinion says that there are two main methods used in industry to recognize revenue: the critical event approach and the accretion approach.

The critical event approach. Most popular of the two methods of recognizing revenue, this approach allows recognition of revenue in full at the time when the significant risks and rewards of ownership have been passed on to the purchaser.

An example of this would be an individual's purchase of an item in a store. The risks and rewards of ownership have been passed on to the purchaser at the point of sale, and the revenue has been recognized by the store. Other companies may decide to recognize revenue at the signing of a contract or even at completion of production (mostly in the production of commodities).

The accretion approach. In the services industry, this approach would be adopted on long-term contracts. This method is most commonly referred to as the percentage-of-completion method. A method of measuring the contract performance is used, and revenues are recorded based on that contract performance.

Therefore, it becomes critical to keep track of costs in a given project, be they time or expenses. An organization can compare actual time and expenses spent on a project to its budget to help determine the percentage of completion.

Notice that in this particular case invoicing has little to do with the revenue recognized for the project. In fact, the comparison of invoiced time and expenses to noninvoiced time and expenses only help in the determination of the WIP.

Automating Revenue Recognition

Depending on the terms and conditions, revenue for contracts can be recognized at different stages of the project. Revenue can be recognized incrementally as work is performed, when the client approves work performed, when the work is invoiced, or even when payment is received.

The benefit of automating revenue recognition is that the criteria can be set out at the onset of the project on a company-wide or even a project-by-project basis, and the accounting department will not have to keep referring to the actual contract to determine at which point revenue should be recognized.

Imagine a company that has 50 different projects in progress at any given time, with each project having a different set of criteria to determine the point of revenue recognition. In a system without automated revenue recognition, the accounting department would have to keep referring to the actual contracts for each project to determine the revenue to be recognized. The benefit of an automated system is that the administrative work is reduced once again for the accounting department. It can set the criteria at the start of the project (e.g., recognize revenue when client approves time) and never have to refer back to the contract. When the time comes to determine WIP at the end of the month, it has the assurance that the PSA solution has already been given the proper guidelines with respect to revenue recognition and that the WIP amount returned by the system is accurate.

In the case of fixed price contracts, a periodic evaluation of the percentage of completion must be performed to determine the total revenue to be recognized, as well as any amounts that must be written off. This is the more difficult part of contract accounting and is not as easily automated. Budgets must be compared to actuals, and amounts exceeding budget must be written off in the period they are discovered. Therefore, the PSA solution used to track this type of project should have a strong budgeting capability to be able to automate this process.

■ ASSET MANAGEMENT

Asset management (AM) is used in companies that build items that are capital in nature. In essence, AM is simply an extension of project management, with the notions of purchasing and depreciation added.

➤ Building an Asset

In the wireless telecommunications industry, companies spend a considerable amount of capital to roll out their infrastructure. Base stations are built in strategic locations in order to provide the optimum service for subscribers. Each one of these assets takes a considerable amount of time and money to complete, and those amounts are usually capitalized on the books of the company as an asset to be depreciated over time.

Most project management systems can handle the actual building of the asset; costs and time are attributed to a specific project, and, once completed, the project is closed. An AM system will be of use when the asset is ready for use but the project is not fully completed. Depreciation of an asset begins when the asset is ready for use, and without the concept of depreciation an AM system cannot compute the depreciation on a given project.

The advantage of an AM system is that if a project can be marked as a depreciable asset and one can specify the time at which the asset should begin to depreciate, one can accurately compute the depreciation of the asset for financial statement purposes. For example, if Company A builds an asset costing $1,000,000 and the asset is ready for use in July, depreciation starts to accumulate as of that date. If in the month of October an additional $100,000 in improvements is added to the project, then the depreciation as of December 31 should be six months of depreciation on the first $1,000,000 and three months of depreciation on the additional $100,000.

Many companies do not have an effective AM system and as a result must follow these additions on a spreadsheet. Projects are completed and closed, and any additions to that project are entered in a spreadsheet for tracking purposes.

The advantage a good AM system provides is that all costs are entered in a centralized database and depreciation is calculated accurately and with little manual intervention. In addition, the journal entries to capitalize and depreciate the asset can be automated and directly entered in the GL.

■ SUMMARY

A PSA solution can undoubtedly help to streamline a company's operations by automating key business processes. By reducing the amount of time a company spends on time tracking, expense reporting, purchasing, invoicing, and similar administrative tasks, it can improve the company's bottom line and free up time to focus on revenue-generating operations. A key concept that is often poorly addressed by most PSA solutions is accounting system integration. This chapter describes various accounting principles, such as tracking payables and receivables, invoicing, WIP, SOP-98, and revenue recognition. The importance of these concepts as they relate to a PSA solution and accounting systems was presented and discussed. The return on investment of a well-integrated PSA and accounting system, as described in other chapters, can be significant to a company almost immediately.

Part

3

Selection and Implementation

Chapter 18

Evaluating a Professional Services Automation Solution

Choosing an enterprise system solely on the basis of product features and functionality will not yield the most effective solution for any organization; nor will choosing solely on the basis of price or return on investment. Which solution will be most effective depends on various factors. Thus, basing a decision on any one or two factors will lead to a less than optimal result. As discussed, there are a wide variety of PSA solutions to choose from. Corporate objective processes ultimately determine which solution should be adopted. There are specific factors to consider to properly evaluate any PSA solution:

> **Evaluate a PSA solution on its functionality, consistency, affordability, usability, corporate focus, and vendor viability**

➤ *Functionality:* This has been described in previous sections.

➤ *Consistency and integration:* Although PSA solutions are offered on a modular basis, some modules may lack integration, especially if they were assembled through acquisition of the original software developer by another organization.

The automation of business processes is not enough; all modules within a PSA solution must be tuned and integrated to meet the needs of the organization using the application.

➤ *Affordability:* Cost is always a consideration. Proper industry research will uncover cost considerations, including license fees, support, hardware, and consulting and customization costs.

➤ *Usability:* Any system is only as good as its usability. Users, managers, and executives will adopt applications that are straightforward and intuitive to use. The trend today is to adopt applications that require little to no training for the average user, thus enabling a quicker ROI. The quickest or most powerful solutions will not be effective if they are too complicated or cumbersome to use. It is to be hoped that the days of forcing all users to suffer through primitive, archaic, and convoluted user interfaces that require extensive and expensive training are over.

➤ *Corporate focus:* PSA solutions offer a variety of features and components. Determining which are more important to you is key to choosing the right system.

➤ *Vendor viability:* Evaluate whether vendors will be around in a few years to continue supporting and developing their solutions. Many PSA vendors emerged onto the market over the past two or three years. The key to longevity is a clear business focus and a focus on technology improvements and application. Is the vendor presently profitable and therefore likely to be around in a few years? How many client installations does the vendor have?

Please refer to Appendix B for a template request for proposal that can be used when searching for a PSA solution.

Chapter 19

A Best-of-Breed Approach

Any organization has to consider when implementing an enterprise software (ES) solution whether to adopt a best-of-breed strategy or a single-vendor approach. A single-vendor solution is really a collection of distinct elements or components that has been built into one unit. A best-of-breed solution is the best product (for that specific organization) in its category. Organizations often purchase software from different vendors in order to achieve the best of breed for each application area; for example, an organization may buy an HR package from one vendor and an accounting package from another. Although ERP vendors provide a wealth of applications for the enterprise and tout their integrated systems as the superior solution, all modules are rarely best of breed. No single company and product can excel in every niche.

A best-of-breed solution can be an attractive and viable solution for any organization because it has many benefits over a single-vendor offering. Some benefits associated with rolling out a best-of-breed solution include

> *Lower costs:* Best-of-breed vendors compete extensively against each other.

> *Faster ROI:* Modules can be phased in and result in immediate efficiencies.

> *Incremental adoption:* The organization does not have to bet on a single product or vendor, large budget, or multiyear IT project; the project can consist of distinct milestones

and smaller projects with predefined measurable metrics of success.

Benefits for each application include the following:

➤ It presents users with the best look and feel for the type of work it entails.

➤ It can be deployed independently, and once it is rolled out, the next solution can be implemented and integrated.

➤ It is more rapidly enhanced to address important system design, stability, and scalability issues.

➤ It includes a more specialized level of support due to the intimate vendor knowledge and implementation experience.

Nevertheless, it is important to identify the right solution set from different vendors that truly offer a fully integrated solution and actively work to enhance interoperability and seamless data exchange between their applications.

In these times of globalization, rapid technological change, and extreme competition, many organizations tend to adopt a best-of-breed approach, selecting software based on current needs that addresses a specific niche requirement. For some, this multivendor enterprise software strategy is a preferred way of dealing with change and achieving rapid and increased ROI in IT infrastructure investments.

Most PSORGs have already invested in traditional enterprise applications such as CRM, project management, ERP, or accounting systems. Implementing a complete end-to-end PSA solution (from CRM to enterprise accounting) for these organizations is not an option because they have already invested considerable resources in implementing and maintaining their current enterprise systems. Their best option is to implement a PSA solution that can leverage the functionality of their existing enterprise systems to achieve complete end-to-end PSA functionality and thus eliminate the need to replace existing systems.

At the other end of the spectrum are organizations seeking to implement new enterprise-wide applications. Implementing a best-of-breed approach for these organizations will result in extensive PSA functionality across all enterprise systems. Implementing a best-of-breed approach would consist of the following:

Best-of-breed CRM solution + Best-of-breed PM solution + Best-of-breed PSA solution + Best-of-breed ERP/Accounting (a best-of-breed HR system can also be included)

This multivendor approach can create islands of data, which are difficult for other business applications to access. However, rarely can one application or vendor excel at all its embedded components. Enterprise Resource Planning, accounting, and project management systems certainly do not so excel. The timesheet and expense industries, for example, have flourished due to the inadequacies of existing ERPs, accounting, and project management systems to effectively address these requirements.

For any one vendor, there are too many changing technologies, market needs, areas of domain-specific know-how, features, attributes, functionalities, and components within all major enterprise systems to upgrade, support, enhance, and develop.

Adopting a best-of-breed strategy will enable an organization to enjoy the most advanced functionality within each enterprise software category. A best-of-breed PSA solution focuses on developing its core competencies. Despite the claim of many PSA vendors that they "do it all," the fact is that most excel only in certain areas of the application. All PSA solutions have their strengths and weaknesses. The challenge is to determine which strengths an organization wishes to focus on and then to adopt that PSA solution within a best-of-breed strategy.

The core competencies of PSA solutions are resource management, project management, timesheet and expense report management, and project accounting. However, as described earlier, the most overlooked areas within PSA solutions are those of timesheet expense and project accounting. Most vendors have only included basic functionality here. Those vendors who offer extensive features and functionality within these areas understand the importance of these components in delivering a more complete solution to the service- or project-oriented organization.

The following table summarizes the differences between single-vendor and best-of-breed applications:

Characteristic	Best-of-Breed	Integrated
Architecture	Three-tier	Three-tier
Data tables	Duplicated in each application	Shared across all modules
Functionality	Deep	Shallow and broad
Integration	Optimal, if provided by vendor; may have to be provided by customer	Provided by vendor
OLAP	Less likely to be able to drill down unless data warehousing is used	More likely to drill down
Support	Multivendor, each with significant domain expertise	Single-vendor; often very expensive; slow response times; difficult or impossible to reach domain experts
Upgrades	Applications can be upgraded as needed, but this also means there may be too many upgrades from too many vendors	Must wait for single vendor to release the entire suite
User interface	Each application designed to fit its unique purpose	Consistent across all modules
Users	Defined in every application	Defined once
Workflow	Events unlikely to trigger cross-module action	Events likely to traverse modules

By leveraging the best and most powerful tool for each system, a PSORG may be able to gain a competitive advantage over another organization that rolls out a large, expensive, multiyear-implementation single-vendor end-to-end system.

Chapter 20

Technology Considerations

■ INTRODUCTION

Investing in any enterprise software product, no matter what its benefits and feature set, also represents an investment in its technology. Solutions that initially seem complete and sophisticated can later be found to be based on inefficient technologies, which can lead to substantial IT infrastructure spending, unproductive use of critical IT resources and expertise, and rapid obsolescence.[1]

Although large and small ES[2] projects fail for a variety of reasons, such as scope creep, lack of a business case,

> When choosing enterprise systems, technology is an important consideration to avoid obsolescence and achieve maximum benefit

---

1. In ERP installation, technology often plays a small role because the inexperienced user community plays a large role in decision making. Therefore, more often than not, old technology is being installed, which results in high implementation, training, and maintenance costs. There are very high initial and ongoing costs to overcome before a positive contribution can be made to the bottom line.

2. For our purposes, ES software refers to any multi-user concurrent access software that includes a database component such as project management, PSA, time and express management, accounting, ERP, CRM, and supply chain management applications.

inadequate planning, and insufficient support from management, technology choices also play a vital role in their success. The more proprietary, inflexible, and customized the technologies are (such as large in-house developed software), the more likely they are to quickly lead to huge expenses and result in diminishing returns.

It is for this reason that the careful evaluation of the technology employed in the development of an ES system must be performed prior to any investment in such applications. The purpose of this section is to outline the critical factors surrounding the assessment of ES technology and describe how such technology can either limit or enhance the utility of the enterprise system implemented, given the particular organizational requirements.

Many software vendors claim that their product incorporates the right technology to satisfy businesses' long-term needs; however, there is no silver bullet. Managing and tracking today's mobile and dispersed work force and communicating effectively with customers and suppliers worldwide require a set of interoperating and cohesive tools and technologies. Before choosing any ES software, carefully consider the following points.

Questions on access:

➤ Do most of the resources (employees and consultants) work in a single site?

➤ If there are multiple sites, can data reside in a central location?

➤ What are the security requirements of a multisite organization? Does every site have access to a single global client and project list, or should each site see only information specific to that site?

➤ How often must resources submit timesheets, expense reports, status reports, and other business data from remote locations?

➤ Are remote users connected to the web, or are they completely offline?

➤ Are wireless devices used by the company? Would support for wireless access be a requirement?

Questions on usage:

➤ Maximum burst simultaneous load: What percentage of resources will simultaneously access the system?

➤ Maximum data rates: What percentage of resources will be generating reports, and how often?

➤ Depending on the size of the installation:

• Will the web server and database server reside on the same computer hardware?

• Are there two independent database and web servers? If so, what is the network between the two systems?

• Are multiple web servers required to handle the load? If so, does the software used support such a configuration?

Questions on IT infrastructure and expertise:

➤ Does the organization have an in-house IT staff?

➤ If so, is there any database administration expertise?

The answers to the above questions determine the types of technologies and tools an organization should choose to invest in.

■ CLIENT/SERVER TECHNOLOGIES

Enterprise software must be designed to *scale*, so that usage grows without reaching artificial technical or manual bottlenecks. A critical factor for scalability is decoupling user interface, business logic, and database management components. The sections that follow describe various computing architectures that are in use today and compare these technologies' scalability.

➤ Two-Tier Architecture

In a two-tier architecture, the database resides on one computer and business logic and user interface reside on a second computer. Each computer represents one of the tiers. Groupware software with a

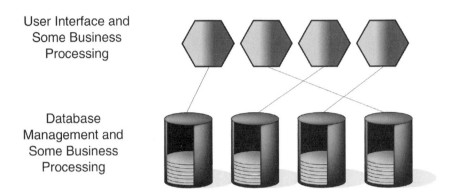

User Interface and
Some Business
Processing

Database
Management and
Some Business
Processing

Figure 20.1 Two-Tier Architecture

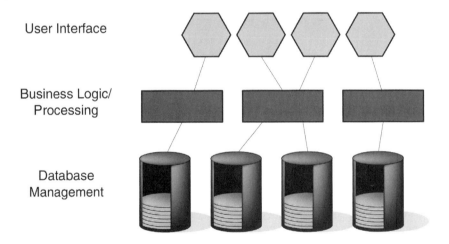

User Interface

Business Logic/
Processing

Database
Management

Figure 20.2 Three-Tier Architecture

two-tier architecture is acceptable for smaller organizations or teams with 5 to 20 users all working in the same office.

➤ Three-Tier Architecture

In a three-tier architecture, the computer hosting the database server represents one tier; the computer(s) hosting the business logic represent(s) a second tier, and the computer(s) hosting the user interface represent(s) the third tier.

Factor	Two Tier	Three Tier
Acquisition costs	Low initially, but will increase over time because client systems must be upgraded and maintained constantly	High initially, but significantly lower over time because client workstations require minimal maintenance; especially true for organizations with more than than 10 to 20 client workstations
Maintenance issues/costs	High, since every client workstation contains a copy of the application software which must be updated when bug fixes or upgrades are required	Low, since client workstations require minimal updates; mainly, business logic and database servers will need to be maintained
Security	Low; client workstations contain some business logic processing, a potential source of security breach	High; all business processing is done on the server, and users do not have access to any critical systems
Reliability	Low; client software can be outdated or out of sync with server software, leading to instability, even data corruption	High
Scalability	Low; it is very difficult to scale using a two-tier architecture; requires tremendous IT resources to upgrade and maintain client workstations	High; client software contains nothing but user interface (usually just a set of web pages viewed using a browser); system can be scaled to thousands of users

➤ Web

Web-based architectures are usually classified as two- or three-tier architectures, depending on the amount of processing on the client tier.

➤ Windows Application to Web Server (Also Known as Fat Client)

> There are many ways to access software functionality. Web access is often the least expensive to maintain and roll out to the user base

In this scenario, the client is known as a fat or heavy client. The client software usually must be manually installed on user workstations, and, as a consequence, major revisions in the software would often require the software to be reinstalled on client workstations.

➤ Java Application to Web Server (Fat Client)

This is almost the same scenario as the previous one. A Java application and, potentially, a Java virtual machine are installed on the client workstation. The client software must usually be manually installed on user workstations. Again, major revisions in the software would often require that the software be reinstalled on client workstations.

➤ ActiveX Components to Web Server (Fat Client)

In this scenario, the user loads a web page that contains an ActiveX component. The ActiveX component (usually 2 to 10 MB in size) is downloaded from the server to the client and installed. Installation usually takes place without user intervention and occurs the moment the web page that embeds the component is accessed. The amount of time required for the installation process can vary from a few seconds to a few minutes. The installation process occurs one time. Subsequent installs can be triggered again if the version of the ActiveX components residing on the server changes. In general, adopting ES systems based on ActiveX technology can be a dangerous proposition due to the long download times, ActiveX component upgrades, ActiveX installation failures on client systems, lack of support for non-Microsoft browsers, conflicts with firewall security rules (which prevent users from downloading ActiveX components), and incompatibility of ActiveX components with other client software. Therefore, similar issues should be given serious consideration when one evaluates applications that employ this technology. In general, although ActiveX technology is suitable for specific use (in a few targeted functions) or smaller applications, it is not recommended as the core client interface architecture of an ES system.

➤ Java Applets to Web Server (Thin Client)

The client consists of a web browser and Java applets that contain some data validation and some business logic. The client collects and validates the data based on the business rules stored in the applet. The information is then sent to the server. Java applets originally created a great deal of hype as a platform-independent and powerful language that is supported by all web browsers. However, security constraints, long and repeated download times, and performance issues have considerably limited the use and effectiveness of this architecture.

➤ Web Pages to Web Server (Zero Client)

The client consists of a web browser and web pages with scripting that contains some data validation. The client provides simple data validation. The information is then sent to the server. In this case, even the web pages are downloaded from the server upon request.

➤ Summary

Advantages of a Zero Client

Maintenance	Only server must be managed or maintained; zero client installation means substantially lower network administration costs and user training or access problems.
Transparent software maintenance and upgrades	With no client install, software upgrades are much easier. Only the software on the servers needs to be updated. This makes it more likely for organizations to upgrade more quickly and take advantage of the latest version of an application.

Advantages of a Fat Client

User interface	With a client installation, one can create sophisticated user interfaces that incorporate complex elements such as drag and drop, clickable charts, graphs, and other sophisticated rich controls. In addition, the user interface is fast and responsive because it does not consist of a set of web pages. Server-based web pages imply a server access for every new page load or user interface action.
Network usage	With a Fat client, every new page that is displayed to the user does not necessarily involve data transfer between the client computer and the server. This can greatly reduce network traffic and therefore network costs.
Offline access	With a full client, it is easier to develop and support offline entry. Users can enter information when offline; the information is then synchronized with the server when a connection can be established.

Client Technology	Comments	Advantages	Disadvantages
Windows desktop	Native executable program developed using C++, Visual Basic, or other tools	Can create powerful apps and user interfaces; offline access	Fat client; requires installation
Java application	Java program + Java runtime machine developed using Java development tools	Object-oriented; can create powerful apps and user interfaces	Fat client; requires installation; slow
Java applets	Java program; assumes client machine includes a Java virtual machine	Can create appealing and small user interface components	Repeated download on every visit to page; can only be used for simple apps; Microsoft will not support Java in future browsers and OS
ActiveX components in web pages	Native executable component developed using C++, Visual Basic, or other tools	Can create powerful user interface components embedded in web pages	Large download and potential auto installation problems
Active server pages (ASP)	Web pages with server-side business logic written in VBScript or JavaScript	Very flexible and customizable; can create large web-based applications	Every user interface action may trigger server access to load next web page
E-mail	Can be used to collect data, download reports	Ubiquitous; virtually every modern device supports at least text-based e-mail; supported on wireless devices	Can have only limited functionality, only entry and reports

■ DATABASE MANAGEMENT SYSTEMS

A critical choice in any enterprise software is the database management system (DBMS) that is chosen. Processing speeds, scalability, general availability of expertise, acquisition, deployment, and maintenance costs are the primary issues to consider.

The following sections describe some of the major relational DBMSs that are widely in use today. A simple rating system has also been provided in order to compare the various choices. The rating is based on our own unscientific but real-world and hands-on experience with these database systems in more than 500 installations over the last 10 years.

➤ Microsoft Database Engine

Microsoft Database Engine (MSDE) offers a powerful entry-level database for organizations that wish to deploy enterprise software on an inexpensive but reliable database platform. This is a royalty-free, stripped-down version of Microsoft SQL Server, which can be obtained either directly from Microsoft (for example, by purchasing certain development tools) or through third-party enterprise software vendors that ship their product with this database system.

Factor	Score (5 = High, 1 = Low)
Reliability	3
Scalability	2
Performance	2
Acquisition costs	1
Maintenance costs	1

➤ Microsoft SQL Server

Microsoft SQL Server is mostly perceived as a powerful DBMS targeting smaller organizations with 100 to 1,000 users. However, Microsoft has been making significant improvements to its database system, and SQL Server is rapidly becoming a major contender for installations of any size. It offers a very reasonable price-performance ratio and should definitely be considered carefully.

Factor	Score (5 = High, 1 = Low)
Reliability	4
Scalability	4
Performance	4
Acquisition costs	2
Maintenance costs	2

➤ Sybase SQL Anywhere

Generally considered a mid-range DBMS, this system is in many ways comparable to Microsoft SQL Server. Sybase is a proven and powerful DBMS that at the right price point should be considered for smaller organizations (100 to 1,000 users).

Factor	Score (5 = High, 1 = Low)
Reliability	3
Scalability	3
Performance	3
Acquisition costs	2
Maintenance costs	2

➤ Oracle

Oracle is the leading DBMS vendor. It runs on virtually every platform in existence and is a proven, scalable, and reliable DBMS that is used by a large number of Fortune 1000 companies. Oracle is the safe (although more expensive) choice when very large installations, high concurrent access, and scalability are the main issues. Both IBM DB2 and Microsoft SQL Server are strong contenders that should also be given serious consideration under the same evaluation scenario.

Factor	Score (5 = High, 1 = Low)
Reliability	5
Scalability	5
Performance	4
Acquisition costs	4
Maintenance costs	4

➤ IBM DB2

IBM DB2 has achieved resurgence in the last few years. IBM has invested heavily in enhancing and marketing its DBMS and has positioned DB2 directly against Oracle. Many of the comparisons of these two products suggest that DB2 is cheaper and easier to configure and administer than Oracle (although not as easy as Microsoft SQL Server).

Factor	Score (5 = High, 1 = Low)
Reliability	5
Scalability	5
Performance	4
Acquisition costs	2
Maintenance costs	2

■ SECURITY

Enterprise software vendors and purchasers pay close attention to the user experience, user interface, performance, scalability, and reliability. However, the same focus, resources, and analysis are not invested on the security considerations of an ES project.

The process of selecting an ES often involves an in-depth review of the feature set and most often includes assessment of application security. However, application security is but one of the safeguards that secure enterprise software should provide.

> **Any enterprise software should contain the following security levels: application security, data security, web server security, database security, business intelligence and reporting security, and network security**

This section presents the concepts of application, data, database, web server, business intelligence, and network security, and describes what to look for in an ES system in order to ensure that the selected system incorporates a comprehensive, scalable, reliable, and flexible security structure.

Enterprise software must incorporate configurable and sophisticated security features that provide a complete security solution for your enterprise. The system security architecture must be designed with an emphasis on scalability, reliability, and flexibility, allowing you to set up the security policies and measures that your organization requires.

Any enterprise software should contain the following security levels: application security, data security, web server security, database security, business intelligence and reporting security, and network security.

➤ Application Security

Application security specifies which system components, screens or pages, and fields a specific user or profile has access to.

Login Password

Users can have a login name and password to gain access to the system. The login name and password are stored in the ES database, and the passwords are encrypted. Application passwords can optionally adhere to strict password aging and format policies to improve security and reduce the possibility of hackers' breaking user passwords.

Windows NT and Windows 2000 Authentication

Using Windows NT or Windows 2000 authentication, the user can gain access to the software without explicitly providing a login name and password. This convenient and secure feature alleviates the need to define a second set of user logins and passwords.

Security Profiles

Users can play various roles in an enterprise system. A user can be a consultant, manager, team leader, or senior executive. Based on his or her security profile, a user gains access to or is restricted from accessing certain ES modules. An ES should provide default access rights for every security profile and allow one to define new profiles or to customize existing profiles to fit the needs of a particular organization.

Audit Trail

Auditing is a critical security feature. In effect, it provides a digital footprint of all user activities. All user actions—such as completion of a timesheet, expense report, or purchase order; approval, rejection, or alteration of timesheets, expense reports, or invoices; and project start and end dates and budgets— are recorded. Every audit record includes who performed the action, when the action took place, and the details of the action. The audit information can be accessed later to verify or track inappropriate or invalid entries and data changes.

Time and Date Server

An optional feature directs all time and date queries to a dedicated time and date server. When this feature is enabled, users will be restricted to using the server-provided date and time. Users will be unable to change their workstations' time and date to make the system think the current date is a few weeks ago. Time and date servers are also used to account for multi–time zone server access.

➤ Data Security

In addition to application security, which controls system access, ES systems must support data security. Data security defines what data a specific user can view or access. In contrast to application security, which controls access to entire subsystems or specific screens or fields within a web page, data security controls what portions of data can be viewed, accessed, and modified by a user. This can be achieved using scoping, filtering, and document approval processes.

Scoping and Filtering

Organizations with large data sets (such as hundreds or thousands of clients, projects, tasks, and users) must have some sort of scoping and filtering mechanism. *Scoping* allows administrators to define real or virtual classes. One or more classes can be associated with groups, teams, users, clients, portfolios, and projects. Users can only see the public items (items that are not assigned to any specific classes) and items that have been associated with at least one of the classes that is also associated with the user. Scoping is used to ensure that specific teams, regional offices, and similar subgroups have access only to pertinent data.

For example, a company's global client list may be accessible by a senior executive working from the head office. However, a regional manager should have access only to the client list specific to his or her region. Therefore, the ES system should have a mechanism for specifying which clients, projects, activities, expenses, and purchase orders can be accessed based on user types or specific users.

Filtering is similar to scoping. Site-specific managers and executives can further specify the activity list available to individual team members by limiting activities to specific clients and projects. This feature is essential for offices that still have a large number of clients and projects to manage even after scoping.

Approval and Processing of Workflows

Approval is a specific form of scoping. Every organization has various approval workflows. Documents that require approval are routed to specific individuals or users with a specified role. Managers should only see the timesheets, expense reports, purchase orders, and issues that require their approval.

An ES should support customizable workflows for the approval and processing of such documents. Users should only see documents such as expense reports, purchase orders, and issues based on the current state of the workflow. That is, the state of the workflow will determine what documents the user will be able to view or access.

Web Server Security

Web server security ensures that only authorized users have access to the web server and that their access rights are extremely limited, so that, even if their user ID and password are compromised, intruders can not cause any damage to the web server or gain access to the enterprise network.

With web-based ES systems (a zero client architecture), nothing is installed on client workstations. Users access the ES server via web pages. All web pages are pure HTML and can operate within the most stringent network and firewall security rules and settings.

Firewalls

A firewall is a system designed to prevent unauthorized access to or from a private network. Firewalls are implemented in both hardware and software, or in a combination of both. Firewalls are frequently used to prevent unauthorized Internet users from accessing private networks connected to the Internet, especially Intranets.

All messages entering or exiting the Intranet pass through the firewall, which examines each message and blocks those that do not meet the specified security criteria.

There are several types of firewall techniques:

➤ Packet filter: Examines each packet entering or leaving the network and accepts or rejects it based on user-defined rules. Packet filtering is fairly effective and transparent to users, but it is difficult to configure. In addition, it is susceptible to IP spoofing.

➤ Application gateway: Applies security mechanisms to specific applications, such as FTP and Telnet servers. This is very effective, but it can impose performance degradation.

➤ Circuit-level gateway: Applies security mechanisms when a TCP or UDP connection is established. Once the connection has been achieved, packets can flow between the hosts without further checking.

➤ Proxy server: Intercepts all messages entering and leaving the network. The proxy server effectively hides the true network addresses.

➤ Two or more of these techniques.

A firewall is considered the first line of defense for protecting private information. For greater security, data must be encrypted.

Many organizations protect their networks with some sort of firewall technology. ES software must provide a safe and secure mechanism for data access for those inside and outside the firewall. It is critical to verify with the ES vendor and with the internal IT staff that the ES software has been proven to work with the organization's firewall.

Firewalls are usually configured to prevent anything but HTTP access (in some cases, a few other protocols such as FTP are also enabled). The more protocols and ports used by the ES that must be enabled by the firewall, the more security is compromised. It is highly recommended to use an ES system that does not require any special configuration change at the firewall level.

Active Server Pages Security

Some ES systems are built on active server pages (ASP) technology, which provides an excellent security model for controlling server-side scripting. To ensure application security, all database and business logic access information must be kept out of the server-side scripts in encrypted and secure files. This eliminates the possibility of intruders' accessing any sensitive information such as database or application passwords even if they are able to break into the web server.

An ES uses ASP to provide entry, management, and administration user interface functionality. Active server pages should not contain any business logic or database access calls; all business logic must be implemented in binary server modules, which usually consist of a set of dynamic libraries.

Active server pages can be further secured in several ways:

➤ Setting permissions on the virtual directory on the web server that contains the ASP pages

➤ Setting file access permissions, if using the Windows NT/ 2000 file system (NTFS), to determine which users can access the ASP pages

➤ Using client certificates (encrypted numbers the browser sends to the server when it requests an ASP page) through two protocols known as secure sockets layer (SSL) 3.0 or through private communications technology (PCT).

➤ Database Security

Access

Database security ensures that only authorized users are actually allowed to access the database. Databases usually support two types of security: named users or operating system (OS) authentication. With both methods, named users or OS-defined users (or groups) can be given read/write/create/delete/execute rights on various database objects such as tables, views, and stored procedures. All database accesses performed by an ES system must use specialized users and password protection. Any database passwords used by an ES system must be encrypted to prevent unauthorized access.

Stored Procedures

It is highly recommended that all application-initiated database access be performed through stored procedures. A stored procedure is equivalent to a database function and usually consists of one or more series of SQL commands encapsulated into a single module with specific input parameters and return values. The advantages of using stored procedures are

➤ *Speed:* Stored procedures are optimized by the DBMS. For example, database accesses usually involve joins between two or more database tables. A DBMS compiles the stored procedure so that such joins are executed more quickly than in a standard SQL statement, which is interpreted and parsed at runtime.

➤ *Encapsulation and maintenance:* If all database access is performed at the stored-procedure level, then the business logic (code) components of the system do not have any dependency on the database tables and views. This significantly facilitates database maintenance and system changes (such as table or field renames and table relationship changes).

➤ *Security:* With all database accesses performed through stored procedures, it is no longer necessary to allow any user to have modify/delete access rights on any database tables. This significantly simplifies security considerations because users would only need execute rights to specific classes of stored procedures (instead of the more powerful and dangerous) modify/delete privileges. This eliminates the need to grant users any access to database tables, thus preventing unauthorized access to the database.

➤ *Database independence:* Most databases use custom extensions of the SQL language. These extensions provide powerful data management, manipulation, and processing functions. Using these functions can greatly enhance the performance and functionality of the database access routines. Embedding SQL statements in the application business logic can cause a maintenance nightmare when supporting multiple databases or porting an application from one database platform to another. With stored procedures, all the database-specific functions are stored in the database rather than in the application business logic. This provides the infrastructure for maintaining a single code base while supporting multiple DBMSs.

An ES should take full advantage of stored procedures, using them to perform all database operations and queries.

➤ Network Security

Most issues concerning network security are independent of the enterprise software being used. However, certain organizations may decide to run their ES systems over secure HTTP and SSL. In such cases, one must make sure that the ES server software has support for this level of network security.

➤ Business Intelligence and Reporting Security

For BI and ad hoc reporting, enterprise systems usually embed a BI tool. Most ES systems simply use their existing security system as described to secure the BI tool, but this is insufficient.

The BI tool should have security access for the following:

➤ The data universe (the collection of ES elements that can be reported on)

➤ BI access rights (the specified users who can create, delete, and modify BI documents of various types—public, private, or shared among various teams)

➤ BI document classification (the specific document type for each BI tool)

➤ User access (restricted to certain reports, universes, dimensions, measures, and menus, and prohibiting the use of certain "objects," and access to table rows to protect sensitive information)

An ES system should allow the assignment of BI security rights described above to specific user roles.

➤ Summary

Enterprise system security is not a matter to be taken lightly. All of the savings, benefits, and efficiencies that result from using an ES system can be wiped out by a single instance of compromised security. Valuable enterprises data can be leaked or modified or can fall into the wrong hands. An organization that adopts an ES without careful planning, analysis, and audit of its security features is jeopardizing the project's ultimate success.

Complete and secure enterprise software must use a combination of application, data, web server, BI, database and network protection, encryption, and auditing features to provide a comprehensive security infrastructure that can address any organization's requirements.

■ CUSTOMIZATION

No software system can satisfy 100% of an organization's requirements. Although any sophisticated ES is usually accompanied by a substantial amount of "out-of-the-box" functionality, the issue of how customizable the system is often determines its long-term viability and the benefits that will be obtained with the rollout of such a system.

➤ Software Development Kit

A major valuable offering by an ES includes a well-documented software development kit (SDK). This is even more true if the SDK is also used by the vendor's internal development team to enhance and extend the ES product. Larger organizations that adopt ES solutions will most likely have in-house IT staff or engage consultants that can use the SDK to

➤ Integrate the ES with other corporate information systems

➤ Generate important custom reports, triggers, and notifications that the core ES product does not include

➤ Build custom add-on modules and web sites using the SDK, for example, to tie in the ES with a full-fledged corporate portal

➤ Web Pages

Fully web-based ES systems often consist of a set of web pages. If the ES is serious about providing third-party support, then these product web pages should be designed to use the SDK. Such web pages would be a great example source code for the use of the SDK.

➤ Integration

Time and again in the last twenty years, most organizations have chosen to adopt a best-of-breed information technology strategy as opposed to single-vendor fully integrated behemoth software products. Single-vendor integrated software often implies the following:

- ➤ Implementation cycles are long, extending over years.

- ➤ Major up-front investment, both in terms of money and resources, is required.

- ➤ Return on investment takes several years and is often difficult to measure.

- ➤ The organization is betting on that single vendor (putting all its eggs in one basket).

- ➤ A single vendor is being relied on to innovate and stay ahead of the curve for all of the functionality it provides—making it a jack of all trades and master of none.

- ➤ Upgrading huge pieces of software is a large and expensive undertaking; therefore, most organizations that select a single vendor often choose to continue using obsolete and inefficient software rather than suffer the pain and expenses of an upgrade.

Because most organizations select accounting, HR, project management, time, expense, and other such systems from different vendors, it is essential that each of the selected enterprise systems has a well-documented and -supported data exchange strategy to allow information to be easily shared among them. Having well-documented and proven SDKs is a clear sign that the ES vendors are serious about integration and want to assist the customer in being as independent as possible. Some vendors may go as far as defining application programming interface (API) for plug-ins so that these different software systems can be seamlessly integrated.

■ IMPLEMENTATION ISSUES

➤ Programming Languages/Tools

Many vendors may use terms such as *scalable, reliable, high through-put, multithreaded,* and *transactional.* It is important to be able to differentiate marketing hype from reality. For example, vendors that use a third-generation development tool such as Oracle Forms, Borland Delphi, or Microsoft FoxPro most likely have primitive architectures that are limited to the constraints of the runtime environment in which they operate. In addition, such systems are often used by developers that do not have sufficient experience to quickly develop a solution.[3]

In contrast, solutions developed using programming languages such as C++, C#, Visual Basic, C, and Java are developed using object-oriented methodologies, sophisticated memory management, thread management, and database access tools and technologies. It is far more likely that an enterprise system developed in these languages (especially C++) can support substantially higher concurrent access, scalability, and faster response times.

In general, interpreted languages with virtual machines are a factor of 10 to 100 times slower than software components developed in native languages such as C and C++. The following table highlights the key advantages and disadvantages of some mainstream programming languages.

---

3. Often high-level programming languages and environments are appealing to managers because of expected productivity gains, and these environments often attract less skilled technical people or are used directly by untrained end users. The result is often systems that run poorly and are difficult to maintain. Often the lack of flexibility in the products and the use of tools by unsophisticated developers result in few actual savings.

Programming Tools	Comments	Advantages	Disadvantages
C	Generates native executable components.	Fast; can be used to develop very complex and powerful software.	Not object oriented; hard to maintain; tough bugs such as memory leaks and crashes are possible, especially for larger products.
C++	Generates native executable components.	Fast; can be used to develop very complex and powerful software.	Tough bugs such as memory leaks and crashes are possible, especially for larger products.
C#	Generates native executable components.	Fast; can be used to develop very complex and powerful software.	A Microsoft language; this language has not been adopted as a standard yet.
Java	Runs in a virtual machine and is interpreted at runtime.	Powerful object-oriented language; garbage collection system; excellent exception handling.	Slow; anything that needs to be done quickly must be done in C++ and then accessed with Java; Microsoft no longer supports Java in its operating systems and browsers.
Visual Basic	Is interpreted at runtime; no virtual environment.	Excellent easy language for user interface validation; straight-forward server business logic and database access.	Not as object-oriented as C++/Java; some things, such as algorithms or extensive processing routines, are better handled in C/C++.
VBScript/ JavaScript	Runs in a special "session" and is interpreted at runtime.	The languages for code used in web pages; should mostly be used to process user interface actions and simple data validation.	Should be used only for UI validation and message processing; not type safe; cannot be used for any complex programming.
Microsoft FoxPro Borland Delphi Oracle Forms	Runs in a virtual machine and is interpreted at runtime.	Easy to create a lot of functionality fast.	Cannot optimize; used for rapid development; unacceptable constraints and limitations for a truly sophisticated enterprise software system.

➤ Third-Party Controls

No ES software developer should take on the almost impossible challenge of building everything from scratch. All ES software requires the following:

- ➤ User interface elements such as grids, trees, data masks, and calendars

- ➤ E-mail client

- ➤ Reporting engine

- ➤ Business intelligence tools (OLAP)

It is important to note what third party tools are used by the vendor, especially if any of these additional components requires licensing fees and payments that must be paid by the ES purchaser.

➤ Transactions

An important issue for multiuser simultaneous access systems such as an ES system to address is the manner in which data integrity is ensured. For example, let's take the task of reserving staff based on resource planning for a contract. Assume that the information is stored in multiple database tables and the system would need to run several queries to update the information. What happens if two different clients access the server simultaneously to reserve the same resources?

If a multithreaded server software (which is usually the case for ES servers) receives the list of queries in sequence from each client and then executes the two requests in parallel, the result would be that some of the resources intended to be reserved for one contract would be overloaded by the other reservation request. Both clients would receive a success message, whereas neither query really accomplished its goal.

Transactions allow business logic components to execute multiple queries as a single atomic instruction. Either the entire instruction set is successful, or the system performs a rollback and the data are returned to their exact state just before the command was initiated. Transactions prevent data corruption and integrity violations. Because all of the DBMSs listed in these sections fully support database transactions, an excellent and simple method with which to guarantee data integrity is to use stored procedures for database updates. Multiple SQL commands embedded within a stored procedure are treated as a transaction, wherein either the stored procedure executes in its entirety or the data are rolled back to their original state.

ES SDK	Source Code
A complete API.	No API, or APIs designed mainly for internal development.
Designed to be used by third parties for product modifications and enhancements.	Source code's primary purpose is to make the product work, not to be used by third parties.
Extensive documentations.	Poor to no documentation.
Numerous sample programs.	No samples.
Third-party development remains valid and requires minimal or no change as the application is enhanced (compatible with future releases).	Source code owner will modify the code for future releases. Third party users would have to redo and retest any custom work for every new release of the software.
SDK is used internally to develop new features and modules and also by many third parties to enhance and extend the core feature set. Therefore, SDK is proven, scalable, and robust.	Source code is used and modified only by internal programmers and those who license it. There is no foundation on which to build but the source code itself. With no consistent base, each party has its own flavor of the original work, with poor possibility of an eventual merge.
SDK is treated as a product. The SDK has its own documentation, installation program, and sample set. It is tested, installed, and documented right alongside every major product release.	Source code is not a product. Rather, it is the set of instructions that created the product.
Using the SDK is easy. Just follow the documentation, samples, and web pages of the product itself.	Modifying source code requires a great deal of domain and technical expertise. In case of this sample ES SDK, the source code consists of over 2 million lines of code developed in C++ and Visual Basic, with Visual C++, VB and ASP forms, and web pages. The source code is a result of many years' engineering work and extensive development. Very few people have a full grasp of the product's reach and complexity and the impact of changes made in various key modules.

➤ Open Source versus Open Architecture

The open source movement has recently drawn serious interest. The open source philosophy asserts that all software should be free and that the source code for all software should be available to the public. Open source licenses state that the source code for any open source product can be modified as long as all such modifications are shared and made publicly available.

Open source software (mainly Linux) has attracted some interest by corporations. However, currently there is no major open source ES (although there are some prototypes and active projects currently under way).

Some small vendors with primitive and niche-oriented products do offer to sell or provide their source code. These vendors are not in the open source camp; rather, they sell source codes as part of their offerings. In the table at left we compare a sample ES vendor that supports a full SDK to an ES that provides or sells its source code.

■ ACCESS

An ES should be accessible from anywhere and by using any device. This is particularly important when the organization has employees and consultants who travel, work off site, telecommute, or have clients or partners who need to access the ES remotely (as the following diagram depicts). Given today's ubiquitous worldwide availability of Internet protocol-based Internet, an ES should support access via a variety of Internet-enabled devices such as PCs, wireless laptops, palm and handheld devices, standard and cellular phones, WAP phones, and access terminals.

> An ES should be accessible from anywhere and by using any device

■ EMERGING TECHNOLOGIES

➤ XML

Recently, there has been a great deal of attention to and investment in XML and .NET technologies. XML is a data definition language. It is a generic way of defining how the data stored in a file, on a web site, or in a database will appear (also known as data structure or

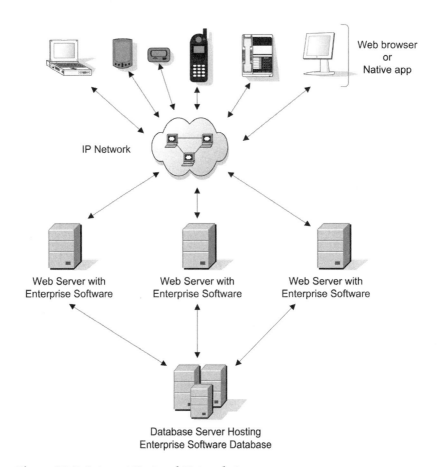

Figure 20.3 Internet Protocol Network Access

data format). XML is rapidly emerging as a widely adopted standard for data exchange and interprocess communication. Several ES systems use the XML protocol to exchange information with suppliers of equipment and services.

➤ .NET

Microsoft appears to have wholeheartedly adopted the XML standard. As a result, Microsoft is actively working on supporting this protocol across all its development tools, browsers, and operating systems. The .NET technology is equal to a set of web-based services using the XML protocol to communicate with each other.

An example of a .NET service is Microsoft Passport. Users are authenticated by the Passport service, which any application can use.

➤ Application Service Providers

Software as a service is also a major recent trend. In an application service provider (ASP) model, the ES is installed and managed at a remote server by a third party (commonly the ES vendor itself). The client pays a monthly fee (and an initial setup fee) to use the ES over the Internet. The only software the user is required to install is the ES administrative and client applications. With some ES vendors, no installation is required and all can be achieved over the web using server web pages.

The ASP model is an option for organizations that do not have the internal IT resources and expertise or simply do not want to invest in the IT resources that are required to install and manage an enterprise software system (since it is outside their core competency). Application service provider has not proven to be a compelling and valuable proposition for many larger organizations with in-house IT staff and server infrastructures.

For a comparison of purchasing and hosting enterprise software, please refer to Chapter 20.

■ SAMPLE ARCHITECTURE

When choosing an ES, it is important to understand how decoupled the various system components are, what tools have been used to develop the system, and how these components interact. Vendors who are unable to provide clear and convincing answers to such questions may be weak in crucial areas such as reliability, scalability, and performance. There should be clear decoupling and distinction between the application layer, server components, business logic, and generic services. In theory, one can develop a single executable module that contains all of these features and functionality. However, such a strategy would quickly lead to an unmanageable piece of software that would soon become obsolete. This is especially true when the ES represents millions of lines of computer code.

The above architecture also highlights the importance of supporting multiple communication or data transfer protocols. The following diagram shows that

➤ ODBC can be used in local area networks (LANs).

➤ Remote data service (RDS), which is based on HTTP or SSL, can be used when connecting via the Internet; either through a secure virtual private network (VPN) connection or direct connection to an IP address available over the Internet.

➤ WAP is used to communicate with web-enabled cellular phones.

➤ HTML can be used by client computers with web browsers that access ES servers via HTML commands and active server pages (ASP).

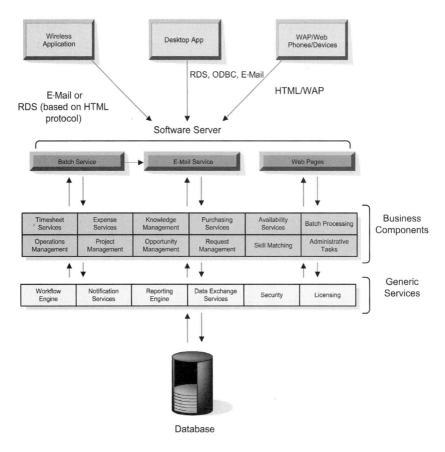

Figure 20.4 Sample Architecture

➤ E-mail can be used from devices such as personal digital assistants (PDAs) to access ES servers (for example, e-mail submissions of timesheets, expense reports, and customer issues). E-mails should be autoprocessed and checked against the organization's policies, and exceptions should be handled automatically by ES software services without any human intervention.

■ SUMMARY

Choosing an ES product and vendor is not simply a matter of matching requirements and features to an organization's current needs; it is also a matter of properly and systematically investing in the technologies of the enterprise systems being considered. Enterprise software is complex in that it represents an enormous amount of functionality aimed at facilitating and automating many detailed organizational processes. Consequently, such a system not only enables the organization to become more efficient and effective, but also becomes critical to any organization's daily operations. Will this system lose its utility shortly after it is finally up and running? Will new needs and changing business environments be beyond the capabilities of the system that has already commanded a considerable investment in time and money? How easily and effectively can this system be upgraded to address new needs and new functionality? Investing in the right technology can greatly affect the success of an ES implementation, the desired ROI, and long-term viability. Like many other business decisions, an investment in critical technology should be accomplished with the future in mind.

Chapter 21

Integration

A critical decision that every enterprise faces is whether to adopt an ES from a single vendor or to assemble a best-of-breed solution by integrating products from several different vendors. Here we discuss some of the strategies and options available.

The following terms are used in this section:

Term	Description
Source app	Items from the source application are exported into a file or directly to destination application (if the integration is live).
Destination app	Items from a file or from the source application (if the integration is live) are imported into the destination application.
Integrator	A developer who works on integrating source and destination applications

Seamless integration is most often bidirectional. Therefore, the same application can be considered a source or destination app depending on the operation.

■ METHODS OF INTEGRATION

There are three types of integration: file-based, batch, and live.

➤ File-Based Integration

With file-based integration, the information from one application is exported into a file with a specific file format. The file is then imported into the other application. Standard file formats include tab delimited text file, SGML, and, most recently XML file formats.

➤ Batch Integration

Most corporate applications allow for scheduled launch and import of data from other information systems. With this method, the integrator must write a data exchange module that uses the destination app API supported and documented by the destination app vendor.

Many vendors do not support an integration API, and the destination app must use import data using the source app database. Using the database directly for integration is less desirable than using APIs because it is more limited and the database structure is more likely to change than the API, thus breaking the integration module.

➤ Live Integration

In a live integration, both source app and destination app have documented APIs. In the Microsoft Windows platform, this API is most likely in the form of COM objects, Visual Basic for Applications (VBA), or XML. Regardless of the API type, the integrator has to

➤ Learn how source and destination apps work.

➤ Determine and document object mappings. Each application may have its own client, project, and product concepts. The mapping determines how objects map to one another in the two systems. In addition, the mapping defines what needs to be done (or not done) if no equivalent object exists.

➤ Design the user interface to allow users to select data exchange defaults and import/export options.

➤ Develop code that uses both APIs together to import/export the objects.

With live integration, data exchange is instant. The data from one system are instantly transferred to the destination app and are immediately available for further processing.

■ APPLICATION REQUIREMENTS

The following three tables describe the characteristics of various types of integration available.

➤ File-Based

Source Application Requirement	Description
Export facility	Ability to select and export various types of items into a file.
Mark as exported	Mechanism for marking critical data (time, expenses, invoices, purchase orders) as exported so that it is not exported again.

Destination Application Requirement	Description
Import facility	Ability to import items from a file.
Overwrite policy	If the item already exists, the application should either replace its contents or generate a warning message that it already exists before the import process continues.

➤ Batch

Source Application Requirement	Description
SDK	Software development kit—source application should have clearly defined database structure or API so that an integration module can be developed.
Custom integration component	A batch plug component (or script) can be developed using the SDK or technical database information.

Destination Application Requirement	Description
Batch manager	The destination app should have a batch manager in which applications can be registered for batch execution.
Scheduled or manual execution	Batch execution can be manual (upon user request) or scheduled.

➤ Live

Source Application Requirement	Description
SDK	Software development kit—source application should have clearly defined database structure or API so that an integration module can be developed.
Custom integration component	Custom integration component uses the SDK to extract the information needed to provide the mapping and exporting of the data to the destination app.

Destination Application Requirement	Description
SDK	Software development kit—source application should have clearly defined database structure or API so that an integration module can be developed.
Custom integration component	Custom integration component uses the SDK to extract the information needed to provide the mapping and importing of the data from the source app.

■ HOW TO AVOID DUPLICATIONS AND CONFLICTS

A critical problem to address is how to avoid duplicated entries and other synchronization errors that can result in conflicts. For example, an invoice for Client A for $5,000 is exported from source application (such as a time and billing software) to destination app (such as an accounting application). How can one make sure that the same invoice is not re-exported as a new invoice to the destination app?

➤ File-Based

If the source application does not support any marking, then a file naming convention can be used to prevent duplicated export. For example, the exported invoice file name may consist of CLIENT_NAME + STARTDATE + ENDDATE. In this case, the file name would provide a warning mechanism in order to avoid double exports.

➤ Live

The most effective mechanism marks all successfully exported entries as "exported" so that they will not be exported again. For example, the invoice for Client A of $5,000 is marked as issued and all the services (time entries) and expenses (expense entries) are marked as billed. Using this marking mechanism will prevent duplication, even if a new invoice is created for the same date interval.

Chapter **22**

Implementation Strategy

■ INTRODUCTION

Enterprise software implementation can potentially affect several processes in the organization. A well-thought-out implementation plan executed by an experienced team is a determining factor in the successful adoption of enterprise software and for attaining the goals and objectives set for the project.

> **Best-of-breed PSA + CRM + PM + ERP/accounting = integrated approach to achieving service and project efficiency**

To take full advantage of ES, you must have clear objectives and a timeline for achieving them. You must also document the scope of the implementation and the impact it may have on your existing processes. Based on your analysis, you can assemble the appropriate team of internal and external resources to complete the project successfully, on time, and within budget.

This chapter presents the process and methodology for successful ES implementation. It describes in detail the workflow a typical organization must follow. It also identifies the key roles and participants required at each stage of the implementation process.

Enterprise system deployment is a manageable process that has a workflow with well-defined states and outcomes that you can reliably anticipate and measure at each step to ensure maximum success. Each stage in the implementation workflow must be fully analyzed by the proper resources so that the required actions are

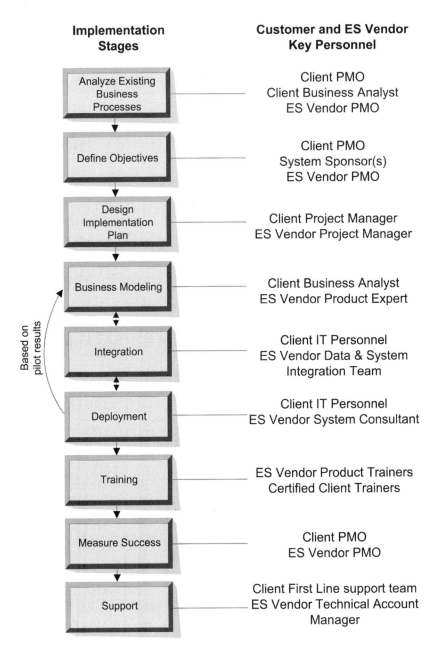

Figure 22.1 Enterprise Software Implementation Workflow

taken. The impact of each step on the organization varies depending on the state of the existing processes, number of employees affected, and the implementation time frame.

This implementation process helps project managers to anticipate the unexpected and manage each step in a well-defined manner.

The implementation workflow consists of the following steps:

➤ *Analyze* your business needs and identify the right solution or solutions for achieving your goals.

➤ *Define* objectives and project deliverables.

➤ *Plan* your organization's implementation.

➤ *Model* the enterprise software to fit your business processes.

➤ *Integrate* the ES into your existing processes and systems. Look at the total picture.

➤ *Deploy* the solution across the organization.

➤ *Train* users and teams to achieve user acceptance.

➤ *Support* the software to ensure continued success.

➤ *Measure* the success of the initiative at specific intervals.

■ ANALYZE YOUR ORGANIZATION'S NEEDS

You must analyze your existing business processes to determine what processes you need to optimize and when, as well as the desired outcome of each process.

> Existing business processes must be carefully reviewed, analyzed, and optimized before the implementation of a new software

You must interview key personnel and collect data to make sure that the right needs have been identified and to determine how they will be addressed by the new ES. Business analysis helps identify what can be optimized, automated, streamlined, completed, or redesigned. Often, the apparent problem is a symptom of a more serious underlying inefficiency. An in-depth analysis can determine the root cause. Many organizations address the symptoms while ignoring the source of the problem. For example, if you are having problems invoicing clients on time, you should determine the cause. Is it the accounting system? Is it the time tracking system? Is it the lack of integration between the two systems? Is it inaccuracies and double entries? Is it too many manual steps in between?

■ DEFINE OBJECTIVES

Based on the detailed analysis of your business processes, and after determining which ones you need to optimize, you can set the goals and objectives to be attained. It is important to clearly define the objectives of the enterprise software project. The objectives must be clear and quantifiable because your goals are the major metrics used to measure success. Examples of objectives include reducing the invoice cycle by two weeks; improving project accounting by consolidating budgets, expense, and labor cost reporting; increasing billable time by 3%; increasing customer retention rate by 10%; and improving employee productivity by 5%.

At each stage of the implementation process, you must ensure that the goals and objectives are respected. For example, if your goals include shortening the invoice cycle by two weeks, you must make sure you analyze your existing processes for time tracking, billing, and invoicing. In addition, in the integration stage make sure that your accounting system, time tracking, expense tracking, and invoicing systems are well integrated to provide fast access to the data for final client invoicing.

■ PLAN THE IMPLEMENTATION

After defining needs and processes that can be optimized, you need to explore the various modules the ES offers and decide on the functionality and features that are required.

You need to make the decision when to roll out each module based on your business priorities. A good ES must offer the flexibility for phased and scaled deployment without affecting the overall system. For example, if you decide that there is an urgent need for a resource planning module to ensure all your users are optimally utilized, you should be able to implement a resource planning (RP) module without having to use the vendor's timesheet management or project management module at the same time.

■ MODEL THE ENTERPRISE SOFTWARE TO YOUR BUSINESS PROCESSES

After deciding on the implementation plan, you need to fully integrate the ES within your organization. Based on the modules you install and the features you use, you need to map the associated business objects to your organization and its processes.

Business modeling is an extremely important step in the implementation process. You must work closely with application experts who have a strong knowledge of your business domain. When analyzing your business process requirements, make sure you clearly identify your reporting requirements and the level of detail you need to track and analyze. There is always a very delicate balance between ease of use, minimum overhead, and capture of important and vital information for proper process management and control. Every business's needs are different. With the help of an application expert who has strong industry knowledge, you will be able to achieve the right balance between ease of use and your organization's requirements. It is important to fully test your ES business model during the predeployment pilot to make sure it offers without overhead the required detail.

This business modeling process consists of several steps:

➤ Organization breakdown structure (OBS) maps your organization, including sites, departments, business units (or cost centers), teams, and employees.

➤ Work breakdown structure (WBS) maps your work hierarchy, such as customers, engagements, products, projects, and tasks.

➤ Resource breakdown structure (RBS) is a hierarchical organization of resources that facilitates both roll-up reporting and summary resource scheduling by enabling you to schedule at the detailed requirement level and roll up both requirements and availabilities to a higher level.

➤ Terminology maps ES terminology for OBS, WBS, RBS, and

document terms to fit your organization's standards. This step minimizes the learning curve of the new application and increases the comfort level of using the ES on a daily basis.

➤ User roles define the different roles required to successfully use the new processes. They also define access rights to the system. Roles can include standard user, project manager, team leader, accountant, and executive.

➤ System configuration options are usually defined for the entire organization; examples include system start date and type of billing cycle.

➤ Alerts and notifications are a crucial part of an ES. You must understand the existing alert and notification functions and how they apply to your business processes. Alerts and notifications can indicate budget overruns, timesheet rejections, a high-priority customer issue, and so on.

When modeling the ES to your business processes, a one-size-fits-all approach does not always work. You must identify the different groups within your organization and target your efforts to each group. During the modeling phase, you should personalize the ES structure for each group to best fit its model. The level of personalization depends on the nature of the process and the scope of the implementation.

For example, if you are implementing time tracking across several departments, such as development and support, you must be aware that these groups have different requirements for a time tracking system. Members of a support group may be assigned work automatically by a ticketing or issue tracking system and may not have the right to assign work to anyone. On the other hand, a development team member may have more freedom in selecting which activities to perform or whom to assign work to at any specific time.

At the end of this phase, you will be able to determine how to tailor and personalize the training content to fit the different groups in order to achieve the best results from the training sessions. It is important to include your new ES model in the training material to ensure a complete understanding of the structure and the proper information that must be captured.

■ INTEGRATION AND THE PREDEPLOYMENT PLANNING

➤ Predeployment

At this stage, you need to identify existing processes and systems that will need to interact with the new ES or that can benefit from the information available from the new processes.

If not handled correctly, integration between the new and existing processes can be a major point of failure. Most processes do not operate in a vacuum—they are linked to other processes in some way. As a first step, it is essential that you identify how the new ES affects all the dependent processes and eliminate inconsistencies or redundancies. A critical part of process integration is eliminating redundant data and repeated entries in multiple systems. All processes must tightly integrate, and data must seamlessly flow across the different processes. For example, let's assume that your organization is using an HR system to track employees and you want to implement a time and expense tracking system. You should not reenter the user information in the new system but rather integrate it with your existing HR system (as the master source of employee information).

Integration of the ES with your corporate security standards is an important predeployment activity that is often overlooked. You must analyze the impact of the new ES system in full detail and consider your security processes to ensure that it will function correctly with your security rules. Discovering security issues after deployment is usually too late and can jeopardize your project.

Enhanced business intelligence and reporting is usually one of the main benefits of ES implementation. You must take the time to analyze data captured by the new processes and determine how they can integrate with existing data to improve accuracy and timeliness of reports. For example, implementing a new time tracking system with advanced cost and billing capabilities can instantly generate valuable data that can be used for better project status, cost, revenue, and WIP reporting.

Finally, you will develop a detailed deployment plan that schedules and assigns all the critical components for a successful implementation based on your organization's requirements.

➤ Site Planning

The IT group should carefully review the site planning document provided by the ES vendor. The following sections highlight the key issues in the site planning process.

Database Server Requirements

Most ES software incorporates a central database server with database software from one of the better-known database providers, such as Microsoft, Oracle, or IBM. The database server is the most critical computer for any organization taking on an ES project. The larger the user base, the more concurrent requests and transactions will occur. The memory, hard disk space, and processing power of this computer should be carefully calculated in collaboration with ES vendor experts.

The database server must also be in a highly secure location accessible only by key personnel. In addition, as mentioned in a section that follows, from the onset, backup and other disaster recovery measures must be implemented.

Web Server Requirements

Sophisticated ES solutions allow replicated installation of business logic components on one or more web servers. All web servers communicate with the same central ES database server. This distributed web architecture is required for larger installations and organizations with multiple sites. The memory, hard disk space, and processing power of the web server should be carefully calculated in collaboration with ES vendor experts.

Client Requirements

Most ES software offers web access through clients running web browsers or requires installation of client software (usually on a Windows platform). There are advantages to each of these approaches. However, the most desirable scenario would be to use ES software that supports both zero client (no installations on the client computer, pure HTML web access) and client software running on the Windows platform.

Size Estimates

An ES database can grow very rapidly. This is especially true if it is used on a regular basis to manage timesheets, expense reports, purchase orders, service requests, and other business processes. Corporate data, including audit information, can run into tens and hundreds of megabytes in a very short time. In collaboration with ES vendor experts, it is very important to estimate initial database size and database growth on a weekly and monthly basis. In addition, system administrators must use archiving to purge data entry information that is no longer needed on an annual basis.

➤ Backup and Disaster Recovery

Another important predeployment activity is the integration of the new ES into your backup and disaster recovery procedures. Enterprise software systems usually store extremely valuable data in central databases, and database disasters are bound to happen. It is not uncommon for computers to fail, power to be interrupted, or natural disasters to hit. Without adequate preparation, server downtime is costly to an organization, especially when information is lost. Frustration can grow among employees and especially among customers, who expect round-the-clock server availability.

■ DEPLOYMENT

Based on the actions taken in the previous steps and the integration requirements you may have, it is recommended to test the configuration under various scenarios and evaluate the results. You can make such a test by rolling out the change to a test group and by running pilot programs. Select your pilot group carefully to make sure it truly represents the organization. You must communicate the strategic importance of the project to the pilot group. Make sure that you provide enough training to the pilot group to ensure that they are at ease with the new software process. Also, set up clear communication channels for user feedback and comments during the pilot process.

The pilot will allow you to find the weak spots in your planning and resolve them before complete rollout. This can also improve user acceptance of the new processes, because users will feel that they have participated in the process and that the solution was not imposed on them.

The next step is for you to put all your preplanning to the test. Depending on the size of the installation and the number of new modules being installed, it may be more beneficial to follow a phased deployment approach. Implementing an ES in a phased manner can provide you with quick wins and initial momentum. In addition, users can learn the new system more efficiently in smaller increments, resulting in immediate productivity gains.

The phased approach also gives you more time to understand and assess your future requirements and allows you to make changes more easily during the implementation process. Phasing the project also reduces risk, partly because risk is easier to manage in smaller subprojects. Moreover, defining the scope of the project well in advance and breaking it down into phases minimizes surprises and isolates potential problems.

➤ Training

Training scenarios can vary based on your requirements, the number of employees to be trained, and the modules you are implementing. You can follow a train-the-trainer scenario wherein an internal resource is trained on the product by the vendor so that they can then train other users in the organization. This is usually more cost effective for end user training in which the functionality required to be learned is limited. However, training by certified trainers is recommended for administrators, support personnel, and power users.

Training materials should be tailored as much as possible to match your organization and work structure. They should also include real-life scenarios based on your business processes. These features make the training sessions more effective and relevant.

To achieve maximum results, you must rapidly train everyone affected by the new solution. Entire teams must receive training together, and all teams within a group should receive training during the same time frame. Experience has shown that team-focused as opposed to employee-focused training can create excitement and reduce resistance to the new process. Teamwork also increases and encourages the utilization of the ES because everyone starts using it at the same time and follows the same track.

Support personnel must be trained so that they will be able to respond to management requests for reporting and business intelligence in a timely fashion. In order to provide advanced reporting and business intelligence and to take full advantage of the ES data warehouse, they must be fully trained. Training should cover areas such as detailed data model analysis, software development kits, and any third-party tools that may be employed.

As part of the training preparation, make sure you set up clear training programs for new employees who join after the initial implementation. In addition, if you adopt a phased implementation approach, you must include adequate training on the new modules implemented at each phase.

■ MEASURING SUCCESS

Throughout the implementation, project management office (PMO) consultants will measure the success of the project at every milestone against the goals and objectives set at the start of the implementation project. After the completion of each phase, PMO consultants will analyze the results achieved and compare them to the initial goals. They will also analyze the improvement in the process and the savings achieved due to the use of the new software.

Organization requirements change over time and new requirements arise that were not considered during the initial install. To ensure that the ES is producing optimal results for the current business environment, the PMO must continuously monitor, evaluate, and communicate what needs to be changed (this is typically done once every six months). The main objective of the periodical evaluation is to recommend changes or realignments in the system, the process, or the staff that may be necessary to increase efficiency.

The ES vendor learns a great deal about the organization and its processes during implementation. The vendor, in collaboration with the PMO team, will be able to provide you with an analysis and recommendation of processes that can be streamlined or that may require closer scrutiny to further improve efficiency, drive down cost, and improve revenue.

■ SUPPORT

To ensure successful implementation and optimal usage of the software, you must invest in resources that will help you reach the desired outcome. In order to reduce resistance and guarantee success, you should make sure that feedback from end users is dealt with quickly and that any issues or problems that arise are handled in a timely fashion.

Support is usually divided into three categories.

➤ *End user support:* Usually handled internally by the product support group. It is recommended that the support personnel undergo detailed training to be able to offer quality support.

➤ *Operational support:* Includes the activities necessary to day-to-day operation of the system, such as OBS, WBS, and RBS configuration, security profile setup, and the like. These operations are usually managed by the ES administrator(s). Administrators must follow extensive training to ensure proper system administration.

➤ *Reporting support:* Includes BI, ad hoc reporting support, and the customization of existing reports or the creation of new ones. Technical staff with the proper training and experience in the reporting tools employed—the ES data model and the ES SDK—handle reporting support.

■ SUMMARY

Enterprise system implementation should not be undertaken lightly. All of the cost savings, benefits, and efficiencies that result from using an ES cannot be realized unless the implementation is achieved through methodical and proven techniques. To attain your goals on time and within budget, you must follow a well-defined and proven workflow with measurable results at each milestone. This will ensure the full and seamless integration of the software into the organization.

The following processes can be critical points of failure if poorly planned and executed: modeling the ES to your business processes, integration, and predeployment planning. These processes require critical attention in order to ensure the success of an ES project.

The preceding sections presented the process and methodology for successful ES deployment. They described in detail the workflow a typical organization follows and identified the key roles and participants required at each stage of the implementation.

Chapter 23

Operations

■ INTRODUCTION

The implementation of an ES can result in significant tangible and intangible benefits and has the potential for tremendous savings and improvements in efficiency. However, ES systems are sophisticated and complex products that require careful planning, management, and tracking from an operational point of view.

> **Enterprise software systems are sophisticated and complex products that require careful planning, management, and tracking from an operational point of view**

This section examines the operational aspect of an ES system, describes some of the features that would be required to streamline operations, and recommends actions by the organization that would ensure that the ES system is used and managed optimally.

There is a substantial body of knowledge regarding ES benefits, selection criteria, feature sets, and implementation guidelines. However, a vital topic that is often ignored is the day-to-day operation of an ES system. Careful prepurchase analysis and a comprehensive selection process do not guarantee success. It is the routine management, procedures and processes that make all the difference between a failed ES project and the one that reaps extensive benefits.

All processes managed by an ES should be regularly reviewed and software capabilities revisited to determine if best practices are

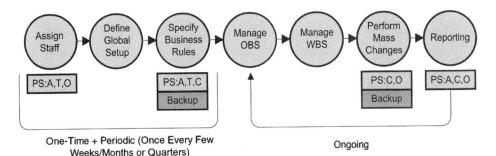

One-Time + Periodic (Once Every Few Weeks/Months or Quarters)

Ongoing

PS (Professional Services)
1. Analysis: The ES vendor has substantial domain experience and can help you quickly identify resource needs
2. Training: The ES vendor's PS team can provide training for various administrative staff and high-power users
3. Customization: Power ES systems provide a documented software development kit and descriptive database model; this information can be used to customize the ES for integration or custom needs.
4. Outsourcing: The ES vendor can provide remote management services, customization and integration services and other IT services related to its area of expertise. The ES vendor's expertise in these domains will lead to quick wins, fast ROI, and immediate visible benefits that would be difficult to acheive otherwise.

Backup: Disaster recovery is often ignored. Even larger organizations sometimes neglect to make frequent backups of their ES database. We cannot emphasize enough how critical it is to perform full backups at every critical milestone in ES project and to perform incremental backups on a regular basis (at least once a week).

Figure 23.1 Enterprise Software Operation Process

being applied and documented, and also to detect any features that are overlooked, not fully implemented, or in need of further enhancement by the vendor. Also, if the ES has an SDK, then it can be used to tailor the features that require customization.

The sections that follow review the internal and external resource and software requirements. This chapter also provides recommendations for each and describes some of the features and processes that make an operationally efficient ES implementation a possibility.

■ DESIGNATED IT AND BUSINESS PERSONNEL

Regardless of the size of the budget, an ES project has a significant impact on an organization. However, one cannot just throw software at problems. Before, during, and long after an ES system is implemented, in order to address a specific need, the organization should carefully select the operations team.

It is important to document all processes in case key personnel leave an organization. This will ensure proper and efficient knowledge transfer of internal data on operations, which the ES vendor would not be able to provide.

➤ Consulting Staff

An ES project should also be perceived as a conduit of knowledge and experience. The organization that implements an ES solution has certain core areas of expertise, which it uses to serve its customers. Similarly, the ES vendor has extensive expertise in its own domain. To maximize the investment of implementing the enterprise software, in terms of time, money, and allocated resources, the organization should insist on a close cooperation with ES consultants. The following areas of ES expertise are required in the operational phase:

➤ ES project manager (ESPM): The project manager can be a consultant assigned to this project by the ES vendor or one of its partners. The ESPM's responsibility is to ensure that the project is as successful as possible. The ESPM works with the organization's internal staff to analyze, plan, and deploy the enterprise software. Regular conference calls or meetings throughout the implementation and operation phase can result in tremendous insight and benefits in optimal use of the software and associated resources.

➤ ES trainer(s): Learning how to manage and operate enterprise software is not just learning about the function of each screen and button. Concepts such as project management, timesheet management, expense report tracking, purchasing, and BI involve a tremendous amount of domain knowledge. The ES trainers have the difficult task of conveying this information in a limited time to the organization's IT staff and executives. Experience has shown that extensive, focused multiple training sessions will significantly affect the probability of success and cost savings for an ES project.

➤ ES consultants: With frequent and regular use of ES, many

organizations will require some customizations and specific reports on the vast amount of data stored in the ES database. ES consultants, managed by the ESPM, can quickly and efficiently provide such services or find the appropriate alternatives for obtaining the information being sought.

➤ Internal Staff

At least two internal project managers should be designated.

➤ ES business case project manager: This manager's responsibility is to prepare a brief list of tangible and intangible benefits of implementing the ES system; this manager is also responsible for providing periodic status reports and comparing achieved results with the initial expectations' baseline.

➤ ES IT project manager: The IT manager must make sure that the ES is running smoothly, the server is secured, backups are maintained, and the IT team is responding promptly to requests for training, custom reports, and other action items approved by the ES business case PM.

In addition to project managers that have primary management responsibilities, an ES system requires some administrative services. These may include the following:

➤ Organization-related items: creating users and groups; defining and enforcing policies.

➤ Work-related items: creating projects and activities; defining thresholds and notifications.

➤ Requests: Users will request to create/modify organization- or work-related items or make special requests, such as questions related to procedures, policies, and the performance of certain tasks within the ES system.

Therefore, someone in the organization must be designated as the ES administrator, to provide all these administrative services.

Depending on the organization's size and the complexity of its business processes, the above responsibilities can represent a part-time assignment for a single staff member or full-time assignments for a number of dedicated people. The organization must determine and define this function based on an assessment of the amount of work that is involved. Based on our experience, the following is a suggested first approach:

Number of Users	ES Personnel
10 to 50	One ES manager for all operational functions; can be part-time.
50 to 100	Two ES managers: a business manager and an IT/administrative manager; can be part-time.
100 to 500	Three ES managers: a business manager, an IT manager, and an administrative assistant; the managers can be part-time, but the administrative assistant is full-time.
500 to 1,000	Four ES managers: a business manager, an IT manager, and two administrative assistants; the managers can be part-time, but the administrative assistants are full-time.
1,000 and above	The needs vary substantially, depending on the industry in which the organization operates and the degree of ES use for carrying out day-to-day operations and tasks.

■ GLOBAL SETUP

Every organization defines a set of standards and guidelines to specify the manner in which its teams are managed, work is performed, and processes are tracked. This information is defined at the global level and is established as the company's default policy to meet its goals. Depending on a variety of parameters, some of the global settings can be overridden on a case-by-case basis (for example, a base currency for the organization can be replaced by different local site currencies for geographically dispersed offices).

➤ Formats

The organization should adopt a uniform format for dates (for example: two-digit month/two-digit day/four-digit year), decimal/thousand separators, numbers (for example: XXX.xx), and telephone numbers; a uniform ES login id length and naming conventions; a password policy; and other related formatting, reporting, and display issues and conventions.

➤ System Parameters

The organization must also define system-wide parameters such as the system base currency, reporting cycles (timesheet, expense report submission dates), and payroll and invoicing cycles. The ES system should have mechanisms for defining and enforcing such parameters and cycles in order to formalize, facilitate, and streamline the data collection and reporting process.

➤ Terminology

Every organization may use different business terms for such items as *client* (customer, account), *project* (job), *employee* (consultant), or *task* (activity). Part of the operational process is to adjust ES terminology for the organization and its functions to fit the organization's terms and standards. This step minimizes the learning curve of the new system and increases the comfort level of using the ES on a daily basis.

➤ Custom Fields

No ES system can provide a 100% match to the organization's requirements. Enterprise software systems that support custom fields offer a simple and efficient way for organizations to add their own specialized fields. More sophisticated ES systems that include multiple integrated components such as timesheets, expense reports, service desk software, and purchasing software should support the concept of common custom fields that can be defined once and used in multiple modules.

➤ Application Security

Enterprise software has extensive application security features that define what modules a user has access to, specifying, for example, setup, entry, reporting, and BI functions for each core system function such as timesheet, expense report, and issue and purchasing management. Standard user profiles that an ES system may define include accountant, administrator, customer care, developer, manager, marketing, project manager, purchasing agent, buyer, quality assurance (QA), engineer, sales, secretary, standard user, support, and team leader.

■ BUSINESS RULES

One of the primary advantages of an ES system is that the enforcement of and conformance to government regulations and organizational policies are significantly automated.

➤ Conformance to Government Regulations

Organizations must comply with various regulations for governmental and regional guidelines such as DCAA, FMLA, FLSA, 21 CFR Part 11 on FDA Compliance for Electronic Records, and the European time directives. The ES system must automate this conformance and make it as seamless as possible.

➤ Policies

In addition to government rules and regulations, an organization has its own set of policies and procedures, such as overtime policy (for example, a maximum overtime of three hours per week), expense report submission policy (for example, all expense report entries require a receipt), and timesheet policy (for example, timesheets must be completed by Thursday at 5:00 pm).

➤ Thresholds

An organization may have very strict policies, such as the regulations that no one can work more than eight hours per day, expense reports by standard users cannot exceed $5,000, and certain items cannot be purchased in high quantities. The thresholds can be defined as hard limits, which cannot be exceeded, or soft limits, which are less strict: For example, entries that are above thresholds are colored differently or trigger e-mail notifications.

➤ Notifications

Notifications are a crucial warning and reporting tool that can be used to ensure the ES operation and use conform to defined policies and parameters. For example, repeated policy violations, the exceeding of defined thresholds, late submissions, and invalid access attempts can trigger e-mail notifications to the ES administration and management team for proper action. Moreover, from a project management perspective, completed assignments, issues, consumed budgets, or budget overruns can result in e-mails that notify project managers.

➤ Maintaining History

In today's rapidly changing world of high turnover rates and a dynamic workforce, organizations should use an ES system that maintains history for important changes in such areas as cost and billing, groups, and employees (for example, when an employee moves from part time to full time). Tracking these changes must affect cost and revenue reports. For example, if John was paid $90 per hour from May 1, 2001, to December 31, 2001, and $95 for January 1, 2002, to April 30, 2002, the cost reports generated from May 1, 2001, to April 30, 2002, should consider both rates in their respective date intervals.

■ BATCH PROCESSING

Batch processing is usually a function provided by an ES system. The batch process runs on an enterprise server and monitors for the occurrence of various events such as those given as examples below. If needed, appropriate database updates are performed and notifications sent. The batch process does not interact with the user; all processing is done in the background.

Many ES operations should not or cannot be performed in real time; such as

- ➤ Auto time entry for holidays (as holiday time cannot be entered until a few days in advance of the event)

- ➤ Suspensions or notifications resulting from budget overruns for projects or users

- ➤ Warning e-mails for incomplete expense reports, timesheets, and other such documents

- ➤ Automatic user and project suspension at termination date

- ➤ Administrative task processing (which calculates accrued vacation, personal days, and other off-project times based on the organization's policies)

- ➤ Computing of summarized cost/revenue/profit information

■ ORGANIZATION BREAKDOWN STRUCTURE MANAGEMENT

Organization breakdown structure (OBS) management refers to the setup and administration of sites, business units, groups, teams, and users. It also includes organization-related items such as resource types, skills, titles, workflows, and classes (used to organize information into a hierarchy for knowledge management purposes).

The OBS structure can become quite large and deep in terms of number of levels. Therefore, a tool similar to Windows Explorer that allows one to traverse the entire hierarchy in tree format is quite useful and facilitates OBS management.

➤ General Organization Breakdown Structure Management

Setting up the appropriate level of detail and hierarchy in an organization's OBS is one of the crucial stages of the implementation of an ES system. The initial OBS should be designed in collaboration with the ES vendor's professional services team, and should be carefully reviewed and verified by the organization's management and IT teams. There is a trade-off in that a deep hierarchy is hard to set up and manage but can result in powerful BI reporting and drill-down capabilities, whereas a flatter hierarchy is simpler to set up and use but is less powerful for reporting purposes. After initial setup, general OBS management is usually carried out by the designated ES administrator.

More sophisticated enterprise software provide OBS templates, rollup-or-down capabilities, statistics at every OBS level, rate definition at various OBS levels, and other such features that enable administrators to quickly create new OBS elements based on model elements, verify current status, and create insightful and summarized reports.

➤ Site Management

A site is a physical or virtual office or location that can be used for scoping. Using this scoping, an administrator can specify what sites, clients, portfolios, projects, activities, users, groups, and teams a certain user can view and access. In addition to its security advantages, this powerful scoping function can be used to significantly reduce the number of projects and activities users have to work with on a day-to-day basis in a geographically dispersed organization.

The site concept can work as follows:

➤ Sites, clients, portfolios, projects, teams, and groups (hereinafter referred to as scoping elements) that are not associated with any site can be viewed by all.

➤ Once a scoping element is associated with a site, it can only be viewed by users who are also associated with that site.

➤ Users see all scoping elements that have no site association and all scoping elements that are linked to any of the user's associated sites.

Every user has a master site as well as an active site. The master site can be the primary location of the user and is used to define the user's default currency, holiday set (defined below), and language (all of which can be overridden on a user basis). The active site specifies where the user is currently located (which is usually the master site unless the user is traveling or on assignment). Users can optionally be allowed to change their current active site. Every entry created by the user gets the active site as its place of creation (which can indicate where the work was done, the expense incurred, or the purchase requested). Given proper access rights, the entry's site can be changed later.

➤ Regional Considerations

The system should allow one to define one or more holiday sets. A holiday set defines all the holidays for a given geographic location or specific type of workers. For example, North American and European holiday sets are geographic holiday sets, whereas Hindu and Christian holiday sets are specific to certain groups' religious holidays.

A holiday set can be assigned to any site. Users adopt the same holiday set as their master site's holiday set. The user's holiday set can be overridden on a user basis.

You can define one or more holidays in a holiday set. A holiday is either a hard date (January 1, 2000), a date range (December 25, 2000, to December 26, 2000), or a moving target (the first Monday in

September). A holiday can also be marked as recurring (i.e., it will be in effect every year).

■ WORK BREAKDOWN STRUCTURE MANAGEMENT

➤ General Work Breakdown Structure Management

As with the OBS, setting up the appropriate level of detail and hierarchy in an organization's work breakdown structure (WBS) is one of the crucial stages of the implementation of an ES system. The initial WBS should be designed in collaboration with the ES vendor's professional services team and should be carefully reviewed and verified by the organization's management and IT teams. Also as with the OBS, decision between hierarchy types involves a trade-off between the advantages of a deep hierarchy, which is difficult to set up and manage but can result in powerful BI reporting and drill-down capabilities, and a flatter hierarchy, which is simpler to set up and use but is less powerful for reporting purposes. After initial setup, general WBS management is usually carried out by the designated ES administrator.

The WBS structure can become quite large and deep in terms of number of levels. Therefore, a tool similar to Windows Explorer that allows one to traverse the entire hierarchy in tree format is quite useful and facilitates WBS management.

More sophisticated enterprise software provide WBS templates, rollup or down capabilities, statistics at every WBS level, rate definition at various WBS levels, and other such features that enable administrators to quickly create new WBS elements based on model elements, verify current status, and create insightful and summarized reports.

➤ Administrative Tasks

One of the major sources of revenue leakage and employee inefficiency in any organization is the management, tracking, and processing of off-project or nonwork activities, such as breaks, personal days, sick leave, leaves of absence, vacations, and overtime.

Many companies that adopt ES systems to automate time and expense tracking still use spreadsheets, paper, and the memories of managers or payroll administrators to track this kind of information, leading to errors, inaccuracies, and invisible but expensive administrative overhead. It is far more efficient and productive to choose an ES that allows one to define and enforce vacation, overtime, absence, and work policies.

Administrative tasks must be tracked for users. The organization must manage vacation requests (based on organization's policy) and time banks (for banked overtime, sick leave, or the like), allow negative draws, apply usage rules, display balances and policies in order to avoid unnecessary calls to HR, and eliminate after-the-fact administrative adjustments.

➤ Change Automation

From time to time, large quantities of information must be changed, for example, if all users with standard security must be given access to *Create* activities (assuming it was not the case initially). The following sections describe what bulk update features should be provided by an ES system.

➤ Standard Entries

Default timesheets, shift work, recurring purchases, expense reports, and requests are examples of activities that can be automated by an ES system. Enterprise software administrators should learn about all of the automations provided by the software and take full advantage of them. All such automations should support exceptional entries. For example, take the case of an employee who works 40 hours a week, always on the same three tasks. The employee uses the timesheet automation feature to set up the mechanized creation of timesheets on a weekly basis. The timesheet is auto-approved by the manager. However, one week the employee takes a leave of absence for eight hours without pay. To reflect this exception, the employee edits the timesheet. The timesheet is not auto-approved and the manager is notified of this exception, either through e-mail or via the color-coding of the timesheet.

➤ Mass Updates

Many ES systems recognize the need for mass changes and provide screens and functionality to facilitate such changes. A sample mass update workflow is as follows:

➤ Select users.

➤ Select projects or tasks.

➤ Select date interval.

➤ Lock all days within that date interval to prevent any changes.

The advantages of mass update functionality are that it is very controlled, it is audited by the ES, and special security permissions can be given to specific users.

➤ Special Case Updates

From time to time, information pertaining to work being performed or user and organizational data must be updated for a large number of records. The more the ES is used and the more processes it automates, the more likely it is that special updates or queries will be required. These types of ad hoc requests or updates are usually not supported by the ES system. In such cases, a documented database model and an experienced DBA staff, in collaboration with the ES consultants, can perform the necessary updates.

■ PROFESSIONAL SERVICES

An enterprise software project must be viewed as a solution, and an ES vendor's professional services team must be viewed as a domain expert and a valuable partner. Neither software nor people can be thrown at problems. The calculated and careful mix of enterprise software, internal staff, outsourced projects, and ES consultants' expertise will yield the best results. The following sections describe some of the areas in the organization that can utilize ES-related professional services to maximize the benefits of the solution employed.

➤ Analysis

Professional services with extensive domain expertise can provide valuable insight, analyze requirements and map them into the ES context, explain factors to consider, and highlight opportunities and pitfalls in the following phases of an ES project:

➤ The very early stages of implementation

➤ Prior to operational launch

➤ Business modeling

➤ Reporting and customizations

➤ Training

Most organizations allocate a training budget in the implementation of an ES system. However, training should also be scheduled and considered in the operational phase of such a system. Enterprise software systems continue to improve substantially as new versions are introduced; each new version automates many more processes than the previous versions. Organizations typically do not make full use of an ES system at initial launch. Continued training will ensure that the organization's staff is aware of the latest benefits and new efficiencies and automations provided by the ES. In addition, since the ES is already rolled out and implemented, the incremental cost of additional services and training versus the immediate ROI is a compelling reason to take this course of action.

➤ Customization

Enterprise software usually includes substantial amounts of out-of-the-box functionality and reporting. However, the larger the organization is and the more complex its operations are, the more likely it is that no ES can match all requirements without some customization. Customizations can include the following:

➤ Creating custom reports

➤ Using the ES development kit to integrate the ES with other information or legacy systems

➤ Using the ES development kit to automate additional tasks

➤ Customizing ES web pages to fit the organization's look and feel

➤ Integrating ES services into the corporate portal

➤ Phased Implementation

Powerful yet flexible ES systems should allow an organization to phase in the various features and modules associated. For example, one should be able to automate timesheet collection in Phase I, which may last three months, and follow that with the automation of the expense reporting process. Other modules such as issue tracking and purchasing or custom workflows can be phased in at a later date.

The ES vendor's professional services team should cooperate with and monitor every phase of implementation. Treating the ES as an ongoing project with defined and communicated milestones, scheduled meetings with consultants and project managers, and ROI assessment for every phase will result in substantial payoffs in the degree of ES use and savings and will ultimately guarantee a successful automation.

■ SUMMARY

Many organizations carefully select enterprise software, diligently install and deploy the product, and then forget about it. The preceding sections explained the importance of defining teams, assigning managers, monitoring benefits and ROI, and maintaining a close and consistent communication with ES experts in order to continually phase in additional functionality, automate more processes, and further improve existing operations. Although many ES projects fail in the implementation phase, many more can fail in the operational phase due to management neglect. An ES project should never be perceived as completed, but rather as a long-term project with multiple phases and milestones and a consistent reevaluation of its benefits and ROI for years to come.

Part 4

The Future of Professional Services Automation

The PSA industry has been invented to meet the pressing needs of PSORGs. To a large extent, these organizations have been left behind as the more traditional business sectors have mechanized, using software solutions tailored for them.

The industry is young and fragmented, but is maturing rapidly, with ever more broad solutions. These solutions are evolving with a host of features, so that PSORGs can offer their services in an increasingly competitive and global market. As in many industries in the past, these targeted software solutions will become standard features and will help PSORGs mechanize more and more, even to the point of challenging the automation of the traditionally organized enterprises.

In the next few years we will likely see the following things take place:

➤ PSAs will continue to evolve into more full-featured, specialized ERPs for PSORGs.

➤ More vendors will offer end-to-end solutions, from customer relationship management to full accounting.

➤ Enterprise systems such as project management, HR, ERP, and accounting will enhance their PSA functionality in order to compete within this space.[1]

➤ Consolidation will increase: Large project management, HR, ERP, and accounting vendors that want to offer increased service chain functionalities will merge or acquire some PSA vendors.[2]

➤ More original equipment manufacturer (OEM) relationships will take place: Some PSA vendors will continue to

---

1. The generalized ERP manufacturer will continue to suffer from over generalized modules, antiquated user interfaces, ancient and cumbersome programming languages, and an overemphasis on satisfying the needs of traditional cost center groups within the enterprise (like finance) to the detriment of the revenue-producing project delivery organizations.

2. Here again it is likely that the traditional ERP-type vendors will have acquisition and integration problems since the PSA industry is currently so fast-moving. Most will probably wait to see how the industry is consolidating before they make large inroads in this sector.

acquire software companies or OEMs with the intent of improving specific functionalities such as resource management, project management, time sheet and expense management, collaboration, and the like.

➤ Some PSA vendors will focus on a best-of-breed approach, developing extensive expertise and functionality within core PSA components.

Conclusion

Corporate inefficiency is an ongoing reality. Organizations must always reevaluate business processes and identify procedures that can be optimized. After all, cutting only one dollar of operational costs could have the same impact on the bottom line as increasing the revenue by thirteen dollars.[1] Project- and service-oriented organizations must now turn to PSA solutions as the best means of optimization and to gain a competitive advantage and a better handle on their operations. This includes organizations that service internal clients as well as those servicing external paying customers.

Professional Services Automation is the first class of software that provides a comprehensive end-to-end solution that uniquely addresses the needs and problems of PSORGs. This class of software solutions is rapidly evolving into the ERP for white collar project- or service-driven organizations.

Technological advances such as browser-based solutions and wireless access, coupled with major changes in the global competitive landscape, obliges organizations to keep pace or face dire consequences. These solutions have emerged to address a noticeable deficiency, single-mindedly focusing on bringing mechanization benefits to PSORGs, which are plagued with many manual and semi-mechanized solutions.[2] PSA solutions are the *best of breed* choice to deliver efficiency benefits to these enterprises.

---

1. According to *CFO* Magazine's annual SG&A survey. Randy Myers, survey by Exult Process Intelligence Center, December 2000 issue, p66-80, CFO Publishing Corp

2. By using paper, spreadsheets, or very simple internally developed applications.

Project and Service Orientated Organizations demand a solution that generates fast and significant return on investment, and offers quick implementations. Furthermore, all organizations already have other enterprise software such as an accounting system, project management software, or an ERP. A PSA solution must provide the proper means of customization and connectivity so that the organization can tailor the software to its own specific requirements and terminology and fully integrate the PSA with its other information systems.

PSA solutions are evolving to provide increasing amounts of functionality for project and service oriented organizations. The fundamental benefits of a PSA solution are:

> *End-to-end engagement management:* PSA solutions provide a total and comprehensive engagement management solution for PSORGS. The engagement is tracked and managed from demand, to project delivery, invoicing or charge back, to analysis using business intelligence tools. No other software solution has ever provided such a comprehensive view and approach to project and engagement management for PSORGS.

> *Resource management:* Resource Management enables improved tracking, deployment, matching, and prioritizing of resources based on skills, interests, location, availability, and business practices for a given service engagement. As a key component within a PSA solution, Resource Management enables substantially improved resource utilization.

> *Significantly reduced billing cycles:* Reduces billing cycles by automating the data collection process, reducing error, eliminating rekeying, and by providing integrated billing functionality that can quickly produce accurate and complete invoices. Invoices can be generated at the level of detail demanded by the customer, without regard to the restrictions imposed by an accounting or ERP system. This improves the enterprise's bottom line because it can bill more rapidly and it can collect faster, thereby bringing in cash sooner and further reducing its costs.

➤ *Accurate cost, revenue, and project tracking:* By tracking actuals (time, expenses, purchases, and issues), the PSA system can produce detailed graphical and visual representations of project status, trouble spots, cost, revenue, and profit or loss. This in-depth insight of project status gives managers and executives a powerful and definitive tool to ensure that projects are managed and delivered in a timely and cost effective manner.

PSA vendors use the latest technology to provide ubiquitous connectivity and web access to help further reduce the total cost of ownership of these solutions. Every PSA solution has its unique set of strengths and limitations. Determining which areas are important to your business is the key to selecting the most effective solution. PSA is no longer a way to have software or a means to gain competitive advantage; PSA is rapidly becoming a must-have tool for project and service oriented organizations.

Appendix A

Other Sources
of Information

The following are great sources of information for project- and service-based organizations:

➤ **PSABook.com**

www.psabook.com

Provides online PSA ROI calculators, links to sources and analysts, and the latest news and reports on the PSA industry.

➤ **Project Management Institute (PMI®)**

www.pmi.com

The Project Management Institute is the world's leading not-for-profit project management professional association. It provides global leadership in the development of standards for the practice of the project management profession. Its standards document, *A Guide to the Project Management Body of Knowledge,* is a globally recognized standard for managing projects, and its Project Management Professional (PMP®) certification is the world's most recognized professional credential for individuals associated with project management.

➤ **PMFORUM**

www.pmforum.org

Includes various resources such as a portal to information, resources, and working groups associated with PM accreditation, certification, education, research, and standards; an online publication, which contains the latest notices, reports, news, and information related to project management from around the world; and search engines that include all project management terms and definitions.

➤ PM Boulevard

http://www.pmboulevard.com

An e-commerce solution that delivers project management services over the Internet. As the most comprehensive PM resource on the web, PM Boulevard offers access to a virtual project management office, online training center, extensive knowledge center, and personalized online consulting services. It also provides news, links, and other PM resources to keep you up to date on the industry's latest trends.

➤ Gantthead

http://www.gantthead.com

The experience bridge that fills in the gaps, providing help to project managers in a myriad of ways. It is a community—your community—for IT project managers.

➤ allPM

www.allpm.com

AllPM provides a host of information of use to Project Managers, including forums, scheduled project management events, jobs postings and product reviews.

➤ The Institute of Management and Administration (IOMA)

http://www.ioma.com

IOMA provides a large amount of publications, newsletters, and other resources related to project management.

➤ Association for Services Management International (AFSMI)

http://www.afsmi.org

The only global organization dedicated to furthering the knowledge, understanding, and career development of executives, managers, and professionals in the high-technology services and support industry.

➤ Association of Management Consulting Firms (AMCF)

http://www.amcf.org

The premier international association of firms engaged in the practice of consulting to management. It provides a forum for the exchange of ideas, helping consultants to better understand developments within the profession and to capitalize on new opportunities. Publishes a broad range of high-quality information products for business professionals.

➤ Information Services Financial Management Association (ISFMA)

http://www.isfma.com

A professional association dedicated to the education and advancement of the financial management of information services (IS) organizations in areas such as chargeback, cost allocation, cost control, benchmarking, asset management, contract negotiations, performance measurement, activity-based cost, portfolio management, outsourcing, service-level agreements, and function point analysis.

➤ Information Technology Association of America (ITAA)

http://www.itaa.org

Provides information about the IT industry, its issues, association programs, publications, meetings, seminars, and more, plus links to other valuable web sites. Your best stop on the Internet for industry news and perspective.

➤ Information Management Forum (IMF)

http://www.infomgmtforum.com

Provides a platform for sharing the best past experience, current practices, and future innovative directions. Assists members to identify, understand, and resolve issues and to implement solutions in areas such as IS organization and infrastructure, application development, operations and telecommunications, electronic commerce, measuring and communicating the value of IS, distributed processing, and client/server and knowledge management.

➤ The International Guild of Professional Consultants (IGPC)

http://www.igpc.org

The International Guild of Professional Consultants is dedicated to furthering professionalism among consultants through programs and support services that enhance both the quality of services provided to their clients and the profitability of their consulting practices.

➤ Network of Professional Services Organizations (NPSO)

http://www.npso.com/

Connects the seasoned experience of its members to one another in order to increase the effectiveness of professional services in all.

➤ National Association of Service Managers (NASM)

http://www.nasm.com

Improves the service industry's quality and effectiveness, fosters communications and cooperation among managers in the service industry, and provides quality educational opportunities directly related to the needs of the industry.

➤ Software Productivity Consortium

http://www.software.org

A unique, nonprofit partnership of industry, government, and academia, the Consortium develops processes, methods, tools, and supporting services to help members and affiliates build high-quality, component-based systems and continuously advance their systems and software engineering maturity pursuant to the guidelines of all of the major process and quality frameworks.

➤ Bitpipe, Inc.

http://www.bitpipe.com

The leading syndicator of in-depth IT content, Bitpipe distributes content from over 3,200 leading IT vendors and over 50 top analyst firms. The best way to gain access to the latest and greatest white papers.

➤ **Workflow Management Coalition**
http://www.wfmc.org
Promotes and develops the use of work flow through the establishment of standards for software terminology, interoperability, and connectivity between work flow products.

➤ **Workflow and Reengineering International Association**
http://www.waria.com
Makes sense of what's happening at the intersection of business process management, work flow, knowledge management, and electronic commerce and helps users reach clarity through sharing experiences, product evaluations, networking between users and vendors, education, and training.

➤ **Business Process Management Initiative**
http://www.bpmi.org
Promotes and develops the use of business process management (BPM) through the establishment of standards for process design, deployment, execution, maintenance, and optimization. The Initiative develops open specifications, assists IT vendors in marketing their implementations, and supports businesses for using BPM technologies.

➤ **Analysts who provide objective, complete, and current information on the PSA market:**

- ➤ AMR Research, http://www.amrresearch.com
- ➤ Aberdeen Group, http://www.aberdeen.com
- ➤ Forrester Research, http://www.forrester.com
- ➤ Gartner Group, http://gartner.com
- ➤ Giga Information Group, http://www.gigaweb.com
- ➤ Hurwitz Consulting Group, http://www.hurwitz.com
- ➤ International Data Corp, www.idc.com

➤ Kennedy Information, http://www.kennedyinfo.com

➤ META Group, http://www.metagroup.com

➤ SPEX, http://www.checkspex.com

➤ The Standish Group, http://www.standishgroup.com

➤ The Yankee Group, http://www.yankeegroup.com

App$B$*dix*

Professional Services Automation Request for Proposal Template

This appendix presents a suggested template to help the reader in evaluating PSA solutions. It provides questions about the vendor, the general product, and specifics of features that the reader may be interested in (for example, timesheet management). The reader may find it beneficial to use this template as a starting point when searching for the right PSA software.

So that you can more easily select the ideal solution for your organization, the evaluation guide details what questions should be asked and how they should be formulated to evoke meaningful replies.

Request for Proposal

Vendor Questionnaire

Vendor Information

1. Company Name
2. Contact
3. Address
4. Phone number
5. E-mail

6. Number of employees and total of software support staff
7. Years in operation
8. Total number of software licenses sold
9. Publicly held or private company
10. Approximate annual sales revenues
11. References from customers actively using vendor's products
12. Industry partners

Product Information

1. Product name
2. Operating systems supported
3. Programming language(s) used
4. Third-party packages required by or included with the product
5. Is this system web-based? If web-based, what browsers and web servers does it support?
6. Does it support e-mail–based functionality?
7. Client/server hardware and software requirements
8. Does the system support any wireless devices? If yes please describe which one and what functionality is available.
9. If available, please provide a diagram of the system's architecture.
10. What is the scalability model in terms of users and database sizing? Please attach benchmarks.
11. Have the company's products been reviewed by any publications?
12. Latest release date
13. Frequency of major and minor releases
14. Date of next release and details of planned changes

Requirements

Timesheets

Entry

1. How many timesheet views are included? How does each of them capture work? Can users be limited to different views?
2. Does the system allow a time increment to be specified to capture time (for example, can time entries be no less than 15 minutes)?
3. Can users add comments to their timesheet? Add time

entries? Specify different comment types? Attach documents?

4. Does the system provide a stopwatch to track time and update the timesheet?
5. Can the system fill and submit timesheets automatically for specific users in a specific time frame?
6. How can timesheets be entered offline?
7. Can users submit their timesheets via e-mail? If yes, please explain how this information is entered into the database.
8. Can users submit their timesheets via a swipe card system? If yes, please explain how this information is entered into the database.
9. Can users submit their timesheets via a time clock system? If yes, please explain how this information is entered into the database.
10. Can users enter their time via wireless devices?
11. Does the application support exception time entry? (This feature allows users to specify a default time entry that is entered automatically each week; the user does not need to make any time entry unless it is different from the pre-defined timesheet.)
12. Does the application support definition of holidays and users' eligibility for paid holidays based on their status (e.g., an employee versus a consultant) or their seniority?

Projects

1. What is the number of levels available to capture work? Can it vary based on the user or the work type?
2. Does the system track the project status, start and end dates, and phases?
3. How does the system handle projects not related to clients?
4. Does the system support clients with multiple projects?
5. Can users be limited to the budgeted amount (in time, cost, or billing amount) for a project, task, or assignment? Can their manager be notified when the limit is reached?
6. Can users specify their estimate for completion of the work? Does this information integrate with project management software such as Microsoft Project? If yes, please describe.
7. Can time entries' status be changed for previous work periods

(for example, can time entries in a specified time frame be changed from billable to nonbillable)?

8. Can one specify the status of time entry, activity, task, or project (such as costed, billable, R&D, funded, etc.)? If so, what are the status indicators included? For which items? Does the system security allow designating who has the ability to control this option?

Labor Management

1. Can the system setup allow for business rules to be created on a per-user basis that automatically calculates overtime and banked overtime balances? Can the system control how these overtime or banked overtime hours may be used per day or period? Please explain.
2. Does the system track balances and allow usage rules for non–project-related work such as vacation, sick leave, personal days, and the like?
3. Can users be asked to work a certain number of minimum hours each day, week, or period? Can users be limited to a maximum number of hours each day, week, or period?
4. How does the system handle shifts and rotational shift work?

Management

1. Please describe the timesheet submission process and the number of approval levels.
2. Can the manager reject the user's timesheet? How is the user notified?
3. Does the system support midweek work approval?
4. How does the manager know when it is time to approve a previously rejected timesheet?
5. Can the manager view and approve subordinates' timesheets using e-mail? Wireless devices?

Expense

Entry

1. How many expense views are included? How does each of them capture work? Can users be limited to different views?
2. How can expenses be entered offline?

3. Can expenses be marked up for billing?
4. Can the expense reporting capture and input cycle differ from that of the user timesheet?
5. Can some users be required only to enter expenses, without access to any timesheets?
6. Does the system support multiple currencies? Tax jurisdictions? Multiple tax categories?
7. How are the exchange rates entered and updated in the system?
8. Can users be limited to budgeted or threshold amounts for a user, client, project, task, activity, group, team, site, or expense category?
9. Can expenses be automatically approved for preset amounts?
10. Can expense transactions be imported from Amex or banking transaction files?
11. How does the solution support cash advances? Please elaborate.
12. Can one specify the status of expense entry (such as costed, billable, R&D, funded, etc.)? If so, what are the status indicators included? For which items? Does the system security allow designation of who has the ability to control this option?

Management

1. Please describe the expense report submission process and the number of approval levels.
2. Can the manager reject the user's expense report? How is the user notified?
3. Does the system support midweek work approval?
4. How does the manager know when it is time to approve a previously rejected expense report?

Cost and Revenue Accounting

1. Describe the different types of billing and cost rates supported in the system. Is there support for the "cost plus" concept for automatically generating billing rates from cost rates?
2. Please describe the project cost and billing budget functionality available in the solution.

3. Can multiple cost centers be defined?
4. Does the system allow for multiple hourly rates per employee based on client, project, department, and the like? Please elaborate.
5. Can project and billing amounts be split between various clients?
6. Can rates be defined for overtime and double overtime?
7. Can the system recognize special rates—for example, rates for work performed on weekends or holidays?
8. How does the system handle billable and nonbillable work—for example, in the case of a consultant who works for 10 hours, only some of which are attributed to the total project cost and considered billable? Explain.
9. Can billing rates be date-driven—for example, with automatic start and end dates? Is history kept for past reporting purposes?
10. Can expense and time entries be marked as billable or costed? What else can be included in the billing for a client?
11. Can the system support milestone billing? Percentage-complete billing?
12. Does the solution support multiple currencies?

Invoicing

1. Is there a facility for generating invoices? If so, how does the system recognize what is billed and what has not been billed?
2. Can billing amounts be overridden prior to generation of the invoice?
3. Can invoices be printed? Can they be e-mailed directly from the preview screen?
4. How does the solution handle revenue recognition? How does it handle work in progress?
5. How does the solution handle receivables or payments received and outstanding balances?

Resource Planning

1. Can one apply skills to a user, project, task, or activity?
2. Can one set the resource proficiency level?
3. Can one define the importance of a project, task, or activity and calculate the weight?

4. Does the system allow one to match resources to specific projects based on resource level of expertise and availability?
5. Does the system support resource scheduling, leveling, and forecasting? If so, how?
6. Can one reserve resources or assign work?
7. Can the system track user interests?
8. Can resource planning queries search for offsite users who are willing to travel and relocate?

Workflows and Change Management

1. Is there support for wireless devices?
2. Are any workflows predefined in the application? If so, how many? Please describe the workflows included.
3. Does the application provide for predefined assignment for specific states or stages in a workflow?
4. Can one define issue escalation based on user roles in the system? Please describe.
5. Can issues be organized so that specific users only have access to specific issue types?
6. Can a user build searches based on issue types or queries to analyze issue information?
7. Does the product allow for automatic sequential numbering of issues based on issue type?
8. Does the product allow for free-form text descriptions of specific issues?
9. Does the product allow for document attachments with attachment constraints?
10. Can the product capture ongoing dialogue with business groups?
11. Can the system determine who an issue is assigned to based on the specific problem area?
12. Does the product allow for classifying customer issues in a knowledge base?
13. Can one generate live information on issue statistics? For example, are issues closed or resolved?
14. Is a user able to see the history of an issue and how many days it has been open?
15. Does the product provide the ability to prioritize requests based on urgency?

Purchasing

1. Does the solution include a functionality to help streamline purchasing processes and the issuing of requisitions and purchase orders? Is it workflow-based?
2. Is it web-based?
3. If so, how many workflows can be defined? Are they customizable?
4. Can a workflow be used for multiple purchase types or requests?
5. Does the system support customizable fields?
6. Can fields be designated as mandatory or optional? Can they be validated?
7. Does the application provide for predefined assignment for specific states or stages in a workflow?
8. Can thresholds be defined so that a maximum unit price cannot be exceeded for a specific purchase? Are there any limitations that can be enforced in the application other than unit price?
9. Can there be multiple purchase entries in a requisition or purchase order?
10. Can purchase orders be submitted in multiple currencies? Please describe.
11. Is there a feature that will allow for the listing of specific organizational purchasing policies? Can the policies be linked to specific purchase types so that employees can access them for referential purposes?
12. Does the system support keyword searches?
13. Does the product support document attachment? Please describe different levels of document attachment that are available and where these documents are stored.
14. Does the system provide a facility to store preferred vendors? Can preferred vendors be associated with specific items?
15. Can a user mix dissimilar items on one requisition?
16. Can a user build searches based on purchase types or queries to analyze purchase request information?
17. Does the product allow for automatic sequential numbering of purchase requests based on purchase type?
18. Can you define escalation based on user roles in the system? Please describe.

19. Does the system support an unlimited number of approval levels? Describe.
20. Is an e-mail sent to the originator if a requisition is rejected?
21. Does your solution track stock reorder points?

Knowledge Management

1. Can the knowledge management system be accessed over the web and by wireless devices?
2. How does the product handle document management? At what levels (client, projects, activities, users, timesheets, expense reports, etc.) can documents be attached in the application?
3. Does the system support event-driven e-mail notifications for knowledge articles or documents that are ready for approval?
4. Does the system allow for full-text searches?
5. Does the system allow for key word searches?
6. Please describe support for creating security roles or profiles that define what screens and functions a user can access.

Supervisory Controls and Data Integrity

1. Does the system have the capability to limit who is authorized to set budgets and charge time, expenses, purchases, and issues for certain projects or activities?
2. Can users of the system review their hours, issues, and expense reports on a real-time basis?
3. Can records be created for adjusting entries to past reporting periods (e.g., can records be entered in negative amounts to correct prior reported time in system)? How are changes to prior periods handled?
4. Can managers be limited to creating and viewing only projects for which they are responsible?

Reporting

1. What reporting engine is used in the product?
2. Please describe any standard reports provided and the possibility of creating new reports.
3. Is it possible to roll up report data?
4. Who has the ability to create reports?
5. Can management create reports for their areas?

6. Is it possible to filter data displayed in reports (e.g., can one set filters to show or hide data on the basis of its status as approved or not approved, completed or not completed, billable or nonbillable, posted or not posted, etc.)?
7. Is there a way to provide security to certain reports so that only specific users can make modifications?
8. What are the archiving capabilities for reports?
9. What tools or built-in integrations are available for multi-dimensional data analysis?

Performance Analysis

1. Does the system have an embedded BI OLAP component? If yes, please specify name and brief information.
2. Can the OLAP component be accessed through a pure web interface?
3. Is there a Windows application available for creating OLAP reports and more sophisticated OLAP functions?
4. Does the OLAP component support multiple databases?
5. Is the OLAP tool integrated into the PSA software's application security system?
6. Can BI reports be placed on user, manager, and executive home views?
7. Do the BI component and the PSA software support digital dashboards?
8. Can any user or manager create BI and ad hoc reports using a pure web client?
9. Can any user or manager create BI and ad hoc reports using a Windows client?
10. Does the BI tool support ad hoc queries and reporting?

Security

1. What type of security is built into the system?
2. Is security function-, transaction-, or field-dependent?
3. How can security be assigned to individuals? How is it maintained and controlled?
4. What is involved in adding, deleting, and modifying security?
5. How many levels of security are involved?

6. How are password and user ID checks performed? Can passwords be viewed online? Are they encrypted?
7. Does the system support a minimum password length and password aging options?
8. Once a report is created, can security access be added so that only certain people can print or modify that report?
9. Is there an audit trail or log? Please describe in detail how it is tracked and what its reporting options are.
10. Does the system support Windows NT authentication?

History

1. Can a user enter time or expenses into a previous period?
2. Can a user change time or expenses that were entered into a previous period?
3. What is involved in correcting history?
4. If a user changes groups, does the system keep his or her historical changes?
5. If a user's cost or billing rate changes, does the system keep the historical changes?

Interfaces

1. Please provide information on the system import/export functionality.
2. Please indicate how the system handles general ledger numbers and historical changes.
3. Does each component seamlessly integrate and interoperate with the others (e.g., timesheet tracking, expense reporting, project management, purchasing, invoicing, etc.)?
4. Does the solution ship with built-in integration to accounting packages (e.g., Microsoft Great Plains)? If yes, describe how the information is exchanged.
5. Does the system integrate with ERP software (e.g., SAP)? If yes, describe how the information is exchanged.
6. Does the system integrate with CRM software (e.g., Siebel)? If yes, describe how the information is exchanged.
7. Does the system integrate with payroll software (e.g., ADP Payroll)? If yes, describe how the information is exchanged.
8. Does the system integrate with version control software (e.g.,

Microsoft Visual SourceSafe)? If yes, describe how the information is exchanged.

9. Does the system integrate with flow chart software (e.g., Microsoft Visio)? If yes, describe how the information is exchanged.

10. Does the system integrate with messaging software (e.g., Microsoft Outlook)? If yes, describe how the information is exchanged.

11. Does the system integrate with project management software (e.g., Microsoft Project)? If yes, describe how the information is exchanged.

12. Does the software include any customizable fields?

13. Does the solution support digital dashboard? Please describe the integration.

14. Please indicate if an SDK or API is available for the system.

15. Under what conditions would you build custom interfaces to other company systems?

16. Does the system support telephony integration?

17. Please list any other interfaces.

Other

1. What languages are supported for the user interface?

2. Is the solution entirely web-based? Please describe the technology used.

3. Please describe the various methods through which users receive their assignments, purchase and issue types, and expense categories, or the methods with which managers assign such items. Also describe all associated security functions that govern such access globally and per site, group, employee type, and user.

4. Does the system limit access to data elements based on user site for entities such as groups, client, currency, holidays, and so on?

5. Can the user specify the location for the work performed?

6. Can items such as users, projects, and expenses be suspended, made inaccessible to active users, and removed from view?

7. Please describe all system e-mail notifications or reminders.

8. Does the system support customizable fields? If yes, for which

components? What types of fields can be created (text, pick lists, etc.)?

9. Does the system support customizable notifications? If yes, for which components? Can new e-mail notifications be added to the system through the application interface (as opposed to custom-developed notifications)?
10. Does the solution support client login? If so, what can external clients access?
11. Does the system setup display the information in the database in a tree structure?
12. Can you search and find items in the system from each screen?
13. Can you change the system terminology?
14. Can you add items to the pull-down menus?
15. What languages does the system support?
16. Can the system be hosted?

Software Cost Estimate

Please detail the sales price for a 100-user pilot and an additional quote for another 400 users. Attach to the proposal a recommended schedule for software implementation.

Support

The vendor's service level agreement (SLA) may answer most or all of the questions below, but in cases in which there is no SLA, these are some of the relevant questions that may have a significant impact on your satisfaction with the product.

1. What is the cost of the support plan?
2. Does the support plan include upgrades to the new version of the software?
3. What is the company's SLA?
4. Do customers have access to an online bug reporting system in order to report issues and requests as well as to check the status of reported bugs directly?
5. What is the average response time for bugs with different levels of priority?
6. What is the average time for reported bugs to receive fixes or workaround?

7. Is there access to online knowledge bases, such as FAQs, known bug lists, and patches?

8. Can the help function be expanded or changed to support company-unique requirements? If yes, must these changes be reapplied with each new release?

9. Is there a user group for the system?

10. Please provide the rates for the following:
    - On-site consulting
    - Custom development
    - Report customization
    - Training

Training Information

1. Describe the training offerings.
2. Does computer-based training come with the software?
3. List any charges associated with training (hourly training costs, travel expenses, etc.).
4. Please include a copy of the most recent training schedule.
5. What is the time frame you anticipate for a complete implementation of the system?
6. Describe the online help facility included with the system.
7. What documentation do you provide? In what media?
8. Are the implementation or installation details documented?
9. How current is the documentation? Is it complete with the current release?

User References

Please provide at least three reference accounts that may be contacted.

Appendix C

In-House Software

■ INTRODUCTION

To build or not to build? This is the question many PSORGs face constantly. In particular, PSORGs with internal resources or access to external resources capable of building an in-house PSA system are likely to consider this option. It should also be understood that while such organizations debate this situation, paper, spreadsheet, and small database programs remain the number one remedy when the question of buying or building is left unresolved. Effectively, the specific operational needs that prompted this situation remain unsatisfied, as the temporary fix measures become standard procedures. The purpose of the following sections is therefore to outline the problems and benefits, both short-term and long-term, of purchasing or building a solution that is capable of addressing the PSORG's particular needs.

Why not develop this software using our in-house IT staff? This question is asked each time an organization must decide whether to evaluate commercial software or to build its own in order to automate an element of its business. The problem is that finding the right software is a time-consuming venture. In-house development, a high-risk and low-reward activity, and alternatives such as paper-based and spreadsheet systems or even inaction are sometimes perceived as the easiest way out of this quandary.

■ SOFTWARE EVALUATION

The question is not without merit because evaluating a new software application is a project in and of itself, in most cases a lengthy process that involves several phases, including

➤ Document needs: Consider what each department requires and address the questions and concerns of each team leader as well as each company executive (depending on the scope of the project).

➤ Research: Survey the commercially available software that best meets the requirements.

➤ Filter marketing hype: Sort through the marketing literature and focus on real needs.

➤ Vendor qualifications: Consider not only the software but also corporate profile, experience, and customer base in related industries.

➤ Evaluate products: Review product demos in detail to narrow down best-fit solutions.

➤ Assess functionality: Identify what is lacking in even the best solutions and determine the possibility for further customization and integration, including calculating associated costs in time and money.

➤ Assess technology: Rate product technology or obsolescence that can lead to higher deployment or maintenance costs and discontinued support.

➤ Determine turnaround time for urgent bugs, requests, and support issues.

➤ Understand the particulars of the licensing agreement and what it means for the immediate and future needs of the organization.

➤ Screen: Narrow down potential vendors to the top three, based on the above criteria.

➤ Arrange for presentations: Ask finalists to provide more

detail and present their solutions to the department heads within the organization that will use the software.

➤ Pilot: Select one or two vendors and pilot at least one of the products in a small representative group for at least four weeks.

➤ Deploy: If the pilot is successful, plan the deployment and training schedule, dedicating resources to work with the vendor, and finally roll out the solution.

Clearly, these activities involve precious time and resources that some organizations believe would be best spent actually developing the solution internally. However, the reason most cited for building in-house is the organization's belief that there cannot possibly exist a solution that would meet its specific needs or could be adapted to do so in a cost-effective way.

■ IN-HOUSE DEVELOPMENT: A HIGH-RISK, LOW-REWARD ACTIVITY

By nature, in-house development is a high-risk, low-reward activity. Seventy-five percent of software projects fail because managers underestimate the complexities, user requirements, and long-term consequences of software development.

➤ In most cases, the organization must start from scratch.

➤ The user interface, server components, and database architecture will not be based on any real-life experience or feedback.

➤ To build, test, and stabilize a brand-new application is no simple undertaking.

➤ At the outset, some important resources will have to be dedicated to developing the solution. After the project is over, other resources will have to be trained to learn the software and support it instead of focusing on the company's core business.

➤ If the in-house developers leave, the organization is left with a system that is no longer supported or maintained by its experts, and which may be poorly documented, if at all.

➤ New technological advancements can lead to product obsolescence, and new needs may not be supported by the initial design.

➤ Marketing time is an opportunity cost that cannot be overlooked, because the organization must wait until the custom-developed system is delivered and, depending on the project size, oversimplification, complexity, and missed deliverables, this can be a very lengthy wait period.

■ WHY CHOOSE TO BUY SOFTWARE?

➤ The vendor is a software company, and developing software is its core business and area of expertise.

➤ A reliable, scalable, and proven architecture used by hundreds of organizations for many years already exists.

➤ You will gain complete user documentation and training far superior to what will be available if tools are developed internally.

➤ You gain support for one or more enterprise databases such as Microsoft Database Engine (MSDE), Oracle, SQL Server, and DB2, allowing the solution to scale as necessary.

➤ Commercially developed software usually includes extensive security features.

➤ If customizations are required, enterprise solutions must offer a complete application programming interface or SDK to customize and enhance the software or to integrate with third-party applications.

■ MAIN DISADVANTAGES OF IN-HOUSE SYSTEMS

Some disadvantages of an in-house system include incomplete feature sets and high administrative overhead. In-house systems can also make it difficult to integrate and exchange information with other applications and can be expensive to update, modify, and enhance.

■ AVAILABLE ALTERNATIVES

Some organizations may also consider all the disadvantages of buying or building software and simply decide that it is best to use some combination of paper and spreadsheet software. After all, the time and cost of implementing such systems is minimal. Of course, this means that the organization is simply sweeping the problem under the rug. In addition, the organization may be completely underestimating the administrative and clerical overhead and costs associated with such a system; costs can be deceivingly outrageous.

Using paper and spreadsheets does not resolve the problems. Either the organization will operate inefficiently until a major event leads it back to the realization that a more effective system is necessary, or it will follow the faith of many other organizations that continue operating at lower margins or unprofitably.

Although paper- or spreadsheet software–based systems may seem to be attractive options, some fatal flaws limit their appeal and effectiveness.

■ PAPER-BASED SYSTEMS

Some disadvantageous features associated with a paper-based system include the following:

- ➤ They are not efficient tracking tools.
- ➤ They are manual labor–intensive.
- ➤ They involve huge administrative overhead.
- ➤ They pose inherent storage risks.
- ➤ They provide limited reporting.
- ➤ They lack security, business rules, and validations.

■ SPREADSHEET SYSTEMS

Some disadvantageous features associated with a spreadsheet soft-ware–based system include the following:

- ➤ They are cumbersome to use and not user-friendly.
- ➤ They involve high administrative overhead.
- ➤ They are primitive in design.
- ➤ They lack important analysis and notification features.
- ➤ They provide limited reporting.
- ➤ They lack security, business rules, and validations.

■ COST ANALYSIS

Developing an in-house software system with very basic functionality would require the following investment:

	Year 1	Year 2	Year 3
Development[a]	$30,000.00	$8,000.00	$8,000.00
Programming tools	$5000.00	$0.00	$0.00
Tool upgrades	$0.00	$2,000.00	$2,000.00
Ongoing internal support[b]	$5000.00	$3,000.00	$3,000.00
Support	$0.00	$0.00	$0.00
Upgrades	$0.00	$0.00	$0.00
Total	$40,000.00	$13,000.00	$13,000.00
Cost per user per year (assuming an organization with 100 employees)	$400.00	$130.00	$130.00

Notes: Assume that this system will be running on Microsoft Access, MSDE, SQL Server, Oracle, or DB2 database, to automate one of the following operational processes: workforce management, PSA, change management, customizable workflows, help desk, timesheets, expense reports, billing, invoicing, resource planning, skill matching, budgeting, R&D tracking, project management, purchase order tracking, multidimensional analysis, and data warehousing. It is assumed that in a custom system, only the *minimal* functionality for that organization would be created, not the full functionality of a commercially available product. Development of a feature set comparable to enterprise software designed for a PSA solution would require a multiyear, multimillion-dollar IT project with substantially more expertise and resources. The estimate is for a standard client/server Windows application with some web-based entry functionality. It is assumed that qualified programmers or systems analysis staff are available who already have some understanding of design requirements. There is no allowance for major new enhancements to the system. The system design will not be able to scale to more than 10 to 20 concurrent users and more than 80 to 100 named users in the database; there are critical database and web technology issues that must be taken into account for high concurrent systems and larger databases.

[a]It would take approximately four months to develop even a basic system. The specified amount is based on two full-time programmers salaried at $45,000 each. Development includes system design, programming, testing, minimal online help, and system documentation. Bug fixes and minor system changes are assumed to take five weeks per developer per year for the two next years.

[b]User training—especially due to poor documentation, limited validation, limited automation of administrative functions, and other system complexities—will lead to higher internal support costs. Assume a support position salary of $30,000 and that 15% of a support person's time is spent on support issues for year one and 10% in years two and three.

■ REAL-LIFE EXAMPLE

Should an organization build an enterprise optimization system in-house?

The following is a true account. Persons and company names have been modified at the request of the persons and company involved.

Jane Smith, director of operations of XYZ, Inc., has a problem. She is having trouble tracking the time and costs associated with each of her teams' projects. Project budget overruns and late deliveries are the norm, not the exception. Jane decides to find an appropriate enterprise optimization solution that will help her view a project's current status and track employees' progress in order to schedule and deliver projects on time and within budget.

After weeks of research and evaluating several products, Jane decides that none of the products on the market suit her specific requirements. Finally, she wonders: "How difficult can this be? We will simply use Microsoft® Excel™, Access™, or some other simple database product and build our own in-house system that will do exactly what we want." She hires a very knowledgeable software engineer and two junior programmers to get the job done.

After a review of the requirements, the project was scheduled to be completed within six months. Six months later, the software works, but there are problems; sometimes the system hangs, or the reports come up empty, or the database gets corrupted. The team reviews the problem and promises a fix within four weeks. Three months later, some of the old problems still exist, and now there are new ones.

As the engineers work on these problems, Jane's managers, observant of the new system, start asking questions:

➤ How about linking the data with a project management application such as Microsoft® Project™?

➤ How about a web version, so we do not have to install this on every computer?

➤ How about integration with an accounting system?

➤ How about entering time while we are on the road?

➤ How about sharing information (such as tasks and activities) with other company divisions?

➤ How about some graphs and charts? More reports?

Jane goes back to her team with the list of existing bugs and the new requests. The team's leader says he will need two new programmers that are much more senior and six to eight months to deliver just half of these features. To make matters worse, two weeks later, the team leader finds a better-paying job and leaves. Now Jane is stuck with an undocumented, unreliable piece of software, two junior engineers, and pages of new requests.

Ten months and $120,000 of salaries paid later, she sits down to review the corporation's job cost and time management system. The problems and the in-house system's requirements had far exceeded her wildest imagination. She concludes: "Our company makes widgets. We got into the software business. How did I get us into this?"

She realizes that building a program is not a trivial task and that any system brings the need for further changes, which may not be possible if the right decisions are not made at the onset. She fires the in-house development team and goes back to reviewing the commercial products on the market.

To her absolute surprise, several products already support the features her team had built as well as most of the new requests. In addition, with these products, her cost for tracking her 100-employee organization is less than $15,000. She can even create her own customized reports. One of the companies is also willing to develop extensions and specific customizations at very competitive rates. Jane buys a system and asks for some customization. The total package costs her $30,000.

A few months later, Jane has a total understanding of what each team is working on and how much every project costs. The system tracks time and expense at the task level. It also generates valuable reports with the ability to cross-reference the data to track performance, and it identifies inefficiencies to allow for better forecasting. This new system collects valuable data that would otherwise slip through the cracks and would have been lost forever. Jane and her management team are now able to make far more accurate budget and project delivery estimates. They are also able to bill their customers more accurately and account for time that they previously would never have captured.

After all, *time* is the most important commodity for most businesses. Consequently, it is imperative for corporations to consider many factors before deciding to build an in-house system, factors such as reporting, security, data integrity, supervisory control, approval process, and Internet access. Once all the various aspects are taken into consideration, most companies recognize the tremendous investment of time and money implicated in terms of planning, designing, testing, support, and maintenance.

■ SUMMARY

The dilemma of building in-house software solutions to automate operational processes is here to stay. Any organization that is faced with this question should carefully consider its options. Perhaps it can support a certain process in the short term using a paper- or spreadsheet-based approach, but in the end building in-house should only be a last resort. With substantial innovation and the proliferation of new software, there are, in most cases, commercially available products that will cost much less and do a lot more, and in far less time. Buying is a better short- and long-term investment and allows organizations to focus on their core competencies.

Appendix D

Professional Services Automation and Enterprise Resource Planning

■ INTRODUCTION

There is much about ERPs and similar products that is excellent. They primarily offer the enterprise the hope that all its business processes, or at least its main ones, can be mechanized and perfectly integrated.

Enterprise resource planning systems evolved in the late 1970s to provide *standard* software solutions to large corporate customers and to relieve them of the necessity of building basic business software (for example, accounting software) in-house. The main focus was, and still is, standard office functions such as accounting, human resources, and inventory management—that is, basic, essential services that most enterprises must have. Over the years ERPs have branched out into more and more ancillary business processes and developed more industry-specific solutions.

In recent years, the popularity of enterprise re-engineering and the anticipated Y2K conversion problems have encouraged many large enterprises to radically reorganize their enterprises and install ERP, primarily in their finance or human resource groups. From there, ERPs have often attempted to push out into other parts of the organization.

Often an ERP is installed only with the actual participation and encouragement of the most senior levels of management. Enterprise resource planning often demands a modification of the basic business processes of the enterprise and causes considerable disruption, and because many ERP systems were developed over the last 30 years, their general usability is very low, causing a great deal of resistance to what appear to be antiquated 20-year-old screens and menus (they usually require a considerable amount of training of the user community before they can be rolled out).

More often than not, they are sold from the *top down*, meaning that the CEO level managers brought in the solution (typically upon the recommendation of re-engineering management consultants), leading some wags to remark that any lesser managers would probably have been fired if they brought in anything causing a similar amount of business disruption, escalated consultant budgets, employee grumbling, and increased running cost.

In contrast, many PSA solutions are pushed from the *bottom up* by departments desperate for functionality that will allow them to perform their professional services jobs. Often these departments are part of larger organizations that have already implemented ERPs and have a large number of specialized legacy systems to deal with.

Therefore, PSA solutions are evolving in an environment in which they must interface well with a panoply of ERP and in-house solutions. They are also successful because they do not require major process re-engineering of the professional service department: They simply codify the best practices in the software solution area (often what the professional services organization is trying to do anyway with the primitive tools at hand) and are flexible enough to adapt to the precise way the user provides service.

In addition, PSA minimizes the costs of installation, integration, and rollout. Most customers with ERP solutions always have an option to turn on, purchase, and roll out the ERP's own offering in the professional services area. However, the cost, time pressures, flexibility, heavy training costs, idiosyncratic and nonintuitive user interfaces, and the corporate governance of the ERP implementations in most enterprises mitigate against an ERP solution.

Therefore, in summary, PSA and ERP (and other in-house solutions) easily coexist. Professional Services Automation solutions are optimized to be rapidly installed, easy to use, and nondisruptive, and they provide almost immediate payback and ROI. They follow industry technical standards and are meant to integrate easily with the customer's current and future suite of mechanized systems. The PSA vendors are focused on evolving their solution as rapidly as possible to beat the other specialized, highly competitive PSA developers. Professional Services Automation solutions are these vendors' main focus. It is unlikely that ERP vendors will become dominant in this area unless they themselves force a major industry consolidation by purchasing the major PSA solution providers or reach strategic relationships with them. Indeed, some have already done so in the CRM area, where some have recognized that their own internal CRM offerings were not competitive in the marketplace and have either purchased major specialized CRM software providers or entered into joint marketing programs.

The underlying goals of PSA and ERP systems are fundamentally the same. Although tailored for different organizational structures, both application types share the purpose of reducing corporate inefficiencies through the automation of core business processes. The purpose of these sections is to identify both the ERP and PSA product offerings and aid an understanding of how your company will benefit from the implementation of a PSA solution, with regard to project and service engagements.

For the purpose of this document, three major types of organizational models must be clearly identified:

➤ Product-oriented organizations

➤ Project- and service-oriented organizations

➤ Product-, project-, and service-oriented organizations

Regardless of the products or services offered, every organization relies heavily on mission-critical business applications to keep its operations running smoothly. However, choosing the wrong type of application can place a corporation in the precarious position of absorbing heavy financial losses.

Over the last 20 years, the services industry has seen a tremendous increase in new business. As a result, the services industry has branched off into several subcategories, one of which is the focus of the following sections: professional services.

Professional services can be defined as any specialized service that is provided to internal or external clients. It is ultimately the capitalization on human knowledge and expertise.

Recently many medium-sized and large enterprises have implemented very large and comprehensive software systems called ERP systems. An ERP system is often implemented with the assumption that it will integrate all departments and functions across a company into a single integrated software solution, encompassing, among other things, accounting, billing, human resources, and manufacturing. This system then acts as a central repository for corporate reporting, offering accurate organizational insight for management.

Recently, a new breed of application has surfaced for PSORGs: PSA solutions. In essence, PSA solutions streamline business processes for project and service engagements. They automate and integrate core business processes so that organizations within these industries can increase productivity and, ultimately, profitability.

■ ENTERPRISE RESOURCE PLANNING FOR SOME; PROFESSIONAL SERVICES AUTOMATION FOR OTHERS

Having matured over the last 20 years, ERP vendors have set their focus on the manufacturing and distribution sectors. The emerging project-oriented and services industries (having their own specific set of business processes) were hence put in a position of embracing ERP tools that were ill-adapted for their core business competency or using a multitude of different tracking or planning tools (ranging from paper-based systems to spreadsheets to project management packages, etc.) that were extremely inefficient.

Often, these tools could not be integrated into a master system to provide a corporation with a complete organizational picture for decision makers. This resulted in tedious manual processes, human error, loss of precious billable time, strategic corporate decisions based on erroneous information, inaccurate status reports, prolonged billing cycles, payroll errors, and numerous other disadvantages, all of which drastically cut both productivity and profitability.

The reality is that any organization having to provide any form of professional service cannot rely solely on an ERP system to attain maximum productivity and profitability. The advent of PSA tools has proved to be of great benefit for these organizations, as they have been introduced in today's marketplace with PSORGs in mind. Professional Services Automation applications provide what ERP systems lack. Enterprise resource planning packages tend to be weak in areas in which PSORGs require the streamlining of business processes for their project and service engagements.

■ UNDERSTANDING ENTERPRISE RESOURCE PLANNING SYSTEMS

Enterprise resource planning systems emerged in the early 1980s. However, they were not considered essential to corporate operations until the early 1990s, when ERP implementations swept through systems and were widely adopted by large enterprises worldwide. Over the past decade, ERP systems have positioned themselves to play a key role in a basic business infrastructure.

The focus of ERP systems is the tracking of equipment, machinery, and items for project-related work. The goal of an ERP implementation is to integrate financial data, standardize manufacturing and distribution processes, and standardize HR information.

The ERP offering can be summarized as follows:

➤ Product planning

➤ Parts purchasing

➤ Inventory management

➤ Supplier interaction

➤ Order tracking

➤ Financials

➤ Human resource management

Although ERP application vendors have proven that a centralized system can have its benefits, they have also demonstrated that ERP systems:

➤ Are costly to implement

➤ Have a long implementation timeline

➤ Do not offer a fast ROI

➤ Have a tedious learning curve

➤ Have high hidden costs

➤ Require a massive amount of resources for both implementation and maintenance

➤ Have serious scalability and customization limitations

Regardless of these disadvantages, once in place, ERP systems can offer substantial savings to corporations. One study from Meta group done across 63 companies states that the average implementation time of an ERP system is 8 months, with a median ROI of 1.6 million dollars annually.

It can be concluded from the above that product-oriented corporations will find ERP systems extremely beneficial to their operations, whereas PSORGs will have difficulties adapting the same application to their business processes and requirements.

■ UNDERSTANDING PROFESSIONAL SERVICES AUTOMATION SOLUTIONS

Professional Services Automation solutions have been on the market since the mid-1990s and have recently become a necessity for PSORGs and internal IT departments. The purpose of a PSA solution is to streamline and integrate project and service engagements for corporations that service clients based on both billable and non-billable work.

A PSA can be divided into the following core categories:

➤ Opportunity management

➤ Resource management

➤ Project management

➤ Timesheet and expense management

➤ Knowledge management

➤ Purchasing workflows

➤ Request and issue management

➤ Reporting management

➤ Project/revenue and cost accounting

Some PSA vendors include the following extended components in their product offerings:

➤ Customer relationship management

➤ Human resource management

➤ Complete enterprise accounting

The PSA offering can be summarized as a best-of-breed solution that allows for the tracking of actuals (such as time, expenses, cost, and revenue) and utilization of people assigned to project and service engagements.

In light of this viewpoint, PSA solutions can be viewed as the missing link between customer relationship management (CRM) and ERP systems. Professional Services Automation software is designed to complement these solutions rather than replace them. In a common scenario, opportunity management workflow is the first point of contact, which in turn typically ties into a CRM package. Once work begins, the PSA package matches the proper people to the project and automates the project/service delivery function through the various features described above. Finally, once the project/service engagement is complete, information is transferred to the ERP system for final billing, project accounting, and record maintenance.

■ LEVERAGING PROFESSIONAL SERVICES AUTOMATION AND ENTERPRISE RESOURCE PLANNING AS ONE

Today, the service economy is by far the largest nonautomated market. Project- and services-based corporations are at a disadvantage, because they have not had the luxury of access to product offerings that specifically fit their needs over the last 20 years.

Professional Services Automation is the new area for organizations to achieve massive optimization. The service economy is a growing global phenomenon, and PSA can bring tremendous automation and efficiency to virtually any organization operating in any industry. Many companies have optimized their inventory- and transaction-focused operations (ERP) and their sales procedures (CRM). The new opportunities for major productivity gains can occur from internal improvements from the project and service component of the organization.

Having a PSA solution as a complement to an existing ERP system can offer tremendous benefits to a PSORG. In addition, in terms of streamlining organizational processes, a PSA solution offers direct interaction with the people that are out in the field and the actual completion of the project and service. It acts as a channel of communication, providing feedback to all parties from the end user to managerial staff. Professional Services Automation solutions provide all responsible parties instant access to information with which to assess various critical situations.

Professional Services Automation and ERP packages are implemented for somewhat different purposes. Consequently, incorporating a careful balance of both systems is the best possible solution for companies that are product-, project-, and service-driven. Whereas ERP packages are implemented to solve internal corporate issues, PSA solutions should be viewed as a tool that provides organizations with a competitive edge, driving up a maximal amount of revenue from project and service delivery.

Moreover, it has become a popular trend for corporations to implement PSA solutions to reassure their clientele of their reliability and efficiency. Proactive organizations are determined to show their customers that they are using the latest technology to keep track of work they were commissioned to perform.

■ ENTERPRISE RESOURCE PLANNING AND PROFESSIONAL SERVICES AUTOMATION SYSTEMS INTEGRATION

The underlying principle of an ERP package is that a single-vendor application can streamline operations within a corporation from top to bottom. This is obviously not the case; therefore, more and more corporations are using the best-of-breed approach toward systems implementation.

Additionally, many companies already have established infrastructures, making it a difficult decision to discard the current investment altogether. Implementing a best-of-breed approach for PSOs would consist of the following:

Best-of-breed CRM solution + best-of-breed PM solution + best-of-breed PSA solution + best-of-breed ERP/accounting + best-of-breed HR solution.

The diagram below depicts three common points as a common denominator:

Figure APD.1 How ERP, PSA, and CRM Work Together

➤ Organization breakdown structure (OBS): Maps your organization by such areas as sites, departments, business units (or cost centers), teams, and employees

➤ Work breakdown structure (WBS): Maps your work by hierarchies such as customers, engagement, products, projects, and tasks

➤ Resource breakdown structure (RBS): Facilitates both roll-up reporting and summary resource scheduling by enabling you to schedule at the detailed requirements level and roll up both requirements and availabilities to a higher level

This brings up the issue of systems integration. Because integrations of multiple systems are typically difficult, many argue that embracing a single-vendor philosophy will solve integration issues. Others stress the importance of offering the best functionality possible for every core business area instead of focusing on a single broad application.

It is also important to emphasize the fact that PSA solutions are modern systems using modern tools, techniques, and integration technologies. Consequently, the whole process from the very start of the project to "going live" with them can typically be accomplished with a fraction of the cost and time required to develop an in-house product or to use paper-based process manually entered into an ERP system.

Professional Services Automation solutions offer easily customizable interfaces and easy-to-use application programming interfaces (APIs) that allow for painless and rapid integration to back-office ERP systems.

Hence, implementing a PSA solution as a complement to an ERP package will not only streamline ineffective business processes but will also allow this critical information to be shared across the multiple key systems in place within an organization.

■ SUMMARY

It is important to distinguish PSAs from ERPs. Both of these applications are designed with the same overall objective. However, they optimize different core business processes.

Some ERP vendors are entering the PSA space without covering the necessary core competencies of a PSA solution. Without these core features, these vendors are offering functionally weak solutions, which do not benefit organizations that require PSA solutions.

It would not be surprising to see most large ERP vendors merging and acquiring smaller PSA vendors with the purpose of finally providing an integrated solution that encompasses both the product and project/service engagement sides of companies. Several strategic market moves and corporate mergers or buyouts are already signaling this shift.

A few years from now, it is projected that a new category of software will emerge from these two spaces, encompassing both offerings. Enterprise resource planning systems will truly live up to expectations and will most probably incorporate the necessary tools and functionality to accurately track the efficient utilization of human resources as well as equipment and material resources.

Finally, it can be concluded that the three major organizational models can benefit from automating their business processes differently. Product-oriented corporations will benefit from the implementation of an ERP package; project- and service-oriented corporations will derive tremendous benefits from implementing a PSA solution, and product-, project-, and service-oriented corporations will benefit from a mix of both, having a PSA solution as a complement to the ERP offering. Professional Services Automation software will ultimately assure the delivery of projects and services on time and within budget.

Appendix E

Emerging Standards and Technologies

■ .NET INITIATIVE

No discussion of enterprise software and integration today would be complete without considering .NET's facilitation of live integration and its significant impact on an organization's best-of-breed versus single-vendor strategy.

.NET is a bold and ambitious initiative by Microsoft to achieve seamless integration of best-of-breed software services over the Internet. With .NET, software providers create .NET services, each providing a unique and consistent function (for example, calendar management, contact management, and user authentication services such as Microsoft Passport); .NET services use XML (a standard data definition protocol) to exchange data. These web services are then put together to create complete applications. Since all web services have a common access API, are independent, are accessed over the Internet, and have a unique function, seamless integration may become easier and more practical than ever before. However, as of this writing, .NET remains an unproven platform, and it is probable but still uncertain that Microsoft will be able to standardize and popularize such a comprehensive and all-encompassing Internet-based integration strategy.

■ WIRELESS NETWORK

A number of factors are driving wireless to a convergence of voice and data:

➤ Society is more computer literate.

➤ Internet/Intranet users and trafficare increasing rapidly each year.

➤ PC penetration is increasing worldwide.

➤ The pace of e-commerce is accelerating.

➤ Pressure to become more productive is increasing.

➤ Mobility and use of palmtops, laptops, and the like are increasing.

Moreover, wireless is extending capabilities:

➤ The convergence of wireless and Internet is already a reality.

➤ The rapid adoption of handheld devices and remote applications is driving a new generation of mobile applications.

➤ The third generation of wireless systems consists of key enablers of high-speed data, Internet, voice, and multimedia services.

➤ Wireless devices' throughput and bandwidth are on the increase, while telecommunications costs are spiraling down.

➤ Significant technological improvements are making it possible to manufacture small devices with integrated voice, data, and personal assistant technologies.

These trends indicate that over the course of the next five years, organizations and users will be able to fully access most of the same applications, features, and services that are currently available on wired networks on wireless networks.

Many PSA vendors already offer some form of wireless capabilities, mostly in the form of data collection, alerts, and summarized status reports. The wireless network will drive PSA vendors to offer richer and more complete offerings that can be used entirely over remote connections for their field-level staff, offsite employees, and on-the-road workers in industries such as construction and professional services.

$Appendix$ F

Purchasing Options

These days we have a wealth of options available for acquiring software solutions, and most ES vendors offer them all.

Therefore, the organization looking for ES solutions is likely to be able to arrange an acquisition or purchasing option that exactly meets its purchasing requirements.

It is not unusual for decision makers to adopt an acquisition policy that revolves around how the purchase[1] will be treated from an accounting perspective, and therefore how it will affect the financial statements; EBITDA[2] has recently become a popular measure.

Often a financial analysis will be conducted wherein all the various acquisition options are examined and the principal costs and benefits are attached to their chief characteristics. Usually, a major determinant in the choice between purchase and renting[3] the software will be the number of times the customer will be upgrading

---

1. Of course, software is usually not *purchased* but licensed, in that it still belongs to the vendor, and the "purchaser" has acquired a right of use, sometimes for a specific length of time. For simplicity's sake, we will continue to refer to this transaction as a purchase.

2. This is not an accounting text, and we will not discuss EBITDA further. However, major software license fees do have an impact on an organization's financial statements, and there is often intense internal debate on how these charges should be treated to minimize impact on earnings per share.

3. Renting the software is often referred to as *subscription*. In this publication, we will exclusively use the term *renting*.

software. Considered simplistically, if the customer has *absolutely* no plans to upgrade within the renting period and therefore can avoid paying the yearly upgrade fees, it would be less expensive to purchase the software. Conversely, if the customer will be upgrading within the renting period (which may cover a contract of three years, for example), it is usually more cost effective for the customer to rent the software, because often the right to unlimited upgrades is embedded in the rental agreement.

Frequently, the purchased software will be capitalized and written off over the estimated life of the software version—say, three years—whereas the renting approach would see the full yearly fees written off as they are incurred every year. Sometimes in a very aggressive accounting environment the yearly rental fee may also be capitalized and written off over a period of years.

The major remaining option when acquiring software is for the software solution to be hosted by someone other than the customer. This option often refers to the *extreme* case, in which the whole solution, software, and hardware are actually physically hosted off the customer's premises. However, a more practical hosting solution may simply be for the vendor, or third party, to manage the solution on the customer's premises, thereby providing the customer with all the benefits of remote hosting[4] without the necessity of storing any data offsite and worrying about security, remote communication issues, and so on.

Therefore, in principle, pure[5] software acquisition options consist of the following:

➤ Buy: One-time licensing plus support fees

---

4. Essentially, the customer benefits by having the equipment on his own premises (if indeed he is more comfortable with this arrangement) while having the software vendor's experts manage the environment. This frees up the customer's staff to focus on core business.

5. There are many combinations of these options, one of which may be the best option for the customer. It is not practical to present all the combinations here. However, it should not be too difficult to select the most appealing options from each one and create a unique combination that exactly meets the customer's requirements.

➤ Rent: Monthly or annual fees[6]

➤ Host: Server hosting (application service provider)

Which is the right option for your organization depends on many factors, which are discussed exhaustively in the following table.

Factor	Comments
One-time costs	Purchasing an ES will have high startup or initial one-time costs.
Running costs	Running costs of a purchased ES will be lower than a rented solution; hosted solution running costs may be higher or lower depending on many factors such as the organization's size, IT capabilities, hosting contract, and provider.
IT infrastructure	Organizations that do not have the appropriate IT staff and infrastructure should seriously consider hosting at least initially when implementing an ES solution.
IT expertise	IT expertise must include web server, database server, and network administration expertise and resources that can implement, operate, and support the ES system.
User support	User support includes basic training, troubleshooting, and the ability to respond to more advanced requests and issues.
Maintenance	System maintenance includes performance testing, backup, replication, and ensuring scalability and reliability as more users come online or at peak usage.
Upgrades	ES software upgrades would require server upgrades and possible client workstation upgrades (for non–web-based installations).
Security	Security depends on many factors. If the organization has a complete IT team with extensive resources, then it can provide the best possible security for its own ES project; however, smaller firms with limited IT resources may choose the security measures and infrastructure provided by a hosted solution.
Performance	An ES installed and maintained in an Intranet environment could be much faster because Intranets have a dedicated high bandwidth network. In contrast, the performance of a hosted solution will be limited by the delays and limitations of the servers and by the Internet connection between the organization and ASP servers.

---

6. Often the renting, or subscription, options are part of a multiyear agreement that includes unlimited upgrade privileges and are thereby often quite appealing to the customer.

Software leasing (rental) has several important advantages:

➤ Lower purchase costs: Spread the cost of the software over a one- to three-year period.

➤ Upgrades for free: Automatically receive all the software service release updates and upgrades free of charge.

➤ No annual support fees: Usually, a standard annual support plan is included.

➤ A complete tax write-off: Leasing fees may be declared as a business expense, hence, a complete tax write-off.

Software hosting has the following benefits:

➤ Elimination of the need for extensive hardware, integration, support, and maintenance costs

➤ Lower cost of management and operation

➤ Lower cost of software

➤ Shift of costs to the service provider

➤ Quicker implementation

➤ Freedom to focus on business, not technology

➤ Upgrades to the latest technology

➤ Predictability of costs

➤ Top quality security, backup, disaster recovery, and support systems

➤ Low risk

➤ Increased performance and scalability

➤ Swift implementation and platform independence

➤ Instant upgrades

Enterprise Software	Purchase	Host (ASP)
Cost	High one-time cost; must pay for upgrades over the years.	Monthly cost; will cost more than outright purchase because server is managed and maintained by ASP.
Maintenance	Internal IT staff must be involved in fixes, patches, and upgrades; must train internal resources, internally administer ES.	No internal staff allocated to maintaining the system; fixes and upgrades all handled by ASP.
Security	ES data are stored and housed at corporate facilities; highly secure, especially for larger organizations.	ES data are stored at a data center managed by ES vendor or a third party; data security depends on security provided by the ASP provider.
Reliability	Can be highly reliable because internal IT staff are involved in installation and maintenance; system runs on internal corporate network.	Reliability depends on the Internet connection of the ASP, the Internet connection of client, the stability of the Internet, and the quality of the data center managed by the ASP.
Scalability	Can be highly scalable; internal IT staff will add web and database servers as necessary.	Scalability depends on ASP data center (ASP focus is to cut costs by minimizing servers per customer) and the bandwidth of Internet access by ASP and by the client.
Performance	Can be as fast as the ES permits, since ES is running mostly on private corporate network; system much more likely to be responsive.	Performance depends on ASP's data center (ASP focus is to cut costs by minimizing network bandwidth used per customer) and the bandwidth of Internet access by ASP and by client.

Issues	Installation	Hosting
Data security	Typically no encryption security	May use encryption on all transmissions
Hardware security	Company servers may be compromised if at the company site because of lack of security to limit access.	Servers do not reside at the company site; in general kept under lock and key in an office, which is secure all year round.

continued

Issues	Installation	Hosting
Installation	May lead to deployment delays to find the appropriate equipment, negotiate pricing, in addition to the time required to install hardware and software.	Nominal installation requirements based on the users' data access rights; organization will be up and running immediately.
Scalability	Organization's growth represents added hardware, upgrade, and replacement costs; system may need to be replaced as organization grows.	ASP may be better positioned to bring additional usage capacity online and do so cost effectively.
Down time	Down time from hardware failures and software bug fixes and upgrades.	Typically, no hardware required and limited software upgrades for administrators. Even if internal server goes down, one can still enter time, get reports, and print bills from any computer connected to the Internet; For Web software, system may be continuously upgraded when improvements are available, with no effort required by the customer. Upgrades are typically instantly usable by all people at all locations of the organization without any installation. In general, no redistribution and reinstallation required.
Reliability	Server goes down after hours; needs dedicated IT staff to restore service.	An ASP generally offers systems that are up 24 hours per day, 365 days per year.
Data backups	Effective and reliable data backups may require costly internal oversight and procedures. Restoration of backups may not function.	A typical ASP has strict backup and recovery procedures and processes. Data is backed up continuously, and backups are integrity tested regularly.
Maintenance	Requires valuable technical personnel to install and maintain.	In general, zero installation required; can be used immediately by anyone.
Licensing costs	Added cost of "per seat" database licenses can run in the hundreds of dollars.	Usually, no costs associated with database licenses.
Technical support	Often an additional charge; technical problems may be blamed on hardware, operating system, web server, or database software and thus not covered by the support agreement; resolution often requires involvement of one's technical personnel and other third-party vendors.	Typically included at no additional charge; since the ASP maintains both the hardware and software, issues are resolved quickly.

Index

About the Authors

Rudolf Melik, president and chief executive officer, Tenrox

Rudolf is one of the four original founders of Tenrox. He has over ten years of experience in software engineering and project management. For the first five years of his career, he worked as a software engineer at companies such as Matrox Electronic Systems, ABL Canada, Discreet Logic, Bell International, Jazz Media Networks, and Nortel.

Since the company's inception in 1995, Rudolf has played a major role in making Tenrox an internationally renowned and successful software company focused on enterprise optimization. The company is privately held and has grown at an average rate of 60% annually without any debt or external financing and has always been profitable. The company has six products and more than 600 customers in 40 countries worldwide.

Tenrox is listed in *Software* magazine's World's 500 Largest Software Companies and won Microsoft's Innovation Solution of the Year award in 2001, the Mercad'Or Award in 2001, the Octas Commercial Business Success award in 2000, the CODIE for Best Enterprise Software Debut in 2000, and the Grand Exportation award in Information Technology from Economic Development Canada in 1999. It was included in the Branham Group and National *Post*'s Branham 250 roundup in 2000 and was named one of ten rising stars in the software industry in Quebec by *InfoTech* magazine. Rudolf was also the winner of the 2001 Technology Entrepreneur of the Year award in Quebec, Canada.

Rudolf holds a bachelor's degree in computer engineering, with a minor in management, and a master's in computer engineering (pending thesis attestation) from McGill University.

Ludwig Melik, vice president, sales and marketing, Tenrox

Ludwig was appointed vice president of sales and marketing of Tenrox in September 1999. Since joining the company in 1997, he has played a central role in creating and managing sales, public relations, marketing, creative, and business development teams. Prior to joining Tenrox he held positions within the sales channels of the computer industry.

He has extensive knowledge of the software industry, trends and marketing strategies, promotions, and setting up sales channels and partnerships.

He has established an extremely effective Internet-based marketing and sales strategy that services customers worldwide and has resulted in a 1,000% increase in revenues and profits in 1999, and a more than 60% increase in each succeeding year.

Ludwig was on the administration board of CPLQ Quebec's largest software association in 2000 and received the Entrepreneur of the Year award from the Chamber of Commerce of Laval in 2001 for his accomplishments and his contributions to the community.

Ludwig holds a bachelor's of commerce degree from Concordia University.

Albert S. Bitton, director, business development, Tenrox

Albert's responsibilities since joining Tenrox in December 2000 include establishing, growing, and managing the partner and strategic alliance channels, as well as taking part in developing the overall corporate marketing and business strategy for Tenrox.

Albert has more than seven years of business management, sales management, and marketing management experience within various channels of the computer industry. His experience has been gathered from the mass retailing, corporate sales, distribution, manufacturing, and now software vendor channels of the IT industry. Prior to joining Tenrox, Albert focused on regional operational, sales, and marketing management efforts for a leading Canadian computer distributor and manufacturer.

Albert holds a bachelor's of commerce degree in finance and marketing from Concordia University.

Gus Berdebes, vice president, professional services, Tenrox

Gus joined Tenrox in August 2001 as vice president of professional services. Gus has been successfully creating and re-engineering professional services delivery teams since 1977 within the BCE family of companies.

Using a wide variety of technology, he has created organizations that have planned, built, and integrated large enterprise–scale financial, billing, and customer care information systems, both for internal corporate use and to be marketed nationally and internationally.

Most recently, with the e-commerce company BCE Emergis, he built that company's first MIS IT department, which covered all corporate information systems in the United States and Canada.

Prior to this, he re-engineered and relaunched one of the largest secure commercial IP networks in Canada to safely carry sensitive information for government and commercial enterprises.

His main experience and interest lie in creating organizations that efficiently deliver engineering talent to build and integrate sophisticated information systems.

Gus holds a bachelor's degree in computer science and a master's of business administration (MBA) degree with a major in finance from Concordia University.

Ara Israilian, chief operating officer, Tenrox

Ara is one of the four original founders of Tenrox. He has over ten years of experience in software engineering and business management. Prior to Tenrox, he worked as a software engineer at companies such as Nortel, Bell Northern Research, and BCE.

Since the company's inception in 1995, Ara has been instrumental in aiding the company's growth while increasing the efficiency and productivity of its employees. He has extensive knowledge and experience in software, corporate operations, legal affairs, and corporate investments.

Ara has worked with Global 2000 companies such as ADP, Business Objects, IBM, Microsoft, Oracle, and SAP in establishing partnerships and positioning Tenrox to be a global player in the PSA domain.

Ara holds a bachelor's degree in computer engineering from McGill University.

YOUR FEEDBACK IS IMPORTANT TO US.

We are always interested in your comments, feedback, suggestions, and experiences on the book you've just read. Your insight and contributions help us to better understand your needs and produce more relevant and valuable texts. We might also want to use your feedback for future editions of our textbook to help us deliver the most value-adding and relevant information to the public. Please feel free to email us at info@psabook.com, or photocopy this form and mail it with your comments to Rudolf Melik and coauthors, 600 Armand-Frappier, Montreal, QC, Canada, H7V 4B4.

■ Please note, items indicated by an asterisk (*) are required fields. Thank you.

Name*:_____

Title*:_____

Affiliation:_____

Education:_____

Employer:_____

Industry:_____

Work address (1):_____

_____

Work address (2):_____

Work phone (1):_____

Work phone (2):_____

Fax:_____

Home address (1):_____

_____

Home address (2):_____

_____

Home phone (1):_____

Home phone (2):_____

E-mail (1)*:_____

E-mail (2):_____

■ **General Feedback Area**

_____

_____

_____

_____

Please answer the following questions:

1. Are you currently using any PSA software? ☐ Yes ☐ No

2. If yes, please specify:_____

_____

3. Are you interested in receiving a free monthly newsletter by e-mail?
   ☐ Yes ☐ No

4. Why did you purchase this book? (Please check one.)

   ☐ General interest in the PSA market

   ☐ Interest in PSA software solutions

   ☐ Academic reasons

   ☐ Other (please specify)_____

5. Did this book answer all of your questions on PSA? ☐ Yes ☐ No

6. Would you be interested in furnishing a quote or comment to be used as a reference? ☐ Yes ☐ No

7. Do you have any additional comments or questions?_____

_____

_____

_____

_____

I herewith freely allow and give right and title to Rudolf Melik and coauthors and John Wiley & Sons Inc., or their assigned, to use the following comments, feedback, suggestions, and experiences either to improve this or any of Rudolf Melik and coauthors' books or as a testimonial in the promotion of this book in any advertising medium solely determined by Rudolf Melik and coauthors and John Wiley & Sons Inc. I also agree to allow the use of part or all of a testimonial as determined by Tenrox.

_____

Your signature   Date